Mercedes-Benz
E-Class Owner's Bible™
1986 ▸ 1995

History and Development
Maintenance and Repair
Installing accessories
Performance Tuning
Buyer's Guide

B www.
BentleyPublishers
.com

Table of Contents

1 Introduction to the E-Class   1

General   Chassis and suspension
Body exterior   Body interior
Safety   Model year news

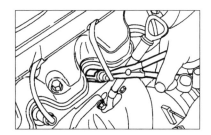

2 Buying an E-Class   25

Before you buy   After you buy

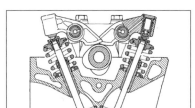
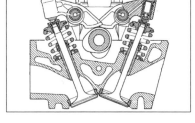

3 Maintenance   39

General   Body and interior
Fluid and lubricant   Wheels, tires and brakes
  specifications   Underside of car
Lubrication service   Engine compartment maintenance
Maintenance service   Trunk area maintenance

4 6-Cylinder Engines   125

General   M104 engine
M103 engine   Tips, maintenance, service

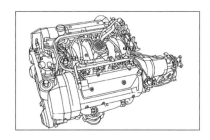

5 V-8 Engine   145

General   Tips, maintenance, service
Engine description

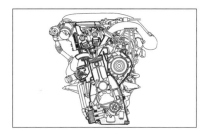

6 Diesel Engines   155

General   Tips, maintenance, service
Engine Technical

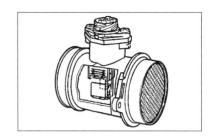

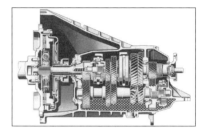

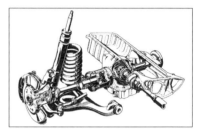

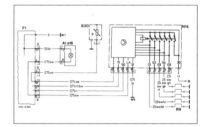

BENTLEY PUBLISHERS | Automotive Books & Manuals

Bentley Publishers, a division of Robert Bentley, Inc.
1734 Massachusetts Avenue
Cambridge, MA 02138 USA   Information that makes
800-423-4595 / 617-547-4170   the difference®

www.
BentleyPublishers
.com

Technical contact information

We value your feedback. Technical comments and suggestions are helpful to us. Please send your comments and thoughts to Bentley Publishers e-mail: tech@BentleyPublishers.com

From time to time, updates may be made to this book. A listing of updates can be found on the web at www.BentleyPublishers.com/updates

Copies of this book may be purchased from most automotive accessories and parts dealers specializing in Mercedes-Benz automobiles, from selected booksellers, or directly from the publisher.

The publisher encourages comments from the reader of this book. These communications have been and will be carefully considered in the preparation of this and other books. Please contact Robert Bentley, Inc., Publishers at the address listed on the top of this page.

This book was published by Robert Bentley, Inc., Publishers. Mercedes-Benz has not reviewed and does not vouch for the accuracy of the technical specifications and procedures described in this book.

Library of Congress Cataloging-in-Publication Data

Mercedes-Benz E-Class owner's bible, 1986-1995 : maintenance, service, and repair tips, technical specifications, shop owner insights.
     p. cm.
   Includes index.
   ISBN 0-8376-0230-0 (pbk. : alk. paper)
    1. Mercedes automobile--Maintenance and repair--Amateurs' manuals.

TL215.M18 M47 2002
629.28'722--dc21   2002066614

Bentley Stock No. GMOB
Editorial closing 04/02

10 09 08 07 06 05 04 03 02   10 9 8 7 6 5 4 3 2 1

The paper used in this publication is acid free and meets the requirements of the National Standard for Information Sciences-Permanence of Paper for Printed Library Materials. ∞

Manufactured in the United States of America

Please read these warnings and cautions before proceeding with maintenance, repair or modification work.

WARNING—

- Some repairs may be beyond your capability. If you lack the skills, tools and equipment, or a suitable workplace for any procedure described in this book, we suggest you leave such repairs to an authorized Mercedes-Benz dealer service department, or other qualified shop.

- Mercedes-Benz is constantly improving its cars. Sometimes these changes, both in parts and specifications, are made applicable to earlier models. Therefore, before starting any major jobs or repairs to components on which passenger safety may depend, consult your authorized Mercedes-Benz dealer about technical bulletins that may have been issued since the editorial closing date of this book.

- Do not re-use any fasteners that are worn or deformed in normal use. Many fasteners are designed to be used only once and become unreliable and may fail when used a second time. This includes, but is not limited to, nuts, bolts, washers, self-locking nuts or bolts, circlips and cotter pins. Always replace these fasteners with new parts.

- Never work under a lifted car unless it is solidly supported on stands designed for the purpose. Do not support a car on cinder blocks, hollow tiles or other props that may crumble under continuous load. Never work under a car that is supported solely by a jack. Never work under the car while the engine is running.

- If you are going to work under a car on the ground, make sure that the ground is level. Block the wheels to keep the car from rolling. Disconnect the battery negative (–) cable (ground strap) to prevent others from starting the car while you are under it.

- Always observe good workshop practices. Wear goggles when you operate machine tools or work with battery acid. Gloves or other protective clothing should be worn whenever the job requires working with harmful substances.

- Do not attempt to work on your car if you do not feel well. You increase the danger of injury to yourself and others if you are tired, upset or have taken medication or any other substance that may keep you from being fully alert.

- Greases, lubricants and other automotive chemicals can contain metals and toxic substances, many of which are absorbed directly through the skin. Before use, read the manufacturer's instructions carefully. Avoid direct skin contact. Always wear hand and eye protection.

- Friction materials such as brake or clutch discs contain asbestos fibers or other particles which are hazardous as dust in the air. Do not create dust by grinding, sanding, or by cleaning with compressed air. Avoid breathing asbestos fibers and asbestos dust. Use an aspirator when working on brake pads. Breathing asbestos can cause serious diseases such as asbestosis or cancer, and may result in death.

- Tie long hair behind your head. Do not wear a necktie, a scarf, loose clothing, or a necklace when you work near machine tools or running engines. Finger rings should be removed so that they cannot cause electrical shorts, get caught in running machinery, or be crushed by heavy parts. If your hair, clothing, or jewelry were to get caught in the machinery, severe injury could result.

- Disconnect the battery negative (–) cable (ground strap) whenever you work on the fuel system or the electrical system. Do not smoke or work near heaters or other fire hazards. Keep an approved fire extinguisher handy.

- Never run the engine unless the work area is well ventilated. Carbon monoxide kills.

- Car batteries produce explosive hydrogen gas. Keep sparks, lighted matches and open flame away from the top of the battery. If hydrogen gas escaping from the cap vents is ignited, it will ignite gas trapped in the cells and cause the battery to explode.

- Connect and disconnect battery cables, jumper cables or a battery charger only with the ignition switched off, to prevent sparks. Do not quick-charge the battery (for boost starting) for longer than one minute, and do not allow charging voltage to exceed 16.5 volts. Wait at least 1 minute before boosting the battery a second time.

- Illuminate your work area adequately but safely. Use a portable safety light for working inside or under the car. Make sure the bulb is enclosed by a wire cage. The hot filament of an accidentally broken bulb can ignite spilled fuel or oil.

- Catch draining fuel, oil, or brake fluid in suitable containers. Do not use food or beverage containers that might mislead someone into drinking from them. Store flammable fluids away from fire hazards. Wipe up spills at once, but do not store the oily rags, which can ignite and burn spontaneously.

- Many air conditioning systems are filled with R-12 refrigerant, which is hazardous to the earth's atmosphere. The A/C system should be serviced only by trained technicians using approved refrigerant recovery and recycling equipment, and trained in related safety precautions, and familiar with regulations governing the discharging and disposal of automotive chemical refrigerants.

- Do not expose any part of the A/C system to high temperatures such as open flame. Excessive heat will increase system pressure and may cause the system to burst.

- Some aerosol tire inflators are highly flammable. Be extremely cautious when repairing a tire that may have been inflated using an aerosol tire inflator. Keep sparks, open flame or other sources of ignition away from the tire repair area. Inflate and deflate the tire at least four times before breaking the bead from the rim. Remove the tire completely from the rim before attempting any repair.

- Do not touch or disconnect any high voltage cables from the coil, distributor, or spark plugs while the engine is running or being cranked by the starter. The ignition system produces high voltages that can be fatal.

- The Mercedes-Benz Supplemental Restraint System (SRS) automatically deploys an airbag in the event of a frontal impact. The airbag is inflated by an explosive device. Handled improperly or without adequate safeguards, the system can be very dangerous. The SRS should be serviced only by an authorized Mercedes-Benz dealer.

- SRS airbags that have been activated during an accident must always be replaced. Only trained personnel should work on or replace the airbag units. Improper removal or installation of the airbag unit or other SRS components may result in inadvertent activation or may render the system useless. The Mercedes-Benz authorized dealer has the proper training, specialized test equipment and repair information to service the SRS.

(continued on next page) v

Please read these warnings and cautions before proceeding with maintenance, repair or modification work.

CAUTION—

*See also **warnings** on previous page*

- Mercedes-Benz offers extensive warranties, especially on components of fuel delivery and emission control systems. Therefore, before deciding to repair a Mercedes-Benz that may still be covered wholly or in part by any warranties issued by Mercedes-Benz USA, LLC, consult your authorized Mercedes-Benz dealer. You may find that he can make the repair for free, or at minimal cost.

- Mercedes-Benz part numbers listed in this book are for identification purposes only, not for ordering. Always check with your authorized Mercedes-Benz dealer to verify part numbers and availability before beginning service work that may require new parts.

- Before starting a job, make certain that you have all the necessary tools and parts on hand. Read all the instructions thoroughly and do not attempt shortcuts. Use tools appropriate to the work and use only original Mercedes-Benz replacement parts or parts that meet Mercedes-Benz specifications. Makeshift tools, parts and procedures will not make good repairs.

- Use pneumatic and electric tools only to loosen threaded parts and fasteners. Never use these tools to tighten fasteners, especially on light alloy parts. Always use a torque wrench to tighten fasteners to the tightening torque specification listed.

- Be mindful of the environment and ecology. Before you drain any fluids from the engine, the transmission, the power steering system, or the brake system, find out the proper way to dispose of the fluid. Do not pour automotive fluids onto the ground, down a drain, or into a stream, pond or lake. Consult local ordinances that govern the disposal of wastes.

- Remove all electronic control units before exposing the car to high temperature, such as from a paint-drying booth or a heat lamp. On-board control units must never be exposed to temperature in excess of 176°F (80°C).

- Before doing any electrical welding, disconnect the battery negative (–) cable (ground strap) and the ABS control unit connector. Also disconnect the airbag control module circuit at the red plug located under the floorboards on the front passenger side.

- Do not connect the battery or switch the ignition on while the airbag unit is removed from the steering wheel. Doing so will register an SRS fault and turn on the SRS warning light. See an authorized Mercedes-Benz dealer to erase the fault memory and reset the SRS.

- Always disconnect the battery cables before quick-charging the battery. Never disconnect the battery while the engine is running. When jump-starting the engine, never use a battery charger or booster battery with voltage greater than 16 volts.

- Disconnecting the battery may erase fault code(s) stored in control unit memory. Check for fault codes prior to disconnecting the battery cables. If the Check Engine light is illuminated, or any other system faults have been detected (indicated by an illuminated warning light), see an authorized Mercedes-Benz dealer.

- Disconnecting the battery will set the radio into code mode. Early radios had to be taken back to the dealer to reset. Later ones come with a code card in the car to reset.

- Do not attempt to disable the ignition system by removing the center coil wire or by removing the distributor cap (where applicable). High voltage may arc to other electrical components causing extensive damage.

- Do not disconnect the battery with the engine running. The electrical system will be damaged.

- Do not run the engine with any of the spark plug wires disconnected. Catalytic converter damage may result.

- When working on diesel fuel injectors, everything must be kept absolutely clean. Clean all pipe unions before disconnecting.

- Diesel fuel is damaging to rubber. Wipe off any fuel that spills on hoses, wiring or rubber steering and suspension parts and wash with soap and water. If coolant hoses are contaminated with diesel fuel, they must be replaced.

Foreword

The intent of this book is to technically inform and educate E-Class owners with aim of enhancing their ownership experience.

The W124 E-Class is considered by many as one of the finest cars in the world. It has stood the test of time for engineering feats, reliability, durability, and design. As you read the technical chapters in this book, it will become clear as to why Mercedes-Benz cars stand head and shoulders above all other automotive offerings.

In the following pages, you will find step-by-step instructions on how to care for your car like the factory intended it to be cared for. You'll discover enlightened buying tips, fascinating technical information, and a wealth of electrical system information, plus lots more practical descriptions and hard to find 'insider's' information. The contents of this book has been distilled from years of shop owner and technician hands-on experiences.

Mercedes-Benz and most accessories and parts sellers specializing in Mercedes cars refer to the E-Class cars covered by this book as the W124 chassis, or simply the 124. Within the 124 classification there are a variety of models referred to by a second set of three digits which pinpoint the chassis design, E320 for example. When ordering parts, knowing this information can be extremely helpful.

Mercedes-Benz uses an internal code for the engines used in its models. One of six engine codes are used to distinguish the powerplants in the W124 E-class. Engine code information is primarily used internally by Mercedes-Benz but will be helpful if you have access to MB technical information. A table on page viii lists the chassis numbers and engine applications for E-Class cars.

The Mercedes-Benz owner who has no intention of working on his or her own car will find that owning and reading this book will make it possible to be better informed and to discuss repairs more intelligently with a professional technician.

The owner intending to do maintenance and repair should have a set of tools including a set of metric wrenches and sockets, screwdrivers, and a torque wrench.

These basic tools will do the majority of the maintenance and repair procedures described in this book. For some of the repairs described in this book, Mercedes technicians use special tools. The text will note when a repair requires these special tools and, where possible, will recommend practical alternatives.

We have endeavored to ensure the highest degree of accuracy possible. When the vast array of data available is taken into account; however, no claim to infallibility can be made. We therefore cannot be responsible for the result of any errors that may have crept into the text.

The publisher encourages comments from the readers of this book with regard to any errors and, also, suggestions for improvement in the presentation of technical material. These communications have been and will be carefully considered in the preparation of future printings of this and other books. Please contact Bentley Publishers using the contact information on the copyright page at the beginning of this book.

Mercedes-Benz offers extensive warranties, especially on components of the fuel delivery and emissions control systems. Therefore, before deciding to repair a Mercedes that may still be covered by any warranties issued by Mercedes-Benz USA, LLC, consult your authorized Mercedes dealer. You may find that he can make the repair either free or at minimum cost.

Regardless of its age and whether or not it is still protected by warranty, your Mercedes is an easy car to get serviced. So if at any time a repair is needed that you feel is too difficult to do yourself, a trained MB technician is ready to do the job for you. Each authorized MB dealer service department has made a significant investment in service and diagnostic test equipment, specials tools, and MB original parts. It is also the best source of the most up-to-date repair and service techniques, which includes factory training and technical literature. Servicing your Mercedes through an authorized Mercedes-Benz dealer will insure that your investment will be protected while maintaining the highest degree of service standards.

Bentley Publishers

USA E-Class model designations
model years 1986 - 1995

Year	Model designation	Chassis number 124.xxx	Engine	Automatic transmission 722.x
1987 - 1992	260E / 300E 2.6	.026	M103.940	.4
1993	300E 2.8	.028	M104.942	.4
1986 - 1992	300E	.030	M103.983	.3
1993 - 1995	300E / E320	.032	M104.992	.3
1992 - 1995	400E / E420	.034	M119.975	.3
1992 - 1995	500E / E500	.036	M119.974	.3
1988 - 1989	300CE	.050	M103.983	.3
1990 - 1992	300CE	.051	M104.980	.3
1993 - 1995	300CE / E320	.052	M104.992	.3
1993 - 1995	300CE / E320 cabriolet	.066	M104.992	.3
1987 - 1992	300TE	.090	M103.983	.3
1993 - 1995	300TE / E320	.092	M104.992	.3
1990 - 1993	300D 2.5 Turbo	.128	M602.962	.4
1994 - 1995	E300 Diesel	.131	M606.910	.4
1986 - 1987	300D Turbo	.133	M603.960	.3
1986 - 1987	300TD Turbo	.193	M603.960	.3
1990 - 1992	300E 4MATIC	.230	M103.985	.3
1990 - 1992	300TE 4MATIC	.290	M103.985	.3

Chapter 1

Introduction to the E-Class

GENERAL

◁ "The Mercedes-Benz 300E, the first new midsized sedan in nine years from the world's oldest automaker and the first Mercedes offered in North America with a 6-cylinder gasoline engine since 1981, arrives this week," read the November 7th, 1985, press release from Mercedes-Benz of North America.

While this sounded like any other automotive press release for a new model, the introduction of the new E-Class marked a permanent change in how buyers and critics alike would look at Mercedes-Benz and its midsized product line.

In 1984 the'W124' chassis was introduced in Europe to an eager motoring public. Only 3,484 cars were built that year, but the car was such an initial sales success that 159,987 were sold in 1985. Orders came in so fast that the European market was sold out for a two-year period.

NOTE—

In Mercedes-Benz literature the E-Class is often referred to as the 'W124' or just the '124' chassis. This is the factory's internal designation for the 1986 through 1995 E-Class series of cars.

The great sales success plus the time needed to develop the North American versions delayed the US introduction until the 1986 model year. Worldwide sales continued to climb, totaling 259,000 in 1986 and 271,339 the following year. Sales were so good that waiting lists developed at Mercedes-Benz retail stores around the United States.

Like the earlier Mercedes-Benz midsized sedans, the E-Class was a premium automobile engineered like no other car in the world. The new model delivered standards of safety and sophistication unmatched by any manufacturer at that time. Performance varied from reasonable to spectacular, depending on the offering.

The new 300E delivered many of the things Mercedes-Benz buyers had been eagerly awaiting. With 177 horsepower and 188 foot-pounds of torque, the silky smooth 6-cylinder gas engine propelled the car from 0 to 55 mph (the national speed limit at the time) in 7.5 seconds, with a top speed over 135 mph. The three-liter engine was the only offering in 1986, but additional powerplants were not far off.

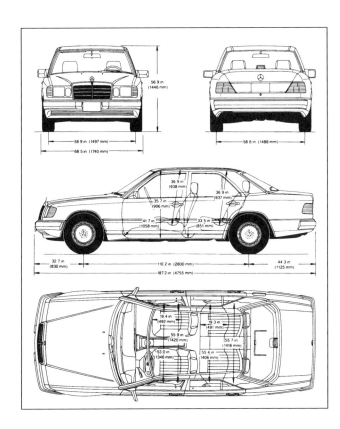

BODY EXTERIOR

◄ The new body shape was smooth, flowing from front to rear with very few 'steps' for the air to tumble over. With the steeply raked front and rear glass, the exterior shape was a pleasing departure from the staid Mercedes-Benz styling cues.

Noise reduction and improved fuel economy were two key design objectives for the new chassis. Detailed wind tunnel work did much to reduce interior noise levels, while simultaneously reducing air resistance to 0.31 C_d (coefficient of drag). The new chassis represented a 27% aerodynamic improvement over the earlier W123 chassis.

The undercarriage was also analyzed in the wind tunnel. The floor pan and other components were designed flat and smooth. This included a protective belly pan under the engine, aerodynamic covers for the lower suspension components, and a panel covering the electric fuel pump assembly. Even the shape of the exhaust system was optimized for drag.

NOTE—

Aerodynamic lift is an important consideration when developing an automotive chassis. When excess under-car lift is present, the car becomes lighter on it axles. This adversely affects vehicle balance, handling, and passenger safety. Through deliberate body design, aerodynamic downforce can counteract the aerodynamic lift. Automotive design engineers constantly seek the ideal balance of lift, down-force and drag, while maintaining a visually attractive design.

SAFETY

Body structure

Many structural safety features were developed for the E-Class chassis:

◄ Side impact protection consists of two structural crossmembers beneath the front seats, one under the rear seat, and one at the base of the windshield (**arrow**).

The crossmember below the windshield also serves to prevent intrusion of the engine.

NOTE—

In 1973 Mercedes-Benz found that most frontal collisions do not occur straight on, but rather as offset impacts where the cars meet at an angle. Collision data revealed that 40% or less of the frontal area of the vehicle is involved in the impact.

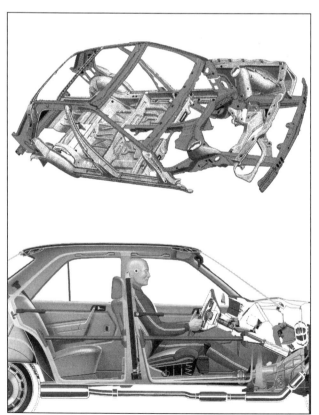

◄ A forked load bearing front end structure was developed to divert impact forces and also help prevent intrusion into the passenger compartment. During an offset-frontal impact, a substructure of reinforced steel panels serves to deform the body progressively and redistribute the kinetic energy. Through this structure, the incoming loads are shared by both sides of the body unit rather than concentrated to one side.

Other features contributing to vehicle safety:

- Fuel tank located above rear axle for rear end impact safety
- Structural body and chassis reinforcements with ten high tensile-strength crossmembers for superior cabin protection
- 'Safety cell' passenger compartment with front and rear body sections designed to crumple and absorb energy
- High-strength low-alloy (HSLA) steel panels and formed stiffeners in the underbody and doors for increased rigidity
- Bumper mounted crossmembers welded to side members for dissipation of offset-frontal impact forces.

Supplemental Restraint System (SRS)

At the time of the model's US debut, the standard Supplemental Restraint System (SRS) included a driver side airbag in the steering wheel and pyrotechnic seat belt tensioners for driver and passenger.

NOTE—
A passenger side airbag was available in later years.

The airbags are the "supplemental" restraint component of the system because the seat belts are the primary restraint in a collision. For airbags to work effectively, seat belts must be worn at all times.

◄ The driver side airbag is located in the hub of the steering wheel. The airbag is constructed of a cloth bag folded in a particular way, inflated by a solid fuel gas generator integrated in the airbag unit. The ignited fuel burns very rapidly to instantaneously inflate the bag. After deployment, the gas rapidly escapes from four vents in the bag.

Beginning in 1990, a passenger side airbag was available as an option and later installed as standard equipment. The passenger airbag uses two gas generators. The generators are not fired in unison. The first is activated simultaneously with the driver's bag and the second 15 milliseconds later.

◄ The main components of the SRS are:

- SRS light in instrument cluster
- SRS impact sensor
- SRS control module
- SRS airbag(s)
- Seat belt tensioners

The SRS light in the instrument cluster illuminates for about two seconds when the vehicle is started. This is a self-check of the SRS circuit. If a problem is found, the indicator light stays on and the SRS system is disabled.

The SRS impact sensor is mounted on the center tunnel of the body, behind the ashtray. The sensor electrically signals the SRS control module when a programmed deceleration threshold is reached. This signal is the basis for activation of the airbag(s). All the electrical contacts of the airbag system are gold plated to eliminate the possibility of corrosion and electrical resistance.

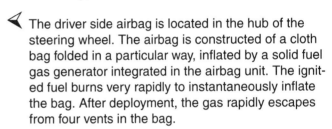

Dual airbags

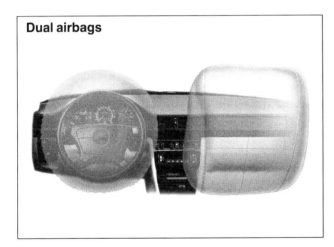

Coupe airbags and seat belts

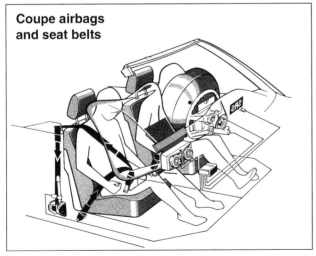

Seat belt tensioner (pyro-technic)

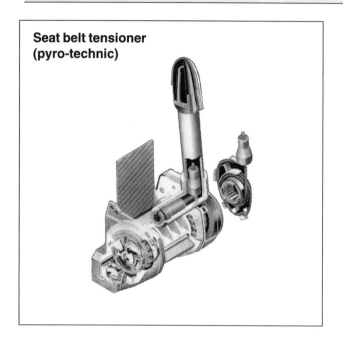

Crash research has shown that static seat belts are inherently loose and seat belts do stretch. Belt slack is also an integral part of the belt retractor design. Crash analysis further revealed that in severe collisions many drivers suffered steering wheel or windshield injuries even when seat belts were worn.

◄ The E-Class features an automatic tensioning system that incorporates gas-generating (pyro-technic) technology. The tensioner retracts up to five inches of belt when the airbag is triggered. The combination of airbags and seat belt tensioning has made the cabin of the E-Class car a safe place to be in today's harried driving environment.

CHASSIS AND SUSPENSION

This heading covers the various integrated electronic braking (ABS) and traction-enhancing systems (4MATIC, ASD and ASR) as well as the front and rear suspension information.

NOTE—
For more detailed information on braking, traction, and suspension systems, see **Chapter 9**.

ABS (antilock braking)

ABS is the German acronym for *Antiblockier System* or anti-block system. ABS was first available in European Mercedes-Benz passenger cars in 1978. ABS became standard equipment on all Mercedes-Benz cars sold in the United States and Canada in 1986. The system has proven to be trouble-free and highly reliable.

◄ ABS components include an electronic control module, a hydraulic control unit, and speed sensors at the wheels.

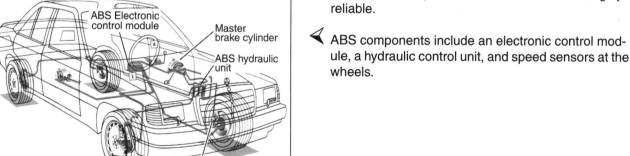

ABS Electronic control module
Master brake cylinder
ABS hydraulic unit
Wheel speed sensor

When the wheel is rotating, the wheel speed sensors output a voltage proportional to wheel speed. The control module uses this signal to calculate wheel acceleration. If a wheel is about to lock up, the brake fluid pressure at the wheel is modified by the hydraulic control unit based on input commands from the ABS control module.

The system either reduces or maintains the brake line pressure during intervention. The ABS system does not have the ability to apply the brakes.

NOTE—
* *The rapid regulation of the brake fluid pressure during ABS intervention is what causes the brake pedal to pulsate and chatter.*

* *4MATIC, ASD, or ASR systems do not conflict with ABS braking.*

4MATIC

4MATIC automatically adds front wheel drive to the normal rear drive mode when road conditions demand it. Depending on the available traction and road conditions, the system operates in one of three power transfer modes: 35:65 front to rear, 50:50 front to rear, and 50:50 front to rear with locked rear differential.

4MATIC models were available from model year 1990 through 1992.

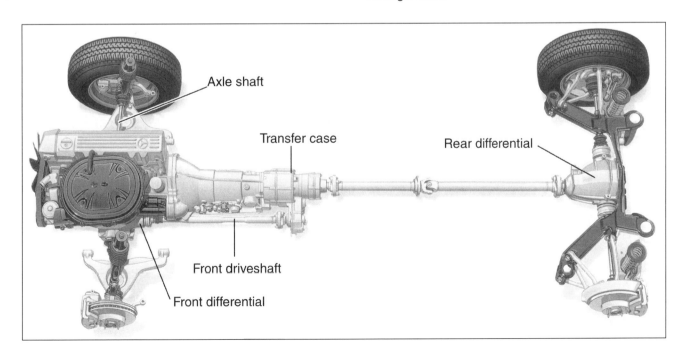

ASR (automatic slip control)

On slippery, adverse road conditions, the ASR system electronically reduces engine power and/or applies the brakes to the driven wheels to maintain the greatest traction possible during acceleration or cornering.

ASR was introduced on gasoline engine cars (except 4MATIC models) as optional equipment from model year 1991. ASR was standard equipment on the 500E.

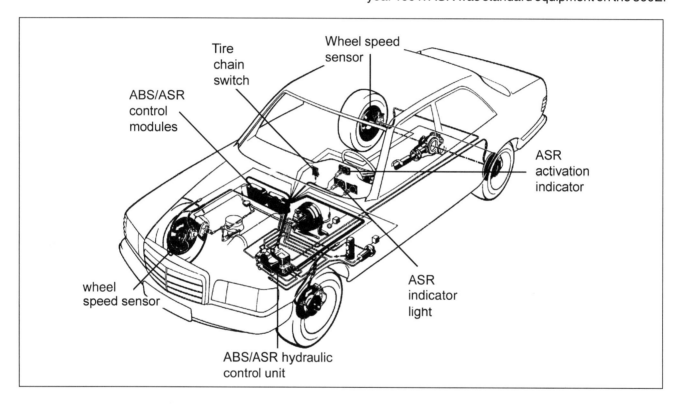

ABS/ASR
control
modules

Tire
chain
switch

Wheel speed
sensor

ASR
activation
indicator

wheel
speed sensor

ASR
indicator
light

ABS/ASR hydraulic
control unit

ASD (automatic locking differential)

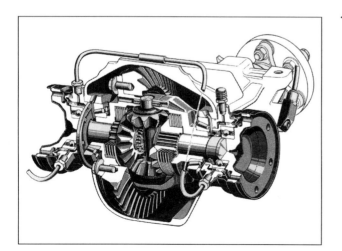

◄ ASD was introduced on diesel engine cars as an option beginning in 1991. This electrohydraulic controlled rear differential automatically transfers driving power to the rear wheel with more grip. ASD is active up to approximately 19 mph.

Suspension

The E-Class suspension was adapted from the earlier Mercedes-Benz 190 series.

◄ Front suspension is a damper-strut system with control arms. The McPherson strut design was not used owing to space restrictions. The spring is mounted separately, inboard of the shock absorber. One resulting benefit of spring separation is the ability to use softer more comfortable spring rates.

In later years a high performance Sportline option was offered that included stiffer, shorter springs, sport shocks, larger diameter sway bars, stiffer rubber bushings and a quick ratio steering box. The Sportline package provides extremely precise handling and weight transfer with minimal body roll.

◄ The E-Class rear suspension looks like it belongs on a modern road-racing car. Movement of the rear wheel is controlled by five links that limit travel within a precisely defined arc.

This rear suspension design endows the car with neutral handling, excellent straight ahead tracking, good lateral stability, good anti-dive and anti-squat, as well as braking or acceleration with no rear wheel steering. Seventy different versions of this rear suspension were tried before the factory decided on the final version.

BODY INTERIOR

Interior comfort

The steering wheel with SRS airbag includes an electrically adjustable steering column. The total fore/aft adjustment range is 2.36 inches and the column mounted controls move with the wheel. On cars with electric seats with memory, the positions of the steering wheel and the driver's seat headrest are automatically stored with the seat position.

Electric seat heaters were offered as an option for the front seats, which in most cases came upholstered in leather. On cars with leather seating, the front and rear center armrests and headrests were leather covered as well. For improved rear visibility, the driver could lower the rear headrests using a switch in the center console if the rear seat was not occupied.

Upholstery options (M-B Tex, leather and velour) were available in black, blue, dark green, palomino, cream beige, burgundy and gray. The interior paneling matched the seat color. The dash panel colors were limited to five and the headliner to three. Zebrano (Zebra) wood was used for the trim in the center console for most models. On 8-cylinder models, a burled walnut was used.

◁ The base AM/FM radio developed 20 watts per channel into speakers at all four corners with a console mounted fader switch. Radio features also included Dolby noise reduction, adjustable signal search levels, metal tape capacity and a visual tone display. A 100-watt, ten speaker system became available in later years, offered as an option on most models.

The radio unit was wired to the vehicle alarm system, rendering the radio inoperable if removed while the alarm was armed.

Becker Grand Prix electronic radio

Dashboard and controls

◁ The analog-design instrument cluster used large clear white-on-black instruments with orange needles. The fuel, oil pressure, water temperature and fuel economy gauge added to the full complement of instruments. Most warning lights are located across the bottom of the cluster for quick, accurate viewing of critical data.

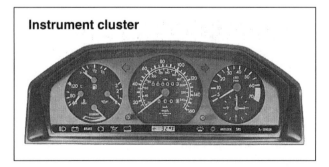

Instrument cluster

◁ Air conditioning was standard equipment and fully integrated with the heating and ventilation components. The automatic climate control system used temperature sensors and automatically selected blower speeds to maintain cabin temperature.

Aerodynamic halogen headlights with a washer-wiper system were standard on all models except the 260E. By selecting the windshield washer with the headlights on, the headlights were washed and wiped.

◁ The temperature sensor for the digital outside temperature display in the instrument console was mounted under the center of the front bumper (**arrow**).

MODEL YEAR NEWS

The W124 E-Class was produced for a ten year run with more than 2 million copies built. It was sold in sedan, station wagon, coupe, convertible and hot-rod versions. It was available with either diesel (turbo and normally-aspirated), 6-cylinder gas, or V-8 gas power.

The information below documents the model's annual product features and technical updates.

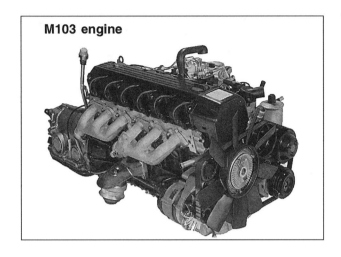

M103 engine

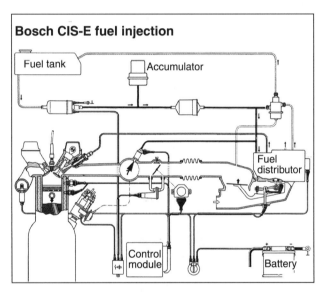

Bosch CIS-E fuel injection

Fuel tank   Accumulator

Fuel distributor

Control module   Battery

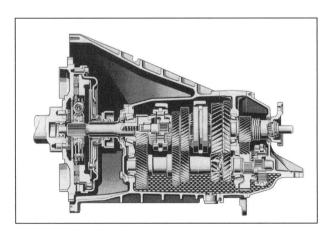

MY86 news

◄ The M103 3.0 liter, single-cam, 6-cylinder gasoline engine was developed specifically for the W124 chassis.

Through the combination of a new cylinder head design, enhanced engine management, and catalytic converter technology, a high compression ratio (9.2: 1) insured good performance, economy, and efficiency.

The M103 engine used an electro-mechanical Bosch CIS-E (KE III) fuel injection system. This system was a technical update of the mechanical K system in use since 1976.

◄ The K in German (C in English) is for continuous fuel injection. When the engine is running, the fuel injectors continuously spray fine atomized fuel into the intake ports of each cylinder. The E indicated electronically controlled mixture adaptation. See **Chapter 7** for detailed information CIS-E.

◄ For the first time since 1972, Mercedes-Benz buyers in the States could order a 6-cylinder 4-door sedan with a manual transmission. This optional 5-speed gearbox featured a direct 1:1 fourth gear and a 0.799 overdrive ratio in fifth. Fewer than three hundred cars were sold with the manual gearbox and the option was dropped after the 1988 model year.

MY87 news

Three new models were offered in 1987; the 260E and two turbo-diesel models.

The 260E was a less expensive version of the 300E. This model used a 2.6 liter M103 engine with a smaller bore (from 88.5 mm to 83 mm) and less horsepower (from 177 hp to 158 hp).

◄ The 300D (sedan) and the 300TD (station wagon) used the OM603 turbo-diesel engine. This engine included many technological refinements for its time. An aluminum cross flow cylinder head, a high compression combustion chamber, and lots of turbo boost pressure yielded 147 hp and 195 ft-lb of torque.

This diesel engines made more low-end torque and higher maximum torque than the 300E gas engine. The toque curve was impressively flat with almost all of the available torque on hand between 1,700 and 4,000 rpm. This 300D was the fastest diesel-powered passenger car in the world, with a top speed of over 125 mph.

The 300D was only available with an automatic transmission and had a 2.65 final drive ratio compared to the 3.07 ratio of the 300E, making for very smooth and quiet high speed touring. Another first for this model was the fuel line and block heaters. EPA mileage ratings were 25 mpg city and 30 mpg highway.

◄ The 300TD wagon used the same hydropneumatic self-leveling system from the earlier W123 chassis 300TD. The self-leveling system maintains rear ride height regardless of vehicle load.

The roofline of the station wagon was almost two inches higher than the sedan, and the standard equipment roof rack brought the overall height increase to three inches.

The 300TD rear seat splits 1/3rd - 2/3rd, allowing for seventy-seven cubic feet of cargo space when folded flat and accommodating objects as long as 9.5 feet. The tailgate hinge design allowed the tailgate to open even if backed close to a wall. The electromechanical closing assist feature drew the tailgate into the closed position once it was in the down position. Standard equipment for the 300TD was identical to the 300E. EPA fuel consumption figures were 23 mpg city and 27 highway for the TD model.

OM603

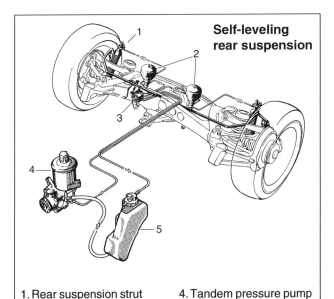

Self-leveling rear suspension

1. Rear suspension strut
2. Pressure accumulators
3. Leveling valve
4. Tandem pressure pump
5. Hydraulic oil reservoir

Unfortunately, the OM603 engine proved to be a disappointment owing to the exhaust system trap oxidizer. The California-mandated oxidizer would physically disintegrate and damage the turbocharger and the engine. Mercedes-Benz did cover these repairs under warranty.

NOTE—

Mercedes-Benz withdrew the diesel models from the North American market because without the oxidizers there could be no diesel sales in California. Since California represented such a large percentage of sales, it made no sense to sell the 300D in the rest of the country.

MY88 news

1988 introduced the 300TE gasoline-powered station wagon and the gasoline-powered coupe. A diesel model was no longer offered.

300CE

◁ The 300CE coupe was the third body variant in the E-Class line. The coupe was designed shorter and lower than the sedan and wagon. The windshield and the rear glass had steeper angles than the sedan and wagon, giving the coupe a streamlined look and a 3% better aerodynamic rating. Color-coordinated side panels further distinguished the 1988 coupe model.

The trunk lid was designed to open a full 90 degrees, with a stop at 60 degrees to protect the trunk contents when it was raining. The coupe did not have a B-pillar, so additional structural reinforcements were added to control body flex and maintain chassis integrity.

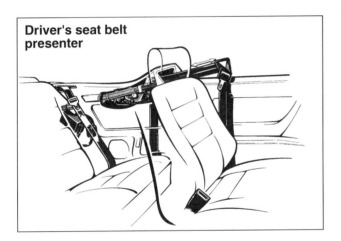

Driver's seat belt presenter

◁ Owing to the long doors on the coupe, a mechanical arm was used to 'present' the seat belt to the driver or front passenger. Once the belt was retrieved, the presenter would retreat into the rear side panel. A sensor in the passenger seat detected whether or not a passenger was present and did not activate the belt presenter when the seat was empty.

As a safety precaution, a vacuum-actuated locking system was employed to lock the seat backs in the upright position when the engine was running and the doors were closed.

Leather seating was standard on the coupe. Velour upholstery was offered as a no-cost option. Another option was the electrically operated rear roll-up sunshade. It was optically transparent, but did a great job in protecting the rear passengers from the full force of the sun.

The 1988 300TE (station wagon) was identical to the discontinued 300TD, excluding the engine. This was the first gasoline powered station wagon to be sold in North America by Mercedes-Benz. Only the automatic transmission was offered in the wagon and the coupe, but the sedan still had a 5-speed manual option. The rear seat of the wagon had three removable headrests.

MY89 news

Changes for the 1989 model year were few. The model line was doing very well and new car sales were brisk.

It was this year that Mercedes-Benz introduced its used car 100,000 miles warranty program, which boosted used car sales.

1989 saw the elimination of the 5-speed manual transmission owing to the low demand.

A small change included a heated windshield washer reservoir bottle (using hot coolant from the engine), and electrically heated spray nozzles.

MY90 news

1990 was the year of the E-Class face lift and technical upgrade.

◁ The 300E 2.6, the 300E, and 300TE received a new exterior look via protective side panels (introduced on the coupe in 1988), body-colored side mirrors and chrome accents on the front, sides and rear.

The interior received newly designed bucket seats with side supports and softer leather. Additional wood trim was used on the dash and doors.

The sunroof and side windows could now be remotely closed using the key in the door and trunk lock. The front windows had a one-touch down 'toll' feature.

1990 E-Class sedan

1990 E-Class station wagon

1990 E-Class coupe

◁ Through the years, the coupe had been the flagship model to demonstrate new technology. In keeping with tradition, the 1990 300CE received the all-new twin overhead cam, 4-valves per cylinder, M104 engine with dynamically adjustable intake cam timing.

With a compression ratio of 10:1, the engine produced 228 hp at 6,200 rpm with a redline of 7,000 rpm. This was a 40 hp 'seat of the pants' increase over the M103 engine.

◁ Diesels returned to the E-Class lineup in 1990 with a 2.5-liter turbocharged diesel engine badged the 300D 2.5 Turbo. The problems faced in 1987 were overcome by a redesigned combustion chamber rather than add-on exhaust pieces.

The new 2.5-liter engine developed 121 hp and 165 ft-lbs of torque at 2,400 rpm. Zero to sixty in 10.7 seconds and a top speed of 121 belied the fuel economy ratings of 27 mpg city and 33 mpg highway.

◁ The only noticeable difference between the 300E and the new 300D was the five-louver air intake (**arrow**) on the front right fender. A diesel-powered wagon was not offered, as the gas version was selling well.

The 300E and 300TE could be ordered with a computer controlled four-wheel-drive system called 4MATIC. The 4MATIC system adapted to changing road conditions by automatically shifting between one of three power transfer modes.

At the first hint of traction loss, the 4MATIC shifts into four-wheel drive by transferring 35% of the drive torque to the front wheels. If the traction loss continues, the front and rear axles are locked (50/50). If additional power transfer is still required, the system will cross-lock all the wheels together. An indicator lamp illuminated when the system was engaged to let the driver know that the car was approaching the limits of adhesion due to changing road conditions.

Passenger side airbag, heated front seats, orthopedic front seat backrest, and an electrically activated rear window shade (introduced on the 1988 300CE) were the available options.

MY91 news

Two traction control systems arrived for 1991. ASR (automatic slip control) was an option on the 300E sedan, 300CE coupe, and 300TE wagon. ASD, an automatic locking differential, could be installed on the 300D 2.5 Turbo diesel.

The ASR option was offered at a cost of $1,975. While it did not equal the traction of the 4MATIC cars, it greatly enhanced winter and wet weather driving.

ASD (*Automatik Sperrdifferential*) was offered at a cost of $1,050. While mechanical limited slip differentials could provide up to 35% locking of the spinning wheel, the ASD system could provide, through electronic controls, 100% locking.

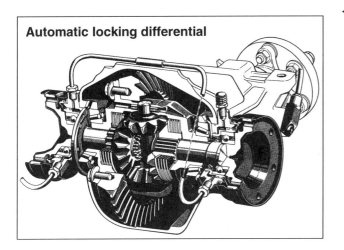

Automatic locking differential

MY92 news

Two special models arrived accommodating V-8 engines; the 400E and the limited edition 500E.

◄ The 400E with its twin-cam 4.2-liter light-alloy V-8 made 268 horsepower with a top speed to 150 mph (electronically limited). Fitting this engine prompted larger front and rear brakes with vented rear discs, modified steering and suspension systems, and structural revisions in the engine compartment and driveshaft tunnel.

With a list price of $55,800 and a $2,600 gas guzzler tax, the 400E came standard with a leather interior, a ten speaker 100-watt sound system, and 8-hole light-alloy wheels.

1992 500E

0058030

1

◀ The 500E 32-valve 5.0 liter V-8 made 315 hp, went zero to sixty in less than six seconds and had a top speed of 150 mph (electronically limited).

The sport suspension package was telegraphed by flared fenders, 8 inch wheels, and 225/55-16 ZR tires.

Almost every option was standard equipment including a Sportline interior with four leather bucket seats. The 500E was fitted with a self-leveling rear suspension, ASR traction control, and dual airbags. Priced at $79,200 with an added $2,600 gas guzzler tax, the 500E was *the* ultra-high-performance 4-door sedan.

Major options for the 1992 model year included a trunk-mounted CD player, a cellular telephone, a passenger side airbag (standard on 500E), ASR traction control (standard on 500E), and a Sportline package.

The Sportline package was available as a $2,000 option. The package included larger wheels with low profile tires, sport suspension with stiffer springs and shocks, and larger sway bars.

E-Class convertible

MY93 news

◄ A convertible and two new engines were the big news for '93. The line now consisted of the 300D 2.5 Turbo; a 300E 2.8 sedan with a new 2.8-liter twin-cam engine; 300E sedan; 300CE coupe; 300TE wagon; and 300CE Cabriolet all having a new 3.2-liter twin-cam 6-cylinder engine. The 400E and 500E rounded out the line.

For 1993, the M104 2.8 liter twin-cam, 4-valve engine replaced the 2.6 liter M103 engine. This engine was only available for one model year. It produced 194 hp, a 40 hp increase from 2.6 liter engine. The new car was badged the 300E 2.8.

The Cabriolet was based on the 300CE coupe, but to retain the rigidity without the roof, the entire chassis had be reinforced.

◄ The Cabriolet featured an integrated rollbar system that automatically deployed within a fraction of a second if the car should start to roll over or in case of a severe front, side or rear impact. The rollbar headrest combination could also be raised and lowered with a switch on the console.

The rear window in the top was made of glass with an electric defroster. Unlatch the convertible top from the windshield, push a button and the fully lined soft-top automatically stowed and all four windows rolled down. This cabriolet had a list price of $76,500.

For 1993, the 400E received a compression ratio boost from 10: 1 to 11: 1. This was possible through advanced engine management systems with knock sensor technology. This horsepower went from 268 up to 275 and improved the fuel mileage enough to remove the 400E from the gas-guzzler list.

NOTE—

In 1993, David E. Davis Jr., of Automobile Magazine chose the 400E as one of the ten best cars in American. Click and Clack, the notorious Cambridge, Massachusetts, public radio personalities considered the 400E the best all-around luxury car built in its day.

1994 E320 sedan

MY94 news

The E-Class lineup was rebadged and the offerings were simplified. Models now included an E320 in all four body styles. The M104 engine in a 3.2 liter version became the base gasoline engine.

Grilles, hoods, headlights, trunk lids and taillamps were all restyled. The new body fittings gave the cars an updated look. The flush grille even mirrored the look of the top-of-the-line S-Class cars.

The 4MATIC models were discontinued.

Mechanically, the 1994 model year was hard to beat, with an engine series that provided greater fuel economy, more power, lower tailpipe emissions and a higher cruising speed.

With increasing economies of scale, Mercedes-Benz decided to lower the prices on the '94 models. The station wagons dropped $8,000, the basic E320 went from $49,900 to $42,500, and the E420 from $56,400 to $51,000. This price reduction was a reaction to slowing sales. The effect was immediate with a 25% sales increase for 1994. Additionally, most of the models in the E-Class lineup were no longer subject to the gas-guzzler tax, making the prices even more attractive.

1

MY95 news

Only a handful of equipment changes marked the 1995 models, as Mercedes-Benz forged ahead with the introduction of the new E-Class (W210 Chassis) for '96.

The limited-production, high-performance E500 sedan was dropped.

1995 E300 Diesel Sedan

The E300 Diesel sedan arrived in the spring of 1994 as an early '95 model, with a new 134 horsepower 3.0 liter diesel 6-cylinder engine. This completely new 6-cylinder engine was developed using the same four-valve technology as the gasoline powered engines, allowing it to meet the very stringent fifty-state diesel emission standards.

The E300 Diesel was the only diesel powered passenger car clean enough to be sold in all 50 states. The E300 Diesel also had the longest cruising range of any automobile sold in the United States: With its 24 gallon fuel tank and a 32 mpg EPA highway rating, the car could go 750 miles between fill-ups.

Chapter 2

Buying an E-Class

BEFORE YOU BUY

Preparing for the purchase

One important service your repair shop can provide is guidance in purchasing a used car. More than just looking at the car during a prepurchase inspection, they can give you technical advice regarding the good model years, why you might consider one model over another, and the things to look for while you are out kicking tires.

Proper care and feeding of a Mercedes-Benz can be an expensive proposition. It makes the most sense to put that money, time and energy into a good car up front.

Once you have made a selection, count on a prepurchase inspection to reveal *most* of the repairs the car needs and what it will cost to make the car right. Once a dollar amount is tallied, see if the total outlay keeps the car within your budget.

As a general rule, try to buy the newest car you can afford with the lowest mileage and the best maintenance records. It is usually a mistake to buy a bargain-priced Mercedes, thinking you will fix the car up as you go. In the long run, this is probably the most expensive way to purchase a car.

◁ If your choice is between a perfect high mileage 1988 with complete service history that only needs windshield wiper blades, or a 1991 model that came from an auction without any records and you can't inspect it before you buy it, go for the 1988 model. The long term satisfaction from buying a used Mercedes-Benz logically instead of emotionally will ultimately be the most rewarding.

Finding the car

Spend the time looking for a good car and don't settle for anything you wouldn't want to live with for ten or fifteen years. It is a fact that Mercedes-Benz buyers are long term owners.

Finding the E-Class you want to buy will take some effort. Going from lot to lot takes time and energy. Going through the newspaper classified advertisements also takes time and energy. There are trade-offs between good price and ease of purchase.

◄ Mercedes-Benz dealers have some of the best used cars available, usually at the highest prices, with the best warranties.

Classified car ads, on the other hand, give you much better pricing, at the cost of time, trouble, and many unknowns.

If you are not familiar with E-Class cars, be sure to read Chapter 1 of this book before venturing out. It would also be beneficial to visit your local Mercedes retail dealer and look at the cars they have for sale. This will give you a benchmark against which to compare other cars. Look at some new cars, and then the used cars. This should establish a scale of quality in your mind.

◄ Owners will often advertise their cars in local newspapers and you can occasionally find excellent, low mileage, well maintained cars. This method puts you more on your own than any other, so beware.

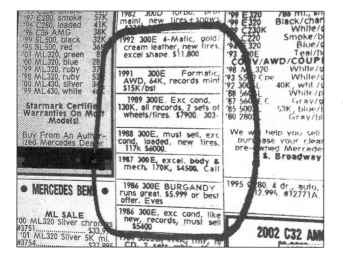

Private sale inspection

Once you have found a car that merits consideration, the inspection process begins.

When you first see the car, try and take it all in. The first impression is very important and usually takes into account the paint, the wheels, the chrome trim, the moldings, the grill and the plastic lenses.

While it is possible to find a well-maintained E-Class with a shabby appearance, it would be a rare event. Unlike some other situations, first impressions do count when buying a car. If the car cries out "dog", politely move on.

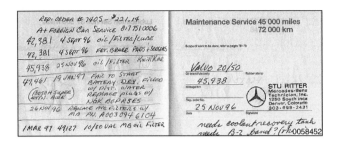

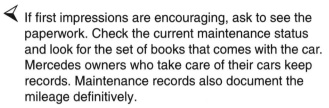

If first impressions are encouraging, ask to see the paperwork. Check the current maintenance status and look for the set of books that comes with the car. Mercedes owners who take care of their cars keep records. Maintenance records also document the mileage definitively.

How many keys does the owner have? There should be two master keys and, depending on the year of the car, two valet keys along with the small wallet key. If there are wheel locks, check that the key is available.

After looking at the exterior, check the interior. Are the mats clean and the carpets underneath like new? Most Mercedes owners keep mats on the floor to protect the original factory carpeting. Look at the upholstery, the dash, the headliner, the ashtrays, the buttons, knobs and wood. Compare their condition to the clean examples you have looked at before. Is the interior clean and odor free? Is the trunk clean, odor and moisture free? Are all the required accessories in place (jack, lug wrench, small tools)? Are the spare wheel and tire properly held in place?

You should use your nose not only on the interior of the car but in the engine compartment as well. Technicians often smell the engine oil for a scent of fuel, or ATF for a burnt odor. So put on the latex gloves, open the hood and examine the engine compartment. How does it look? Are there any oil leaks? Is there any evidence the engine compartment was recently cleaned? While the engine may look nice and clean from the top, sometimes you can look up from the bottom and see half an inch of muck.

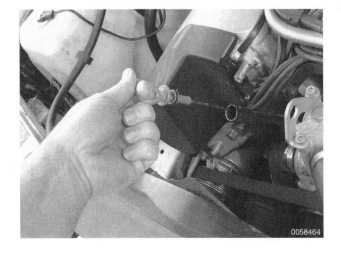

Pull the dipstick, take off the oil filler cap, and use your nose again. Does the oil look and smell fresh without any additional odors? How does the interior of the valve cover smell? Is it a rank odor or does it smell like fresh oil? Are there any signs of emulsified oil on the filler cap? Is the oil at the correct level?

Pull the transmission dip stick out of the filler tube and sniff. It is very important for the transmission oil to have a fresh clean odor and be a bright clear red color. If there is any hint of burnt oil, there is a good chance there is expensive transmission repair in order.

If there is an auxiliary hydraulic system for self-leveling or the 4MATIC system, unscrew the fluid reservoir cap and smell the oil. Again, it should smell clean and oily without any burnt odor.

2

Look into the radiator expansion tank mounted on the passenger side, inner fender. Are there any signs of engine oil? The 6-cylinder engines used in the E-Class cars are known for head gasket failures that leak engine oil into the cooling system. If any engine oil is visible it means either the head gasket is leaking now or it was repaired and the cooling system was not properly cleaned.

◁ Mercedes-Benz has specified the use of its own coolant for many years. It is important to use only the Mercedes-Benz approved product in the cooling system to maintain the pH of the coolant and prevent damage to both aluminum and plastic components. If the maintenance book is available, check to see if coolant changes are up to date.

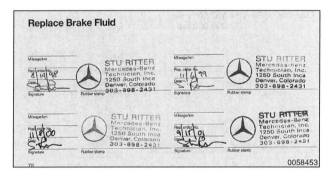

◁ Does the brake fluid look clear or is it dark? Proper Mercedes maintenance requires changing the brake fluid every one or two years, depending on year of manufacture. Dark fluid indicates poor brake system maintenance. Again, look in the maintenance booklet, if available, for evidence of regular services.

If the maintenance booklet is missing or out of date, there should be some other evidence, such as a collection of shop work invoices.

Test-drive

◁ Peel off the gloves, it's time for a test-drive. This is where the time you spent looking at those dealership cars comes into play. You have test-driven some newer cars and know what they feel like. How does your proposed purchase feel?

Is it as tight and crisp as the dealership examples? Are there any noises when going over bumps and railroad tracks? Any irregular noises usually indicates worn suspension components.

Are all of the instruments working properly? Test every switch, knob and lever for function and feel while you drive. From the time you start the engine until you finish your test-drive, is there any smoke visible from the tailpipe or engine compartment? Is there any vibration that was not present on the previously tested cars, either from the road while moving or while sitting with the engine in gear or neutral?

Does the transmission shift smoothly, without delay? Do the odometers seem to read the same mileage during your test drive? Does the tilt function for the sunroof work and is its operation smooth and quiet?

When you return from your test-drive engage the owner in conversation about any problems you found and possible provisions for righting them.

When five or ten minutes have passed, stick your head under the car to check for leaks. While some leaks show up when a car cools down overnight, there are some that only show up right after driving. If everything on this candidate has checked out, it's time for the professional prepurchase inspection. If you owned a Mercedes before, you probably have a shop in mind. If not, the following are some suggestions to help you pick a shop.

Finding a shop

Ask friends for a recommendation. If one repair shop gets mentioned repeatedly, that shop would be a good place to begin. You can also contact the Mercedes-Benz Club of America to ask for recommendations from local members. If you have Internet access, the iATN (international automotive technicians network) has a public site called Shop Finder at www.iatn.net that may also be helpful.

Once you have decided on a shop, get to know the shop manager and allow him or her to get to know you. At the same time you are interviewing the shop manager, he/she is getting the chance to talk to a new customer and explain shop policies and procedures. In your mind, you are deciding if you want this shop to work on your new possession.

Ask to look around the shop, consider the working conditions. Is the shop well-lit with clean working areas or are the technicians working in dark corners with junk piled high on their benches? The working environment will in part establish how your new prize will be cared for. Clean, neat, orderly, well-lit shops tend to do clean, neat, orderly work.

◀ What technical information does the shop have available for its technicians? Is there a complete set of printed Mercedes manuals and a complete service microfiche system? Do they have the Electronic Workshop Information System (WIS)? Without proper technical information, it is almost impossible for a shop to properly repair or maintain your new purchase.

2

Prepurchase inspection

Even if the car looks spectacular, a prepurchase inspection should always be done, but never where you are buying the car. If the inspecting shop expects to service the car after the purchase, they will usually try to find every little thing the car needs.

Most shops schedule between one and two hours for an inspection. It is well worth the charge if the inspection keeps you from purchasing the wrong car.

One actual shop story involves a customer bringing in a beautiful E420 with 40,000 miles. It was out of warranty based on time rather than mileage and was a private sale. The car was spectacular to look at with flawless paint and interior, near new tires and a perfect maintenance history. With three technicians looking at the car, nothing could be found wrong, and the price was right.

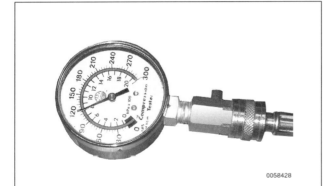

◀ The technician commenced with a compression test. The customer complained about having to pay for a compression test on a car in such perfect condition. The first three cylinders were a perfect 190 psi each, but the fourth was an inadequate 120 psi.

With a prepurchase inspection, you are paying for the experience of the shop. These shops repair and test-drive Mercedes all day long. They have developed an intimate feel for the cars and they know how they should look and feel. Besides looking for body damage, broken parts and taking a compression test, you are getting the benefit of years of experience with the particular model you are buying. At times, a technician only needs to drive a car around the block to find some glaring fault.

Aftermarket warranties

Aftermarket warranties are handled through warranty insurance companies which vary from company to company. If you know a technician, it would be a good idea to have him / her read the warranty to see exactly what you are paying for. Assumptions about what a warranty will cover due to salesman's hype and fast talk need to be examined.

 Warranties are closely guarded profit centers for dealers and salesmen, both for new and used cars. Most Mercedes-Benz salesmen receive commission for selling warranty programs.

Used car lots specializing in Mercedes would be the next step down the ladder. Here you would find a large selection of cars and perhaps service facilities. Aftermarket warranties are usually available but they must be read carefully to see exactly what is covered, and what is considered normal wear and tear.

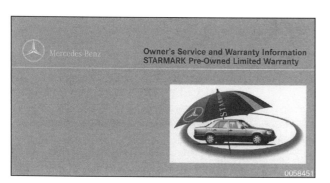

AFTER YOU BUY

Now that you own an E-Class, what do you expect from it and what does it expect from you?

Reading material

First things first—read the publications that came with the car. After reading the books, you will have a clearer understanding of what your new purchase will require.

◄ There should be a pile of books in a black zippered case. The most important one is the owner's manual. If for some reason the owner's manual is missing, you can purchase one from MBUSA publications.

NOTE—
You can order any available Mercedes-Benz publication directly from MBUSA at 800-FOR-MERC (800-367-6372).

Books, publications and identification related items included with the original car are:

- ID card
- Owner's manual
- Maintenance booklet
- Owner's service and warranty information (booklet)
- Radio operation guide (booklet)
- Theft deterrent radio identification card
- Supplemental Restraint System (booklet)
- Roadside assistance book
- Car care guide (booklet)
- Factory Approved Service Products (pamphlet)

If you are interested in maintaining the car yourself, or just want to be more knowledgeable about servicing and repairing your car, MBUSA publications has a CD-ROM that contains all of the manuals (owner, maintenance, service) for the E-Class. It covers all years and models of the E-Class.

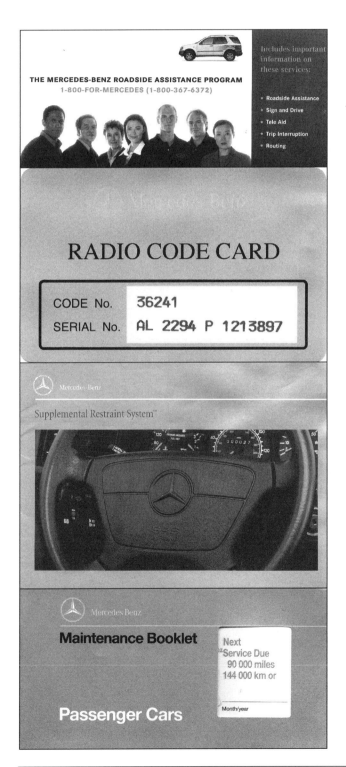

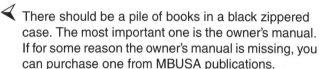

Roadside assistance

The roadside assistance book explains the free 24-hour roadside assistance program. 800-222-0100 is the telephone number that can fetch a can of gas, get a flat tire changed or jump start a dead battery. This service is available within a 30 mile radius of 96 percent of the retail Mercedes dealerships in the US. Roadside Assistance is available to all Mercedes-Benz cars, no matter how old it is or who the driver is. The driver just signs for the service and drives away without any charge. Trip planning is also available through Roadside Assistance without charge.

NOTE—

Many times a breakdown can be fixed at the breakdown site. The charges will be a $25 service call fee plus labor at 1.5 times the dealer's hourly rate with a minimum charge of thirty minutes. If the breakdown is serious and cannot be repaired on site, the program will arrange for towing to the nearest Mercedes dealership. If the car is under warranty there are further benefits such as trip interruption protection that includes a reimbursement for incurred expenses.

Repair and service

Repair shops can be broken down into three categories:

• Mercedes-Benz retail dealership
• Independent Mercedes specialist
• All makes-all models repair shop

Mercedes-Benz dealerships

Mercedes-Benz retail dealerships install original Mercedes-Benz parts and these parts carry a one-year warranty honored at any Mercedes-Benz retailer in the US. The dealer will have the most up to date technical information available and their technicians are factory trained and certified. The dealer is required to maintain a high level of special tools, which helps get the repair work done efficiently and correctly.

In many cases the dealer is the ultimate solution to Mercedes-Benz car care, but the dealership is not always the right place for everyone. Most dealerships are large places that perform many functions. They are involved in new and used car sales, retail and wholesale parts, leasing, financing, car preparation and perhaps even a body shop. There is usually layer upon layer of people between the car owner and the technician, so you rarely talk directly to the person who will be repairing your car. It is also rare to take a test-drive with the technician so you can point out the problems directly and the technician can experience them.

Mercedes-Benz Independent specialists

Independent specialists service only Mercedes. These Mercedes-only specialty shops work on Mercedes all day long and that familiarity will save you time and money

The Independent will usually have most, if not all, of the factory repair information available to them. They normally use a mix of original Mercedes parts and German parts supplied by the aftermarket. Parts suppliers to Daimler-Chrysler often sell the same parts in the aftermarket and these parts are available to the independent shop at a price advantage.

Independent repair shops tend to own a good amount of special tools, based on the different problems they see. While dealerships handle new car running problems and warranty situations, the independent shops deal with unit repair and rebuilding of items like transmissions, steering gear, engines and suspensions.

Mercedes-Benz factory technician training is unavailable to independent repair shops. Most factory training is based on new vehicles. As the cars age, they have different sets of problems. This is where the good independent Mercedes shop shines.

All makes-all models

The all makes-all models shops that work on whatever comes in the door will have little if any factory information. Their references are mostly aftermarket information sources.

These shops will not be familiar with the good Mercedes parts sources and they will count on their American parts houses to find the pieces they need. While NAPA, AutoZone and others might work well for American cars, it's not the best choice for Mercedes-Benz.

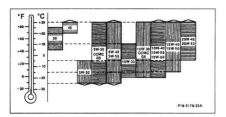

Factory Approved Service Products

Choosing the right fuels, oils, fluids, and greases in your Mercedes-Benz will keep your car running right for a long time.

 Factory Approved Service Products was a pamphlet that explained which liquids to use in your Mercedes. The approved list is no longer used for engine oils but is a useful reference guide.

It went into detail on oil viscosity and listed the oils approved by Mercedes-Benz. Along with an explanation of fuels and oils, the pamphlet covered greases, brake fluid, hydraulic oils, gear oils, and transmission fluids.

When choosing oil and fluids, brand names should rule your choice. In certain instances, only Mercedes products can be used, such as engine coolant.

Fuel

All gasoline powered E-Class cars require premium unleaded fuel at sea level. Above 5,000 feet, you can use the middle grade of gasoline because the effective compression ratio is lower than at sea level. Brand name fuel from high volume stations would be a best choice.

Coolant

The only approved coolant in the US is Mercedes-Benz coolant. Most coolants are chemically very basic with a pH range of 9.5 to 10.5, the Mercedes coolant with its 7.0 pH is unique. A pH of 7.0 means the coolant is neutral, being neither basic nor acidic. This is an important consideration when the cooling system has plastic components.

Both top and bottom radiator tanks are made of plastic and they tend to live much longer if Mercedes coolant is used.

Chapter 3

Maintenance

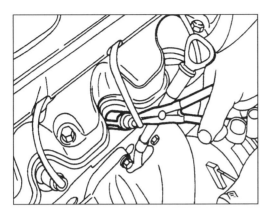

3

Continued on next page

GENERAL

The information given in this chapter includes the routine checks and maintenance steps that are both required by Mercedes-Benz under the terms of the vehicle warranty protection and recommended by Mercedes-Benz to ensure long and reliable vehicle operation.

Scheduled service

There are two services that should be carried out periodically during the life of your Mercedes-Benz.

- Lubrication service
- Maintenance service

Lubrication service is the basic routine maintenance done at every 7,500 miles (12,000 km) for gasoline models or every 5,000 miles (8,000 km) for diesel models. This service consists of an engine oil and filter change along with a few other lubrication items and visual inspections.

Maintenance service is a comprehensive maintenance and inspection service, including spark plug replacement and fluid replacement. Under normal use, this service is performed every 15,000 miles or 24,000 km. The maintenance service is organized logically in this chapter based on the vehicle layout:

- Interior
- Body
- Wheels, tires, and brakes
- Underside of car
- Engine compartment
- Trunk

NOTE—
- *In case of severe operating conditions or heavy use, mainly in city traffic or over short distances (less than 5 miles per trip), frequent mountain driving, poor roads, dusty and muddy conditions, trailer towing or hard driving, it may be necessary to carry out maintenance work at shorter intervals according to the following schedule:*

- *Oil and filter change: Half the recommended interval.*

- *Automatic transmission: Fluid change (without filter change) every 15,000 miles (24,000 km).*

- *Tires: Inspect more frequently.*

- *Air cleaner: Clean or replace as required.*

3

FLUID AND LUBRICANT SPECIFICATIONS

Fluid and lubricant specifications for Mercedes-Benz E-Class cars are listed in **Table a**.

> **WARNING—**
> The use of non-approved fluids may impair performance and reliability, and may void extended warranty coverage.

Table a. Fluids and lubricants

Application	Fluid specification
Engine	
Engine oil, gasoline engines	Multi-grade engine oil API SH / SJ
Engine oil, diesel engines	Multi-grade engine oil API CF-4 or CG-4
Engine coolant	Factory labeled antifreeze, MB part no. Q 1 03 0002
Transmissions	
Manual transmission oil	Factory labeled manual transmission oil or Dexron III / Mercon ATF, MB part no. 000 989 26 03
Automatic transmission fluid (drain and fill)	Factory labeled ATF or Dexron III / Mercon ATF, MB part no. 001 989 21 03
Differential, front or rear	
Non-limited slip (open type) rear differential and 4MATIC front differential oil	MIL-GL5 Hypoid (SAE 90 or 85-90) gear oil. Synthetic oil not approved for use
Limited slip and 4MATIC rear differential oil	Factory labeled oil only, MB part no. 001 989 17 03
Transfer case, 4MATIC	
Transfer case oil	Dexron III / Mercon ATF
Power steering	
Power steering fluid	Factory labeled power steering oil or Mobil ATF D, MB part no. Q 1 46 0001
Brakes	
Brake fluid (change every two years)	SAE DOT 4 Plus, MB part no. 000 989 08 07
Hydraulic system	
Level control Automatic locking differential (ASD) All wheel drive (4MATIC)	MB part no. 000 989 91 03

Engine oil

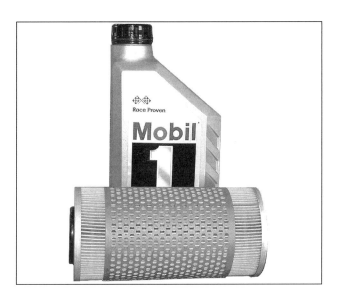

◁ Engine oil is undoubtedly the most important lubricant in your vehicle. Whether you choose mineral-based or synthetic oil, be sure to choose a brand name oil of the correct viscosity and SAE grade.

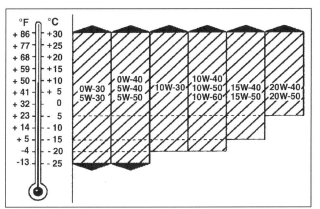

◁ Illustration shows engine oil viscosity (SAE grade) vs. ambient operating temperature range for Mercedes-Benz engines covered in this manual.

Brake fluid

◁ Mercedes-Benz recommends using the factory labeled brake fluid (Mercedes-Benz part no. 000 989 08 07 10). ATE DOT 4 Plus brake fluids may also be used.

Brake fluid absorbs moisture easily. Moisture in the brake fluid lowers the fluid's boiling point, which affects brake performance and reliability. This is why brake fluid should be flushed from the system every one or two years, depending on year of manufacture.

When replacing or adding brake fluid, use only new fluid from a previously unopened container. Do not use brake fluid that has been bled from the system, even if it is brand new. Use only DOT 4 Plus brake fluid.

3

0058423

Engine coolant (antifreeze)

◁ Mercedes-Benz recommends a 50 / 50 mixture of distilled water and Mercedes-Benz anticorrosion / antifreeze. Antifreeze raises the boiling point and lowers the freezing point of the coolant. It also contains additives that help prevent cooling system corrosion.

The water must not be too hard. Usually tap water meets this requirement. If in doubt, substitute distilled water. When mixed at the 50 / 50 ratio the coolant protects the engine against freezing down to −37°C (−35°F). It also raises the boiling point of the mixture.

NOTE—
In very hot climates the mixture can be lowered to 45% antifreeze and 55% water to improve the heat transfer capacity of the mixture.

The corrosion protection of antifreeze diminishes over time and with elevated temperatures.

Coolant should be flushed after a maximum of three years.

Differential gear oil

0058607

◁ On non-limited slip (open type) differentials, Mercedes-Benz recommends using Hypoid gear oil with a viscosity of SAE 90, MIL-GL5 specification. Alternatively, 85W-90 is also approved.

If differential is a limited slip type, a special hypoid oil must be used. To determine if differential is a limited slip type, check identification tag bolted to right lower side of differential (as viewed from rear of car). If it is a limited slip unit, tag will read *Nur Spezial Oel Sperrdifferential* (only special oil, limited slip differential).

NOTE—
On 4MATIC models, the rear differential is a limited-slip type and the front differential is an open type.

CAUTION—
If special hypoid oil is not used in a limited slip differential, the clutches will be severely damaged.

0058650

Power steering fluid

◄ Mercedes-Benz recommends using the factory labeled power steering fluid. The only other approved fluid is Mobil ATF D.

Experience has shown that replacing the fluid in the reservoir greatly increases the service life of the power steering system, including the power steering pump, the steering gearbox, and the fluid lines.

Transmission fluid, automatic

Mercedes-Benz recommends ATF designated Dexron III / Mercon, or preferably the factory labeled automatic transmission oil.

Transmission fluid, manual

The manual transmissions installed in the E-Class cars are filled with MB manual transmission oil and this oil should be used when draining and filling the transmission. Dexron III / Mercon ATF can be substituted if the MB factory labeled oil is not available.

LUBRICATION SERVICE

Lubrication service consists of the maintenance items listed in **Table b**. This is the basic routine maintenance done at every 7,500 miles (12,000 km) for gasoline models or every 5,000 miles (8,000 km) for diesel models.

NOTE—

• *The use of engine oil additives is not recommended.*

• *Mercedes-Benz is constantly upgrading recommended maintenance procedures and requirements. The information contained here is as accurate as possible at the time of publication. If there is any doubt about what procedures apply to a specific model or model year, or what intervals should be followed, remember that an authorized Mercedes-Benz dealer has the latest information on factory-recommended maintenance.*

3

Table b. Lubrication service

Maintenance item	Tools required	New parts / supplies required	Warm engine required
Engine compartment maintenance			
Engine oil, check level			
Engine oil and filter, change	✳	✳	✳
Throttle linkage, lubricate (as applicable)		✳	
Battery electrolyte level, check (except maintenance-free batteries)		✳	
Hood latch and safety catch, lubricate		✳	
Additional maintenance			
Tire pressures, check and correct	✳		

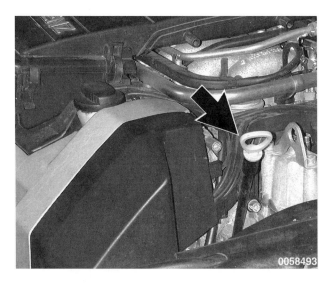

0058493

Engine oil level, checking and correcting

◁ Engine oil level is checked at dipstick (**arrow**) in engine block.

– Check oil level with car on a level surface, after engine has been stopped for at least 2 minutes.

– Check level by pulling out dipstick and wiping it clean. Reinsert it fully, wait 5 seconds, and withdraw it again.

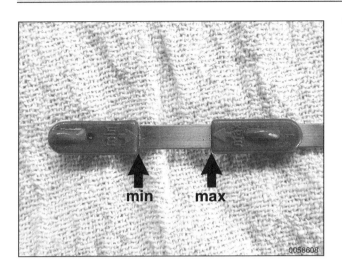

◁ Oil level is correct if it is between **max** and **min** at end of dipstick.

◁ If oil level is below **max** mark on dipstick, add oil through filler cap on top of cylinder head. Add only amount needed to bring oil level to **max** mark on dipstick, using an oil of correct viscosity and grade. Too much oil can be just as harmful as too little.

Engine oil and filter change (M103 6-cylinder gasoline engine)

◁ A complete oil change requires new oil, a new oil filter kit, an oil filter wrench (cap style, 74 mm), and metric sized hand tools.

NOTE—
If using a "fast-lube" service facility for oil changes, ask the technician to hand-start and torque the engine oil drain plug using hand tools. Power tools can strip the threads of the plug and the oil pan.

− Run engine for a few minutes to warm engine oil. Shut engine off. Be sure car is on level ground.

− Place oil drain pan under rear of engine.

◁ Working at rear of engine, unscrew spin-on filter approximately one-quarter turn to allow oil to drain from filter.

– Unscrew filter completely and discard.

– Clean mating surface on oil filter mounting flange.

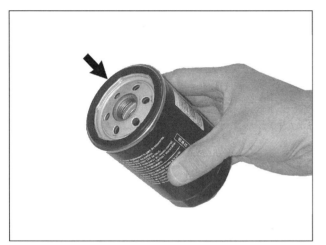

◁ Lightly lubricate gasket (**arrow**) on new filter.

– Screw on new filter until gasket contacts mounting flange.

– Tighten filter an additional ¼ turn (90°) (approximately 20 Nm / 15 ft-lb).

– Place drain pan under oil drain plug. On cars with 4MATIC, place drain pan under drain plug in larger of two oil pans.

◁ Using a 13 mm socket or box wrench, loosen drain plug. Remove plug by hand and let oil drain. On cars with 4MATIC, loosen drain plug only on larger of two oil pans. Remove plug by hand and let oil drain.

> **WARNING—**
> *Pull the loose plug away from the hole quickly to avoid being scalded by hot oil. It will run out quickly when the plug is removed. If possible, use gloves to protect your hands.*

– When oil flow has diminished to an occasional drip, reinstall drain plug with a new metal sealing washer and tighten plug.

Tightening torque

Engine oil drain plug to oil pan . . . . 25 Nm (18 ft-lb)

– Refill crankcase with oil.

Oil and filter change capacity

M103 engine . . . . 6.0 liters (6.34 qts)

M103 engine with 4MATIC . . . . 6.5 liters (6.87 qts)

– Allow engine to run for a few minutes, then check for leaks at drain plug and oil filter. Stop engine, wait 2 minutes, then recheck oil level on dipstick.

Engine oil and filter change (M104 6-cylinder gasoline engine)

A complete oil change requires new oil, a new oil filter kit, an oil filter wrench, and metric sized hand tools.

CAUTION—
If using a "fast-lube" service facility for oil changes, ask the technician to hand-start and torques the engine oil drain plug using hand tools. Power tools can strip the threads of the plug and the oil pan.

– Run engine for a few minutes to warm engine oil. Shut engine off. Be sure car is on level ground.

◀ Working in left rear of engine compartment, unscrew oil filter cap using 74 mm oil filter cap wrench.

– Remove old filter element from housing and discard.

◀ Replace O-ring on threaded filter cap.

3

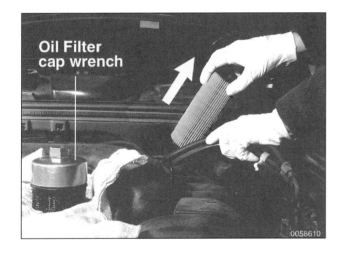

Oil Filter cap wrench

0058610

0058612

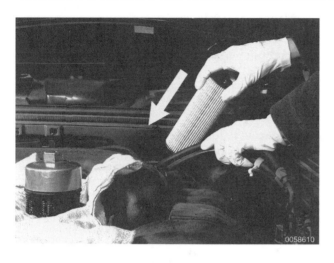

◁ Insert new oil filter element into threaded cap and then insert cap with filter and tighten.

Tightening torque

Oil filter cap to filter housing. . . . . 20 Nm (15 ft-lb)

– Working underneath car, place drain pan under oil pan drain plug.

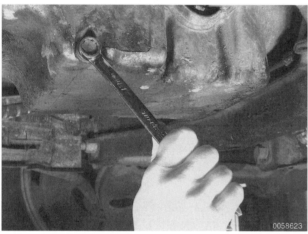

◁ Using a 13 mm socket or box wrench, loosen oil pan drain plug. Remove plug by hand and let oil drain.

> **WARNING—**
> *Pull the loose plug away from the hole quickly to avoid being scalded by hot oil. It will run out quickly when the plug is removed. If possible, use gloves to protect your hands.*

– When oil flow has diminished to an occasional drip, reinstall drain plug with a new metal sealing washer and tighten plug.

Tightening torque

Engine oil drain plug to oil pan . . . . 25 Nm (18 ft-lb)

– Refill crankcase with oil.

Oil and filter change capacity

M104 engine . . . . 7.5 liters (7.93 qts)

– Allow engine to run for a few minutes, then check for leaks at drain plug and oil filter. Stop engine, wait 2 minutes, then recheck oil level on dipstick.

Engine oil and filter change (M119 V-8 gasoline engine)

A complete oil change requires new oil, a new oil filter kit, an oil filter wrench, and metric hand tools.

> **CAUTION—**
> *If using a "fast-lube" service facility for oil changes, ask the technician to hand-start and torques the engine oil drain plug using hand tools. Power tools can strip the threads of the plug and the oil pan.*

3

– Run engine for a few minutes to warm engine oil. Shut engine off. Be sure car is on level ground.

– Working underneath car, place drain pan under oil drain plug.

◀ Disconnect flexible air duct (**arrows**) and remove to access oil filter cover.

◀ Using 13 mm socket, loosen center screw and remove screw together with oil filter cover.

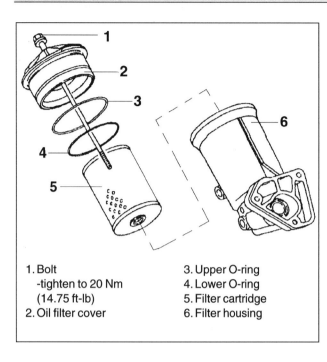

1. Bolt
   -tighten to 20 Nm
   (14.75 ft-lb)
2. Oil filter cover
3. Upper O-ring
4. Lower O-ring
5. Filter cartridge
6. Filter housing

◄ Remove and discard filter cartridge and two O-rings under oil filter cover.

– Using socket or box wrench, loosen drain plug at oil pan. Remove plug by hand and let oil drain into pan.

> **WARNING—**
> *Pull loose plug away from hole quickly to avoid being scalded by hot oil. It will run out quickly when the plug is removed. If possible, use gloves to protect your hands.*

– When oil flow has diminished to an occasional drip, reinstall drain plug with new metal sealing washer and tighten plug.

Tightening torque

Engine oil drain plug to oil pan . . . . 40 Nm (30 ft-lb)

– Working at oil filter housing:
  • Lubricate and install new O-rings.
  • Install new filter cartridge with large rubber seal on cartridge pointing down.
  • Install oil filter cover and tighten center screw.

Tightening torque

Oil filter cover to filter housing . . . . 20 Nm (15 ft-lb)

– Refill crankcase with oil. Approximate oil capacity is listed below. Use dipstick to check correct oil level.

Oil and filter change capacity

M119 engine . . . . 8 liters (8.45 qts)

– Allow engine to run for a few minutes to circulate new oil, then check for leaks at drain plug and oil filter. Stop engine, wait 2 minutes, then recheck oil level.

Engine oil and filter change (diesel engines)

A complete oil change requires new oil, a new oil filter kit, an oil filter wrench and metric hand tools.

> **CAUTION—**
> *If using a "fast-lube" service facility for oil changes, ask the technician to hand-start and torque the engine oil drain plug using hand tools. Power tools can strip the threads of the plug and the oil pan.*

– Run engine for a few minutes to warm engine oil. Shut engine off. Be sure car is on level ground.

– Working underneath car, place drain pan under oil drain plug.

> **NOTE—**
> *On turbocharged engines, it is not necessary to drain the oil from the oil cooler.*

◁ On cars with one-piece filter cover, unscrew nuts (**arrows**) and remove cover.

◁ On cars with two-piece filter cover, unscrew center return pipe (**arrow**) and remove. Then unscrew oil filter cover retaining nuts and remove cover.

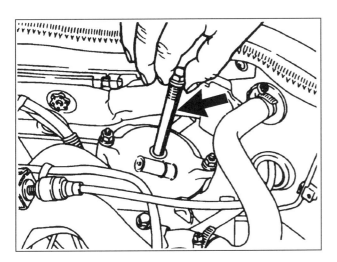

– Using a socket or box wrench, loosen drain plug at oil pan. Remove plug by hand and let oil drain into pan.

> **WARNING—**
> *Pull loose plug away from hole quickly to avoid being scalded by hot oil. It will run out quickly when the plug is removed. If possible, use gloves to protect your hands.*

– When oil flow has diminished to an occasional drip, reinstall drain plug with a new metal sealing washer and tighten plug.

Tightening torques

Engine oil drain plug to oil pan
M12 x 1.5 . . . . 30 Nm (22 ft-lb)
M14 x 1.5 . . . . 25 Nm (18 ft-lb)

> **NOTE—**
> *Slide an open end metric wrench over the threads to determine drain plug size*

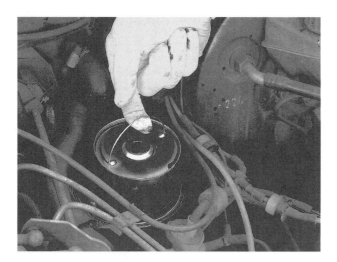

◁ Working at oil filter housing, remove and replace filter cartridge.

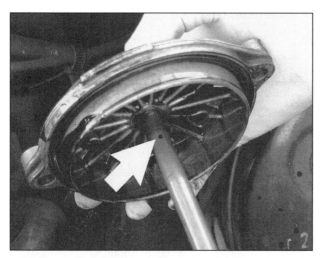

◁ Check oil hole in oil tube (**arrow**). If blocked, clean by hand. If possible, use compressed air to verify that tube is clear.

– Lubricate and install new O-ring into oil filter cover.

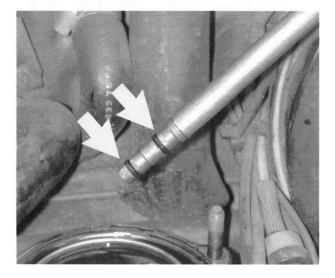

◁ Examine O-rings at bottom of tube (**arrows**) for cracks or hardening. Replace O-rings if required.

– Install oil filter cover and tighten retaining nuts and center return pipe (where applicable).

Tightening torques

Oil filter cover to oil filter housing . . . . 25 Nm (18 ft-lb)

Return pipe to filter cover . . . . 25 Nm (18 ft-lb)

– Refill engine crankcase with oil. Approximate oil capacity is listed below. Use dipstick to check correct oil level.

Oil and filter change capacity

OM602 engine. .7 liters (7.40 qts)

OM603 engine. .8 liters (8.45 qts)

OM606 engine. .7 liters (7.40 qts)

– Allow engine to run for a few minutes to circulate new oil, then check for leaks at drain plug and oil filter. Stop engine and recheck oil level.

3

Throttle linkage, lubricating

– Where necessary, remove air cleaner to access throttle linkage.

◁ Lubricate pivots of control shafts, control levers, throttle linkage joints and control cables (**arrow**) using ATF (M119 engine shown).

– Check control shafts, control levers, guide levers, ball sockets, bowden cable, and throttle linkage for smooth operation and possible wear.

NOTE—

On vehicles with Electronic Accelerator (EA), equipped with ASR, the linkage should only be moved when the ignition is off to avoid setting a Diagnostic Trouble Code (DTC) in the control module memory.

Battery electrolyte level, checking and correcting

> **WARNING—**
> • *Wear goggles, rubber gloves, and a rubber apron when working around batteries and battery acid (electrolyte).*
>
> • *Battery acid contains sulfuric acid and can cause skin irritation and burning. If acid is spilled on your skin or clothing, flush the area at once with large quantities of water. If electrolyte gets into your eyes, flush them with large quantities of clean water for several minutes and call a physician.*
>
> • *Batteries that are being charged or are fully charged give off explosive hydrogen gas. Keep sparks and open flames away. Do not smoke.*

> **CAUTION—**
> • *Prior to disconnecting the battery, read the battery disconnection cautions given at the front of this manual.*
>
> • *Disconnecting the battery cables may erase fault codes stored in ECM memory.*
>
> • *Always disconnect the negative (–) battery cable first and reconnect it last. Cover the battery post with an insulating material whenever the cable is removed.*
>
> • *Never reverse the battery cables. Even a momentary wrong connection can damage the alternator or other electrical components.*
>
> • *Battery cables may be the same color. Label cable before removing.*

On E- Class cars with V-8 engines, the battery is located in the trunk on the passenger side. All 6-cylinder models have the battery in the engine compartment behind the bulkhead.

NOTE—
Check fluid level more often when outside temperatures are high.

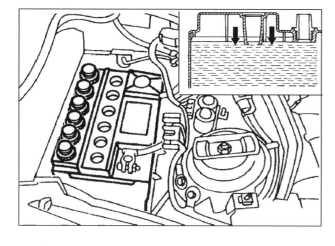

◁ Unscrew or pull out all battery caps.

– Check fluid level and correct if necessary. Fluid level should be at bottom of filler opening (as shown in inset). Do not overfill.

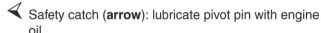

Hood latch and safety catch, lubricating

Lubricate hood safety catch and hood lock. See Illustrations below.

◀ Safety catch (**arrow**): lubricate pivot pin with engine oil.

3

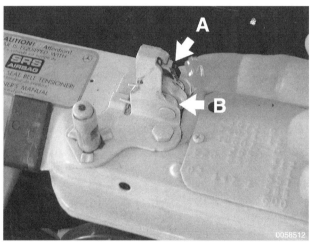

◀ Hood lock: Lubricate contact **A** with general purpose grease and pivot **B** with engine oil.

MAINTENANCE SERVICE

Maintenance service is a comprehensive maintenance and inspection service, including spark plug replacement and fluid replacement. Under normal use, this service is performed every 15,000 miles (24,000 km).

Except where noted, the maintenance items listed in **Table c** apply to all models and model years covered by this manual. The columns on the right side of the table give quick-reference information about the jobs.

Table c. Maintenance service

Maintenance item	Tools required	New parts, fluids, lubricants required	Warm engine required	Dealer service recommended
Body and interior maintenance				
Warning / indicator lamps and horn, check				
Cassette tape head, clean		✳		
Headlights and exterior lights, check operation				
Windshield / rear window / headlight wiper / washer systems, test				
Seat belts, check for damage				
Front seat backrest lock, check operation				
Antenna mast, clean		✳		
Headlight wiper / washer system, check and adjust				
Windshield washer nozzles, check and adjust				
Windshield wiper inserts, replace	✳	✳		
Water drains, clean (every 2 years, up to model year 1993)	✳			
Sliding roof rails, clean and lubricate (every 2 years)	✳	✳		
Body, check for paint damage				
Wheels, tires, brake maintenance				
Brake test, parking brake check (every 15,000 miles or every 2 years)				
Tires, check and rotate	✳			
Tires, check and record tread depth	✳			
Tire pressure, check and correct				
Brake pads and brake rotors, check thickness and condition	✳			
Parking brake, adjust	✳			
Brake fluid, replace (every 1 or 2 years)	✳	✳		✳
Underside of car maintenance				
Fluid lines and hoses, check				
Manual transmission oil level, check and correct	✳	✳		
Manual transmission oil, change	✳	✳		
4MATIC transfer case oil level, check and correct	✳	✳		
4MATIC front differential oil level, check and correct	✳	✳		

Table c. Maintenance service

Maintenance item	Tools required	New parts, fluids, lubricants required	Warm engine required	Dealer service recommended
Underside of car maintenance (continued)				
Rear differential oil level, check and correct	✱	✱		
Rear differential oil, change	✱	✱		
Steering play, check				
Steering gear bolts, check torque	✱			
Body and suspension, check (every 2 years)				
Clutch disc, check for wear (every 30,000 miles)	✱			
Automatic transmission fluid and filter, change (every 30,000 miles)	✱	✱		✱
Driveshaft flex links, check (every 30,000 miles)				
Parking brake cables, check (every 30,000 miles)				
Fuel filter, replace (every 60,000 miles)	✱	✱		
Front suspension ball joint, check for play				
Engine compartment maintenance				
Lines and components, check				
Engine oil and filter, change	✱	✱	✱	
Polyribbed belt, check				
Spark plugs, check and replace	✱	✱		
Coolant / antifreeze level, check and correct		✱		
Coolant / antifreeze, change (every 3 years)	✱	✱		✱
Automatic transmission fluid level, check and correct (up to model year 1993)			✱	
Level control / ASD / 4MATIC fluid level, check and correct				
Brake fluid level, check and correct		✱		
Power steering fluid level, check and correct		✱		
Power steering fluid and filter, change (no factory recommended interval)	✱	✱		
Windshield washer fluid level, check and correct		✱		
Engine throttle linkage, check and lubricate		✱		
Air conditioner, check refrigerant charge level	✱			✱
Ventilation dust filter, replace	✱	✱		

3

Table c. Maintenance service

Maintenance item	Tools required	New parts, fluids, lubricants required	Warm engine required	Dealer service recommended
Engine compartment maintenance (continued)				
Diesel injection timing, check and adjust (once at 30,000 miles for 1995 300D only)	✳			✳
Diesel fuel filter, replace	✳	✳		
Diesel fuel prefilter, replace	✳	✳		
Air cleaner element, replace	✳	✳		
Trunk area maintenance				
Spare tire pressure, check and correct				
Soft top hydraulic fluid level, check and correct (Cabriolet only)		✳		✳

BODY AND INTERIOR

Interior maintenance

The maintenance items listed under this heading can be accomplished without any special tools and can be done in a few minutes.

— Check function of all interior light bulbs.

— Sound horn to verify operation.

— Clean cassette tape head using either a cassette deck cleaning tape or a long swab moistened with pure alcohol.

— Turn on and check parking lights, running lights and headlights. Check all three brake lights and turn signals. Check foglights.

— Check function of windshield, headlight and rear window wiper / washer systems.

— Fully extend all seat belts and examine for abrasion or wear. Test function of seat belt locks and retractors.

– Test front seat backrest lock on coupe and convertible cars:

  • Make sure backrest is locked in upright position with door closed, engine running and unlocked when door open or release button located on outside of seat backrest pressed.

Antenna mast, cleaning

– To clean antenna mast, turn radio on to extend antenna mast.

◀ Wipe mast down with a clean cloth moistened with a light solvent. For best results, use Hirshmann antenna cleaning cloth.

– Turn off radio and allow antenna to fully retract.

– Turn radio on and see if mast extends with a new coating of dirt. If so, repeat cleaning process.

– When mast extends without any dirt, wipe it down with a dry cloth. Turn off radio.

3

Headlight wiper / washer system, checking and adjusting

– Switch on parking lamp and operate headlight cleaning system.

◀ Water spray should hit area just above parked wiper blade (**X**) on headlights.

– Clean jets with suitable sewing needle. Adjust as necessary using needle to reposition jet in housing.

– Pull wiper arm forward and inspect edge of wiping rubber. There should be no sign of cracking or hardening of wiper insert.

NOTE—

Just as with windshield wipers, it is a good idea to wet a clean rag with Windex or its equivalent and wipe down the wiper blade to remove road film, oil and grease that tend to accumulate on wiper inserts.

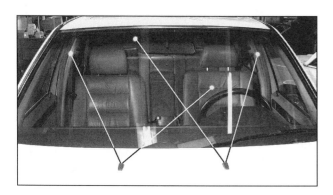

Windshield washer nozzles, checking and adjusting

– Clean nozzles with suitable needle.

◁ Check adjustment (spray pattern) of nozzles. Spray pattern should be approximately as shown.

Windshield wiper inserts, replacing

– Inspect edges of wiper blades for hardening or cracks and replace if necessary.

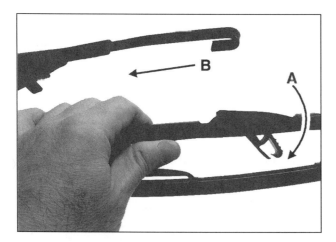

When replacing wiper inserts, it is a good idea to thoroughly clean (degrease) windshield prior to installing new blade. If windshield is pitted and glass cleaner will not remove grease, moisten clean rag with ammonia and wipe down windshield. In severe cases, small amount of Bon-Ami® added to cleaning liquid works well. Accumulated road grease in glass pits will cause new wipers to streak. Use glass cleaner for final wipe down.

◁ To remove wiper blade assembly from wiper arm:

  • Release locking clip by pressing down (arrow **A**).
  • Slide wiper blade assembly toward arm base (arrow **B**) and remove assembly.

◁ Using small pliers, pull both stainless steel strips out of rubber wiper insert (**arrow**). Notice the notch cut into one end of each strip, the end opposite the end you pulled out. These notched ends in strips lock into mating notches in one end of rubber wiper insert.

– Pull rubber wiper insert from wiper assembly.

– Now simply reverse process. Slide new rubber wiper insert into wiper assembly. See that insert engages assembly the same way.

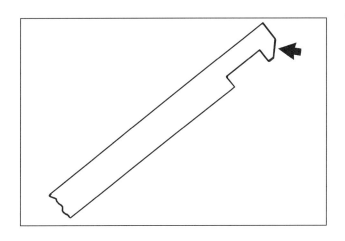

 Slide stainless steel strips into new rubber wiper insert. Strips will engage rubber inserts more easily if corners of notched ends are angled off (**arrow**) and coated with soapy water.

– Reinstall wiper assembly into wiper arm.

– Operate wipers and check that edge of wiper blade flips back and forth. If necessary, gently bend wiper arm so that wiper blade is perpendicular to glass.

3

Water drains, cleaning

There are several drains located around the car that should be cleaned every two years to prevent blockage and accumulated water. These include the fuel filler compartment, rear fenders, spare tire well, side members, air conditioning condenser, front of sunroof well (one on each side), upper A-pillars, front fender component compartment, and engine compartment drains.

Cleaning can be accomplished with compressed air or an old mechanical speedometer cable.

The illustrations given below show most of these drain locations about the vehicle.

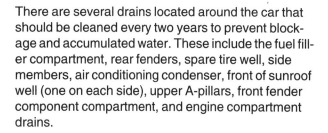 Fuel filler well drain (**arrow**)

Rear fender drain (**arrow**)

◁ Spare tire well drain (**arrow**)

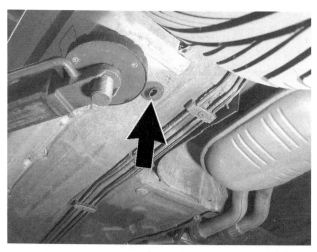

◁ Rear body side member drain (**arrow**)

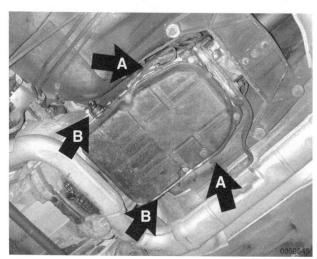

◁ Air conditioning condensation drains (**A**) and air plenum box drains (**B**)

◁ Front of sunroof well (one on each side) (**arrow**)

◁ A-pillar and front component compartment (**arrow**)

Sliding roof rails

While the factory technique calls for removing the sliding roof panel to properly clean and lubricate the slide rails, the job is difficult (even for the professional) and time consuming, requiring some self made tools.

However, unless there is excessive dirt and grit build-up in the area of the slide rails, the rails and the plastic sliding jaws can be effectively cleaned and lubricated with no disassembly.

◁ Open roof and clean sliding area (**arrow**) as thoroughly as possible. A stiff brush followed by compressed air or a powerful vacuum cleaner may be all that is needed.

– Apply a small amount of MB 001 989 14 51 slide paste, as it is waterproof and does not attract dirt and grit. Apply a thin film to all accessible contact surfaces.

– Close roof and reopen it. Examine rails and wipe off any excess. Operate roof several times to spread slide paste.

Body, checking for paint damage

– Carefully examine paint for chips, stars or cracks. To prevent rust formation paint damage should be attended to when found. Touch up paint is available from Mercedes-Benz retail dealers.

WHEELS, TIRES AND BRAKES

Brake test, parking brake check

The parking brake should start to be effective when the pedal is pushed down 4 clicks on cars up to 1989 and 5 clicks for cars 1990 and later. If the parking brake is out of specification it must be adjusted. See **Parking brake, adjusting**.

Tires, checking and rotating

To even out tire wear and prevent heavy wear patterns, tires should be rotated front to rear and rear to front on the same side of the car. Front tires normally wear on the outside edges and rear tires normally wear across the center of the tire. Changing positions will equalize the wear pattern.

– Raise car and remove wheels.

> **WARNING—**
> Make sure car is firmly supported on jack stands designed for the purpose. Place jack stands beneath structural chassis points. Do not place jack stands under suspension parts.

– Keeping wheels on same side of car, reinstall wheels from rear to front and front to rear.

– When rotating wheels, reset tire pressures. Set spare tire to highest specified pressure.

Tires, checking tread depth

◁ Measure tread depth using a tread depth gauge or a steel rule.

– Examine tires for objects that have penetrated tread and for cuts and sidewall bruising.

– Keep track of tread depth to monitor wear looking for any unusual pattern.

3

Tire pressure, checking and correcting

The correct tire pressures are listed on the fuel filler flap. Pressures shown are the minimum allowable pressure for a lightly loaded car. These are also the most comfortable pressures to maintain. The heavy load pressure can be run at all times with a noticeable increase in handling quality. The ride will be firmer. The inflation chart also lists pressure for winter tires.

◁ Tire pressures should be checked when tires are cold to touch (ambient air temperature). Tire pressure increases approximately 0.1 bar (1.5 psi) for each 1°C (1.8°F) of temperature increase. Never adjust pressure in warm tires without taking temperature into consideration.

NOTE—
Remember to check the spare tire pressure. Set the spare tire pressure to the highest allowed.

Brake pads and brake rotors, checking thickness and condition

The brake pad wear indicator light will illuminate when the minimum thickness of the brake friction material is reached, at which point you should replace the brake pads.

Pads should be evenly worn on both sides of the rotor. If one pad is thinner than the other it indicates a brake caliper that requires overhauling.

– Raise car and remove wheels.

Brake pad wear limit

Friction material minimum . . . . 2 mm (0.08 in)

> **WARNING—**
> *Make sure car is firmly supported on jack stands designed for the purpose. Place jack stands beneath structural chassis points. Do not place jack stands under suspension parts.*

◁ Brake rotors should be free from any "blueing", which indicates overheating. Because brake rotors wear from middle of rotor outward it is hard to take an accurate measurement without a brake rotor vernier caliper or a brake rotor micrometer (0 - 25 mm).

Rotors that show cracks longer than 25 mm (1 inch) should be replaced as well as any rotors that exhibit scoring that is deeper than 0.5 mm (0.02 in).

– Check to make sure cooling air passages of vented brake rotor are clear. Use a thin wire to check each passageway.

> **WARNING—**
> *If using compressed air to blow out the vents, be sure to wear approved breathing equipment as the brake dust is toxic and should not be inhaled. A HEPA filter equipped respirator would suffice.*

– On cars with fixed brake calipers (cars with M104 or M119 engines), be sure to clean channels for pads with a stiff wire brush paying careful attention to rubber piston dust seals.

Brake pads

There are two types of brake calipers used on the E-Class:

- **Floating** calipers are used in front on all M103 (6-cylinder single-camshaft gasoline) and diesel equipped cars.
- **Fixed** calipers are used in front on all M104 (6 cylinder twin-camshaft gasoline) and M119 (V-8 gasoline) models. Rear calipers on all models are fixed.

Floating calipers are made by either ATE or Girling / Lucas and are essentially the same design.

Fixed calipers are also manufactured by either ATE or Girling / Lucas. 500E cars made prior to January 1993 have a light alloy caliper manufactured by Brembo. There are slight differences in caliper securing clips and pad retaining pins used by the different manufacturers.

Brake pad replacement procedures for front and rear are similar. The only difference is in the type of caliper used.

Brake pads, replacing
(floating caliper design)

> **CAUTION—**
> *This procedure calls for pushing brake caliper pistons all the way into caliper. To prevent brake fluid overflow at the master cylinder reservoir when caliper pistons are pushed back, use a syringe to remove some fluid from reservoir.*

◁ Using a small screwdriver, pry open brake pad wear sensor cover (**arrow**). Disconnect brake pad wear sensor plug from caliper using needle nose pliers.

> **CAUTION—**
> *Do not use excessive force when prying off the sensor channel cover. Do not pull on sensor wire when disconnecting sensor.*

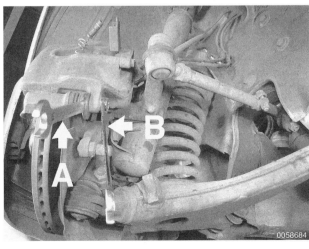

◁ Unscrew and remove lower caliper mounting bolt (**B**, 13 mm) while counterholding sliding pin (**A**, 15 mm).

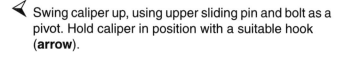
◀ Swing caliper up, using upper sliding pin and bolt as a pivot. Hold caliper in position with a suitable hook (**arrow**).

> **CAUTION—**
> • Do not allow the caliper to hang from the brake hose.
> • While the caliper is hanging up out of its normal position, do not use the caliper to change the steering angle to avoid bending the sliding pin.

◀ Remove brake pads.

– Using a wire brush or other suitable cleaning tool, clean contact surfaces on brake pad carrier.

> **WARNING—**
> Do not breathe brake dust. While brake pads no longer contain asbestos, brake dust will settle in the lower reaches of the lungs and is carcinogenic. Use an appropriate dust respirator, preferably a HEPA unit.

– Remove brake pad wear sensor from inner brake pad.

> **CAUTION—**
> Replace brake pad wear sensor if the insulation is worn through or any part of the sensor is damaged.

– Check condition of dust seals. If they are damaged caliper will have to be rebuilt or replaced.

◀ Using appropriate tool, push piston back until it is flush with caliper bore.

> **CAUTION—**
> Use care to avoid damaging dust seals.

> **NOTE—**
> If the piston is difficult to push in, the piston may have a clearance problem and the caliper may need to be replaced. First try opening the bleeder while applying pressure on the piston. If the piston now moves in easily, the caliper is OK. Close the bleeder before releasing the pressure on the piston.

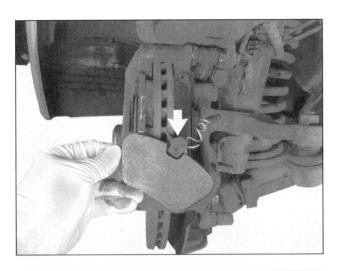

3

> **CAUTION—**
> *Be sure to catch expelled brake fluid in a suitable container and close the bleeder nipple before releasing the piston. Check brake fluid level and top off as necessary.*

− Apply small amount of Mercedes-Benz heat resistant paste to two edges of brake pad that make contact with guide channels in caliper and back of brake pad.

◁ Insert pad wear sensor (**arrow**) in inner pad slot.

− Insert new brake pads into pad carrier.

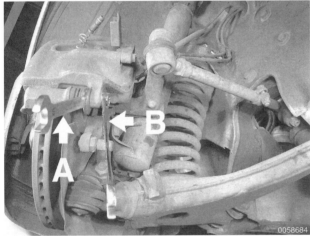

◁ Swing caliper into position and secure with new self locking bolt (**B**) (bolt is supplied with brake pad kit) while counterholding sliding pin (**A**).

Tightening torque

Caliper self locking bolt . . . . 35 Nm (25 ft-lb)

> **WARNING—**
> *Do not reuse self locking bolts.*

◁ Insert brake pad wear sensor wire into plug mounted on brake caliper and install in plastic channel. Close channel cover (**arrow**).

− Pump brake pedal to push pistons against new brake pads. Pump until brake pedal feels normal. Fill or re-move brake fluid to maximum mark on fluid reservoir.

− Reinstall road wheels. Road test.

– Bed in new brake pads:

• Stop 5 to 8 times from 50 to 25 mph (80 to 40 kph) with light brake pedal pressure.
• Allow brakes to cool between each application.
• Avoid hard stops during this procedure.

Brake pads, replacing (fixed caliper design)

> **CAUTION—**
> *This procedure calls for pushing brake caliper pistons all the way into caliper. To prevent brake fluid overflow at the master cylinder reservoir when caliper pistons are pushed back, use a syringe to remove some fluid from reservoir.*

> **NOTE—**
> *This procedure is applicable to both front and rear brake pads.*

– Raise car and remove wheels.

> **WARNING—**
> *Make sure car is firmly supported on jack stands designed for the purpose. Place jack stands beneath structural chassis points. Do not place jack stands under suspension parts.*

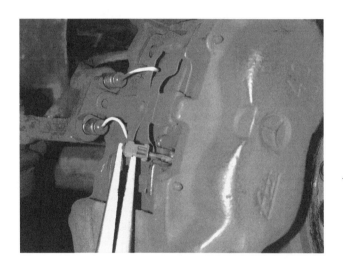

◄ Pull brake pad wear sensors out of pad or backing plate on front brakes.

– On vehicles with ASR (automatic slip control), remove sensors from rear pads as well.

> **NOTE—**
> *To see if your car has ASR, turn on ignition without starting engine and look in instrument cluster for an ASR indicator light: A triangle with an exclamation point inside it.*

◄ Pull sensor wires (**B**) out of plug connections (**A**). Note routing of sensor wires.

> **CAUTION—**
> *Replace brake pad wear sensor if the insulation is worn through or any part of the sensor is damaged.*

– On ATE calipers, use drift or punch to knock out retaining pins. On Girling calipers, remove securing clips and then knock out retaining pins.

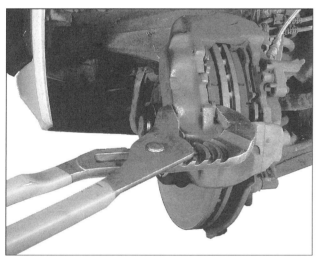

◄ Using a large pair of water pump pliers, squeeze back brake pad to pull it away from brake rotor.

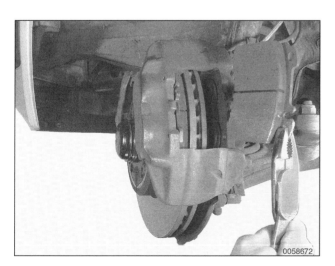

◄ Remove brake pad from caliper with appropriate pulling tool. Repeat for second pad.

> **NOTE—**
> *If pads are to be reused, mark original position.*

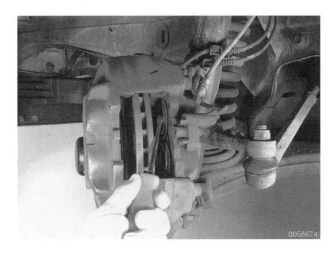

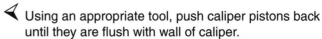

◁ Using an appropriate tool, push caliper pistons back until they are flush with wall of caliper.

> **CAUTION—**
> *Use care to avoid damaging dust seals.*

> **NOTE—**
> *The pistons may be difficult to push in because of the ABS system. In this case, open the caliper bleeder nipple to ease back pressure.*

> **CAUTION—**
> *If you open the bleed nipple, be sure to capture any expelled brake fluid in a suitable container and close the nipple after pushing the piston in. Check brake fluid level and add as needed after you complete this procedure.*

◁ Use wire brush to clean brake pad contact surfaces in calipers.

> **WARNING—**
> *Do not breathe brake dust. While brake pads no longer contain asbestos, brake dust will settle in the lower reaches of the lungs and is carcinogenic. Use an appropriate dust respirator, preferably a HEPA unit.*

– Inspect caliper piston dust seals. Replace any caliper with damaged seals.

– Check vent slots on brake rotor and make sure they are clear.

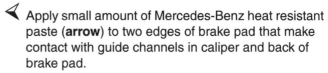

◁ Apply small amount of Mercedes-Benz heat resistant paste (**arrow**) to two edges of brake pad that make contact with guide channels in caliper and back of brake pad.

– Install pads.

– Install retaining spring and pad retaining pins.

– Insert brake pad wear sensor into brake pad and reconnect sensor wire to connector mounted on caliper. Route wire as before.

– Pump brake pedal to push pistons against new brake pads. Pump until brake pedal feels normal. Fill or remove brake fluid to maximum mark on fluid reservoir.

– Reinstall road wheels. Road test.

– Bed in new brake pads:

- Stop five to eight times from 50 to 25 mph (80 to 40 kph) with light brake pedal pressure.
- Allow brakes to cool between each application.
- Avoid hard stops during this procedure.

Brake rotors, replacing

In front, both fixed and floating brake calipers are attached to the steering knuckle with two bolts. In the rear, fixed calipers are bolted to the wheel bearing hub with two bolts. These bolts are fitted with Loctite® and are hard to break loose.

> **CAUTION—**
> *Before starting this job, use stiff wire to construct a pair of hooks that can support the weight of a brake caliper (approximately 20 pounds). Never hang a brake caliper on the brake hose.*

– Raise car and remove wheels.

> **WARNING—**
> *Make sure car is firmly supported on jack stands designed for the purpose. Place jack stands beneath structural chassis points. Do not place jack stands under suspension parts.*

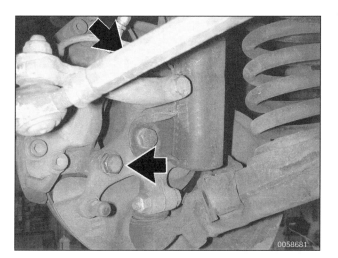

◄ Remove two mounting bolts from caliper (**arrows**).

◁ Remove brake caliper and hang from chassis, using hook you constructed at beginning of this procedure. Make sure brake hose is not unduly pulled or stressed in any way.

> **CAUTION—**
> *Do not hang caliper on brake hose.*

◁ Remove Allen screw from brake rotor.

◁ Remove brake rotor.

> **NOTE—**
> *If corrosion is evident, it may be necessary to use a soft-faced hammer to persuade the rotor off the hub.*

◀ Using wire brush, clean hub mounting surface.

− Remove any anti-corrosive / protective coating from new brake rotor. Lacquer thinner is a good solvent for this job.

> **WARNING—**
> *Lacquer thinner is extremely flammable. Take precautions. Do not work neat heat sources or open flames.*

− Use brake cleaner or similar solvent to clean wheel hub and brake rotor thoroughly, particularly if you used penetrating lubricant to free old rotor.

− Align and install new brake rotor and secure with Allen screw.

3

Tightening torque

Rotor to wheel hub (Allen bolt) . . . . 10 Nm (7 ft-lb)

− Clean threads of caliper bolts. Use Loctite® primer and Loctite® Blue Thread Locker on threads according to manufacturer's instructions.

◀ Reinstall brake caliper using two caliper mounting bolts.

Tightening torque

Front caliper to steering knuckle
(fixed or floating caliper) . . . . 115 Nm (85 ft-lb)

Rear caliper to wheel bearing hub . . . . . . 50 Nm (37 ft-lb)

− Reinstall brake pads using retaining pins along with any securing clips and brake wear sensors. Route brake wear sensor wires in same way they were when you removed them.

− Reinstall road wheels. Road test.

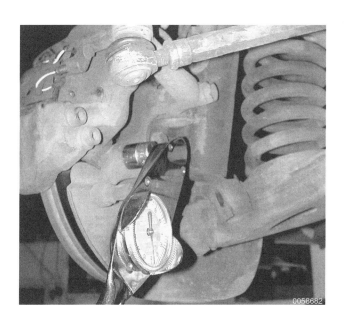

– Bed in new brake pads:

  • Stop several times from 50 to 25 mph (80 to 40 kph) with light brake pedal pressure.
  • Allow brakes to cool between each application.
  • Avoid hard stops during this procedure.

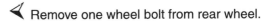

> **CAUTION—**
> New rotors offer less brake efficiency with new pads than old rotors and new pads. Be careful when first driving with this combination.

Parking brake, adjusting

– Raise car and support safely.

> **WARNING—**
> Make sure car is firmly supported on jack stands designed for the purpose. Place jack stands beneath structural chassis points. Do not place jack stands under suspension parts.

◄ Remove one wheel bolt from rear wheel.

– Slowly rotate wheel until star adjuster is visible through open bolt hole.

– Use thin-shank screwdriver to turn star adjuster until brake shoe contacts drum and stops wheel.

> **NOTE—**
> • Left side: Push star adjuster up—pull screwdriver handle down—to tighten.
>
> • Right side: Push star adjuster down—pull screwdriver up—to tighten.

– Back off adjuster 5 - 6 notches so wheel turns freely. There are 15 teeth on adjuster wheel.

– Parking brake cables are only adjusted to remove slack in cable system.

– While road testing car, hold parking brake release and lightly apply parking brake to "bed in" brake shoes to parking brake drum.

> **NOTE—**
> This is a good test to show braking capacity of parking brake if you ever need to use it in an emergency.

Brake fluid, replacing

When replacing or adding brake fluid, use only new fluid from a previously unopened container. Do not use brake fluid that has been bled from the system, even if it is brand new. Use only DOT4 Plus brake fluid.

Brake fluid should be changed once every year for cars produced through March 1991. For cars produced from April 1991, the brake fluid should be changed once every two years. The fluid is best changed during the spring season.

To change brake fluid, you must flush the brake system. Flushing brake system is complete evacuation of old fluid from the system, replacing it with new fluid.

On cars *without* automatic wheel slip control (ASR), bleed and flush the brakes either with or without a power brake bleeder. On cars *with* ASR use a power bleeder capable of maintaining 2 bar (30 psi) pressure.

NOTE—

To see if your car has ASR, turn on ignition without starting engine and look in instrument cluster for an ASR indicator light: A triangle with an exclamation point inside it.

When preparing to the flush brake system, be sure to read the following warnings and cautions.

WARNING—

When working underneath the car, make sure the car is firmly supported on jack stands designed for the purpose. Place jack stands beneath structural chassis points. Do not place jack stands under suspension parts.

3

CAUTION—

• Brake fluid is highly corrosive and dangerous to the environment. Dispose of it properly.

• When adding or replacing brake fluid always add new fluid from a previously unopened container. Do not put anything in the brake fluid system other than new brake fluid.

• It is important to bleed the entire brake system whenever any part of the brake hydraulic system has been opened.

Brake fluid flush (vehicles without ASR)

Using pressure bleeder

◁ Mark fluid level on brake fluid reservoir to maintain fluid level relationship to pad wear.

– Unscrew brake fluid reservoir cap.

◁ Using clean syringe, remove old brake fluid from reservoir until level is approximately 10 mm (0.4 in) above bottom of reservoir.

CAUTION—

Do not empty reservoir completely. If you do, you must then bleed entire system (500 cc or 1 pint brake fluid per wheel).

◄ Connect pressure bleeder unit according to manufacturer's instructions.

– Attach a bleeder hose with fluid receptacle to bleed nipple on right rear brake caliper.

– Open bleed nipple on right rear brake caliper and let approximately 80 cc (1/3 cup) brake fluid flow out, or until clear brake fluid without bubbles appears from bleeder hose.

– Close bleed nipple before removing bleeder hose.

– Repeat previous three steps for each remaining caliper, in sequence:
  • left rear
  • right front
  • left front

All lines and calipers must be pressure-bled with new brake fluid.

– Disconnect pressure bleeder and add new fluid to brake fluid reservoir, matching level previously marked.

– Screw on brake fluid reservoir cap, checking that vent opening is not blocked.

Without pressure bleeder

> *CAUTION—*
> *While flushing the brake system, it is possible to use the brake pedal to manually pump out the brake fluid on a non-ASR equipped car, hence the procedure given here. Only use half of the brake pedal travel. If you push the brake pedal all the way to the floor, the brake master cylinder piston seal will be dragged across areas not normally touched by the seal. These areas may have developed rough spots due to moisture-induced corrosion. This can damage the seal, which may require master cylinder replacement.*

– Mark fluid level on brake fluid reservoir.

– Fill brake fluid reservoir up to MAX mark with brake fluid.

– Attach a bleeder hose with fluid receptacle to bleed nipple on right rear brake caliper. Make sure end of bleed hose is below level of extra brake fluid in receptacle bottle.

— Open bleed nipple on right rear brake caliper and pump old brake fluid out by applying 10 - 15 pump strokes at brake pedal (See **CAUTION** above), or until clear brake fluid without bubbles comes out of bleeder hose.

— Close bleed nipple before removing bleeder hose.

— Check brake fluid level in reservoir. Be sure to keep level up to full mark during bleeding process.

— Repeat previous three steps for each remaining caliper in sequence:
  • left rear
  • right front
  • left front

— Add or remove brake fluid in reservoir to level marked prior to bleeding process.

— Screw on brake fluid reservoir cap. Check that vent opening in cap is not blocked.

Brake fluid flush
(vehicles with ASR)

> **CAUTION—**
> *On cars equipped with ASR, do not attempt to change the brake fluid without using a pressure bleeder capable of maintaining a pressure of 2 bar (30 psi). The fluid and air bubbles cannot be effectively evacuated from the system without a pressure bleeder with 2 bar capacity.*

— Mark fluid level on reservoir.

— Verify that ignition switch is OFF.

— Remove front cover on ABS / ASR unit.

◄ Connect a hose to bleeder valve (marked SP) (**arrow**) on ABS / ASR unit.

◁ Open bleeder valve and empty ASR pressure reservoir. Collect fluid in suitable receptacle.

3

◁ Using clean syringe, remove old brake fluid from reservoir until level is approximately 10 mm (0.4 in) above bottom of reservoir.

> **CAUTION—**
> *Do not empty reservoir completely. If you do, you must then bleed entire system (500 cc or 1 pint brake fluid per wheel).*

– Connect pressure bleeder unit to brake fluid reservoir according to manufacturer's instructions.

– Attach bleeder hose with fluid receptacle to bleed nipple on right rear brake caliper.

– Open bleed nipple on right rear brake caliper and let approximately 80 cc (1/3 cup) brake fluid flow out, or until clear brake fluid without bubbles appears from bleeder hose.

– Close bleed nipple before removing bleeder hose.

– Repeat previous three steps for each remaining caliper, in sequence:
  • left rear
  • right front
  • left front

  All lines and calipers must be pressure-bled with new brake fluid.

– Start engine.

– Open bleeder valve on ASR pressure reservoir until clear brake fluid, free of bubbles, flows out. Collect all discharged fluid in suitable receptacle.

– Close bleeder valve. Allow charging process of ASR pressure reservoir to complete. Charging pump will run audibly for approximately 30 seconds. Replace ABS / ASR front cover.

– Switch engine off.

– Disconnect pressure bleeder unit and fill fluid level in brake fluid reservoir to previous mark.

UNDERSIDE OF CAR

The information under this heading describes routine maintenance that generally involves raising and supporting the car off the ground.

Raising the car

> **WARNING—**
> • Never work under a lifted car unless it is solidly supported on jack stands designed for that purpose.
>
> • When raising the car using a floor jack or a hydraulic lift, carefully position the jack pad to prevent damaging the car body.
>
> • Watch the jack closely. Make sure it stays stable and does not shift or tilt. As the car is raised, it may roll slightly and the jack may shift.
>
> • Do not rely on the transmission or the parking brake to keep the car from rolling. They are not a substitute for positively blocking the opposite wheel.
>
> • Never work under a car that is supported only by a jack. Use jack stands that are designed to support the car.

– Park car on flat, level surface.

– Use the proper jacking points to raise the car safely and avoid damage. Use the jack supplied with the car only at the jack tubes built into the sides of the car.

– Place jack into position. Make sure jack is resting on flat, solid ground. Use a board or other support to provide a firm surface for jack, if necessary.

– Raise car slowly while constantly checking position of jack and car.

– Once car is raised, block wheel that is opposite and farthest from jack to prevent car from unexpectedly rolling.

Fluid lines and hoses, checking

– Raise car enough so you can inspect all lines and hoses under car.

> **WARNING—**
> *When working underneath the car, make sure the car is firmly supported on jack stands designed for the purpose. Place jack stands beneath structural chassis points. Do not place jack stands under suspension parts.*

3

– Check condition and routing of all components, lines and hoses. Look for leaks, often evidenced by a wet or oily appearance.

– Check routing of all hoses and metal lines. Make sure that mounting brackets still have their rubber buffers and that metal clamps are not rubbing through lines.

Oil leaks occur generally when engine is running. These leaks are hard to find. It may be necessary to wash or steam-clean engine. Only then can you start to trace source of leak. Once oil starts to flow it is hard to find source. Between air turbulence caused by engine fan and slipstream, it can be impossible to pinpoint a leak. The source of oil becomes completely obscured. Only cleaning will reveal leak source.

Coolant leaks generally occur as engine cools down to ambient temperature from operating temperature. Puddles are usually found under car. Use a pressure tester to pressurize cooling system to locate coolant leaks.

Manual transmission oil level, checking and filling

For transmission fluid specifications and capacities see **Table a**.

– Raise car enough to gain access to transmission fill plug (**A**).

> **WARNING—**
> *When working underneath the car, make sure the car is firmly supported on jack stands designed for the purpose. Place jack stands beneath structural chassis points. Do not place jack stands under suspension parts.*

◄ Remove transmission fill (**A**) plug using 14 mm Allen wrench.

– If a minimal amount of oil runs out or if level is at lower edge of opening, level is correct. If not, add oil through fill opening.

– Reinstall and tighten fill plug.

Manual transmission fluid

Oil type . . . . ATF

Tightening torque, fill plug . . . . 60 Nm (44 ft-lb)

Manual transmission oil, changing

– Raise car enough to gain access to transmission fill plug.

◄ Remove transmission fill plug (**A**) using 14 mm Allen wrench.

– Place drain pan under drain plug and remove drain plug (**B**).

– When transmission is empty, reinstall drain plug.

– Fill transmission up to level of fill plug opening. Reinstall fill plug.

Manual transmission

Oil type . . . . ATF

Oil capacity . . . . 1.5 liters (1.6 qts)

Tightening torque, drain / fill plugs . . . . . . 60 Nm (44 ft-lb)

4MATIC transfer case oil level, checking and filling

NOTE—
The car must be level when checking fluid level.

– Raise car enough to gain access to transfer case fill plug.

◄ Remove fill plug (**A**).

– Oil should be right at level of fill plug. If more than 50 cc (approx. 2 oz) of oil flows out, check level of hydraulic reservoir in engine compartment.

NOTE—
* *Operating piston bore scoring in the 4MATIC transfer case causes a hydraulic fluid leak into the transfer case. This degrades the lubricating ability of the transfer case oil. The piston originally operated in an aluminum bore. Rebuilt units have been updated with a steel sleeve which prevents fluid cross-over.*

* *Transfer case oil is Dexron III / Mercon ATF.*

Tightening torque

Transfer case drain and fill plugs . . . . 50 Nm (37 ft-lb)

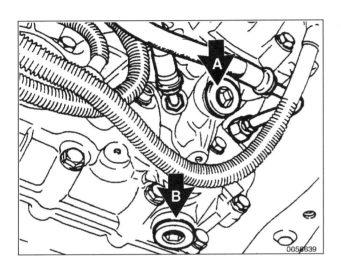

3

4MATIC front differential oil level, checking and filling

NOTE—
Vehicle must be level to check oil.

– Raise car and support safely

– Remove sound encapsulation panel under engine.

◄ Remove differential oil fill plug (**arrow**).

– Oil level should be right at bottom of filler plug. If a small amount of oil runs out it is of no consequence. If level is low, add oil.

Tightening torque

Front differential fill plug . . . . 50 Nm (37 ft-lb)

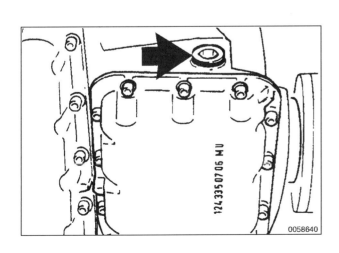

Rear differential oil level, checking and filling

– Raise car enough to gain access to rear differential fill plug.

> **WARNING—**
> *When working underneath the car, make sure the car is firmly supported on jack stands designed for the purpose. Place jack stands beneath structural chassis points. Do not place jack stands under suspension parts.*

◄ Remove fill plug (**B**).

– Oil level should be right at bottom of filler plug. If a small amount of oil runs out it is of no consequence. If level is low, add oil through fill plug opening until oil just begins to run back out, then reinstall fill plug.

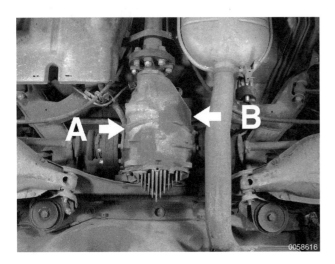

Tightening torque

Rear differential fill plug . . . . 50 Nm (37 ft-lb)

Rear differential oil, changing

While the factory only calls for checking the fluid level at every maintenance service, experience dictates changing the oil every 30,000 miles for long, trouble-free service.

– Raise car enough to gain access to rear differential fill and drain plugs.

– Remove fill plug (**B**).

– Place drain pan in position under drain plug (**A**).

– Remove drain plug, allow oil to drain into pan, then re-install drain plug.

Tightening torque

Rear differential drain plug . . . . 50 Nm (37 ft-lb)

– Add new oil through fill plug opening until oil just begins to run back out, then reinstall fill plug.

Tightening torque

Rear differential fill plug . . . . 50 Nm (37 ft-lb)

Steering play, checking

◄ With steering in straight ahead position, wiggle steering wheel while looking at front wheel.

Steering system play

Maximum steering play (**A**)
with wheels pointing straight ahead . . . . . . 25 mm (1 inch)

— In engine compartment, inspect steering shaft coupling. Examine coupling and its flanges for free play. Correct any play between two pieces of steering column.

— Wiggle idler arm up and down to check for play in its bushings.

Idler arm bushing play

Maximum up / down play . . . . 0.5 mm (0.02 in)

— With car resting on its wheels, move steering right and left while observing tie rod ball joints. Replace any ball joints that show play.

— If any protective boots are damaged, replace affected joint.

Steering gear mounting bolts, checking torque

— Raise left front corner of car and remove left front wheel to gain access to steering gear bolts.

◄ Using a torque wrench, apply 80 Nm (60 ft-lb) to three steering gear bolts (**arrows**) to make sure they are at correct torque.

> *CAUTION—*
> *Do not loosen and retorque the bolts. This is a check-torque only. These are one time bolts and must not be loosened unless you replace them.*

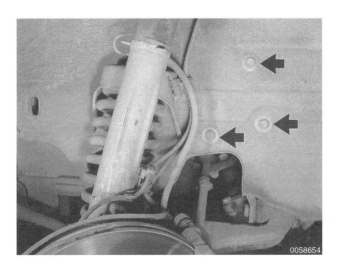

0058654

3

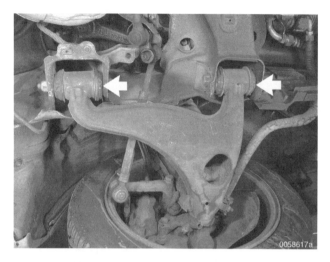

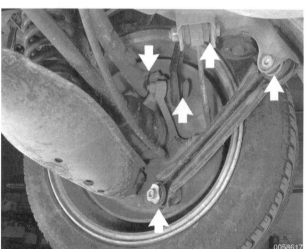

Body and suspension, checking

– Raise car to gain access to suspension components.

> **WARNING—**
> *When working underneath the car, make sure the car is firmly supported on jack stands designed for the purpose. Place jack stands beneath structural chassis points. Do not place jack stands under suspension parts.*

◁ Examine front suspension bushings (**arrows**), looking for cracked or crumbling bushings.

◁ Pay special attention to 5-link rear suspension, looking at condition of bushings (**arrows**). The pulling and pushing links bushings are often worn and require replacement. A symptom of pushing or pulling link bushing deterioration is rear end wander which requires minor steering correction while driving straight ahead.

– Inspect underbody structure looking for damage to undercoating, early signs of rust, and anything else that might need attention.

– Examine rocker panels, bumpers and bumper mounting points.

Clutch disc, checking for wear

– Locate vertical slot on clutch slave cylinder and insert special tool 115 589 07 23 00.

◁ If notch on special tool is visible (**A**), clutch has sufficient lining material. If notch is not visible (**B**), clutch disc is worn and must be replaced.

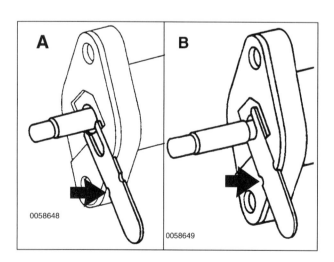

Automatic transmission fluid and filter, changing

NOTE—

• *On vehicles operating under severe conditions (e.g. taxi operation, primarily city operation, trailer operation, or operation in mountainous regions), perform additional ATF change (without filter change) in between normal interval.*

• *Before performing this job, remove engine compartment lower sound encapsulation cover. Replace after completing all maintenance work.*

– Raise car to gain access to transmission.

– Place suitable drain bucket underneath torque converter and transmission oil pan to catch drained ATF.

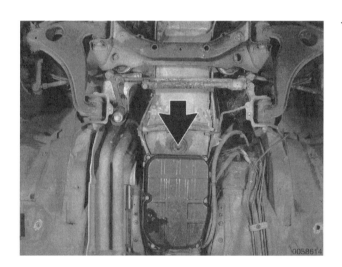

 Working at front of engine, use 27 mm socket on engine crankshaft pulley to turn crankshaft until torque converter drain plug is visible through access hole (**arrow**).

> *CAUTION—*
> *Turn engine only in its normal direction of rotation (clockwise facing engine). Turning an engine backwards can damage timing components.*

NOTE—
This step can be made considerably easier with an assistant to either turn the engine or watch for the torque converter drain plug.

– Remove torque converter drain plug and allow ATF to drain into bucket.

> *WARNING—*
> • *Do not drain the ATF if the engine and / or transmission is hot. Hot ATF can scald. Wear eye protection, protective clothing and gloves.*
>
> • *Perform ATF change with engine stopped and selector lever in **P** position.*

 Remove ATF pan drain plug (**arrow**) and drain ATF.

– Remove transmission pan mounting bolts and remove pan. Leave drain bucket underneath transmission.

3

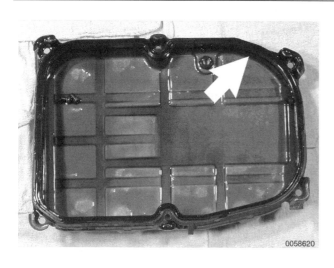

◁ Remove and discard pan gasket (**arrow**) and clean gasket sealing surface.

◁ With oil pan removed, transmission filter becomes visible. Remove filter retaining screws at front and side (**arrows**), but leave rear screw in place until next step.

◁ Now loosen rear filter retaining screw enough so filter hangs down at an angle, allowing excess fluid in filter to drain into drain bucket.

– When excess fluid has drained from filter, remove rear filter screw and discard filter.

– Install new filter using three screws. Tighten securely.

◀ With new pan gasket in place, install pan and torque bolts in sequential order.

Tightening torque

ATF pan to transmission . . . . 8 Nm (6 ft-lb)

— Install ATF pan and torque converter drain plugs.

> *CAUTION—*
> *Always replace drain plug seals, all gaskets and O-rings.*

Tightening torques

Torque converter drain plug. . . . . 14 Nm (10 ft-lb)

ATF pan drain plug . . . . 14 Nm (10 ft-lb)

— Lower car to ground.

— Actuate parking brake.

◀ Insert funnel into dipstick opening and, with engine stopped, pour in 4 liters (4.25 quarts) of ATF.

— Start engine and run at idle with selector lever at position **P**.

— With engine running, gradually add additional ATF until capacity is reached (see **Table d**).

Table d. Automatic transmission capacities

Model	Fluid capacity
260E 300E 2.6	5.5 liters (5.8 qts)
300E 2.8 300E 300CE E320 300TE E320 Wagon 300D Turbo 300TD Turbo 300E 4MATIC 300TE 4MATIC	6.2 liters (6.5 qts)
300D 2.5 Turbo E300 Diesel	6.0 liters (6.3 qts)
400E, E420, 500E, E500	7.7 liters (8.1 qts)

3

– Move selector lever through positions **R-N-D-N-R**, pausing in each position for several seconds, then return to position **P**.

– Allow engine to run for 15 to 20 minutes, after which time transmission oil will be at normal operating temperature (80°C or 176°F).

– Check level of transmission oil and correct as required.

Driveshaft flex discs, checking

– Raise car to gain access to driveshaft.

> **WARNING—**
> *When working underneath the car, make sure the car is firmly supported on jack stands designed for the purpose. Place jack stands beneath structural chassis points. Do not place jack stands under suspension parts.*

◄ Inspect rubberized flex discs (**arrow**) at either end of driveshaft for cracking or separation.

– Check discs for excessive compression by manually rotating driveshaft to make sure there is no play between driveshaft and discs.

– Check discs for distortion such as uneven compression. If any is found, loosen and retorque driveshaft bolts. If distortion remains, replace disc.

Parking brake cables, checking

– Raise car to gain access to parking brake cables.

– Examine sheathing on parking brake cables for wear. Make sure rubber nipples which seal cable to guide tube are in place and not torn.

Fuel filter, replacing

While factory calls for fuel filter replacement every 60,000 miles, experience has shown that fuel filter replacement every 30,000 miles provides better protection to fuel injection system.

– Remove fuel pump protective cover.

– Clamp fuel line to stop fuel flow.

◁ Loosen fuel line fitting (**arrow**) on filter.

> **WARNING—**
> *Fuel will be expelled when the filter is removed. Do not smoke or work near heaters or other fire hazards. Keep a fire extinguisher handy.*

> **CAUTION—**
> *Clean thoroughly around the filter connections before removing them.*

◁ Loosen fuel line fitting (**B**) on filter and filter mounting bracket retaining screw (**C**).

– Replace fuel filter, paying attention to insulating band around filter. Position band so it isolates fuel filter from mounting bracket (to prevent contact corrosion) and tighten retaining screw.

– Reinstall fuel lines.

– Remove clamps from fuel lines and check for leaks.

– Start car and again check for leaks.

– Reinstall fuel pump protective cover.

Front suspension ball joint, checking for play

◁ Have an assistant shake wheel vigorously from side to side (wheels on ground) while holding your hand on lower ball joint (**arrow**). You will feel any free play.

– Replace joint if there is free play.

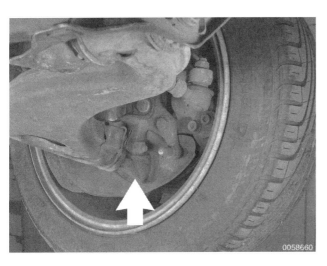

ENGINE COMPARTMENT MAINTENANCE

The information under this heading describes routine maintenance other than oil change done in the engine compartment. It is not necessary for the car to be raised and supported off the ground. Information on oil change is given earlier in this group under **Lubrication Service**.

Lines and components, checking

— Inspect crankcase, front crankshaft seal, valve cover, timing cover, radiator, oil pan and oil filter for leaks.

— Inspect coolant, air conditioning, power steering, oil cooler, heater and transmission hoses for leaks, condition and position or routing.

Polyribbed belt, checking

An automatic belt tensioner is used to keep the polyribbed belt tensioned properly. Unless the tensioner mechanism malfunctions, the polyribbed belt does not require tension adjustment.

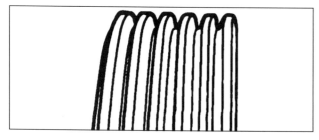

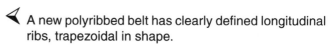 A new polyribbed belt has clearly defined longitudinal ribs, trapezoidal in shape.

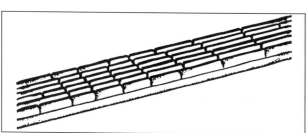

 If existing belt shows signs of wear, cracking (such as lateral cracking across ribbed side as shown), glazing, or missing sections, it should be replaced immediately. To reduce chance of belt failure while driving, replacement of belt every four years is recommended.

NOTE—
When the belt is replaced with a new one, store the old one in the luggage compartment for emergency use, assuming its condition is not too bad.

— To check condition of belt, mark belt with chalk at an easily visible point.

> **WARNING—**
> *Observe care when replacing belts. Personal injury could result if a tensioner springs back into position uncontrollably.*

> **CAUTION—**
> *Mark belt rotation direction if removing and reusing an old belt.*

– Inspect belt while turning engine in steps, using starter. To avoid starting engine, "bump" engine very briefly for each step.

– Look for damage as you turn belt around one complete circuit. Various forms of wear and damage can include:

  • Rubber lumps in rib base
  • Dirt or stone deposits
  • Longitudinal ribs triangular in profile (new belt has trapezoidal ribs)
  • Strand shows through rib base (bright spots)
  • Lateral cracks in ribs
  • Portions of ribs missing
  • Strand pulled out or visibly frayed
  • Lateral cracks on outside of belt (opposite ribs)
  • Ribs separated from belt

– End inspection when chalk mark is visible again (one full turn of belt).

Polyribbed belt, replacing

M103 engine

– Loosen fan shroud from its mounting points and place it back up on fan.

◀ Lock main fan pulley by inserting special tool 103 589 00 40 00 into hole in hub (**arrow**).

– Using special tools 103 589 01 09 00 and 001 589 72 21 00, remove hex socket screw in center of fan hub and remove viscous fan / clutch assembly along with shroud.

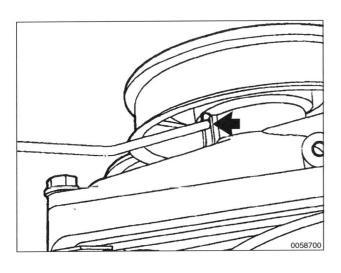

0058700

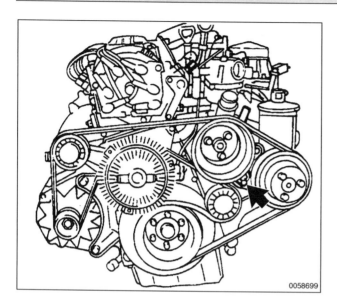

◁ Loosen clamping bolt (**arrow**) at least ½ turn.

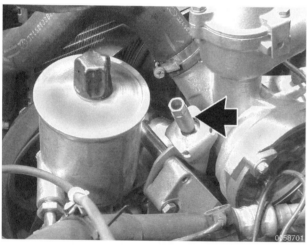

◁ Using tension adjusting screw (**arrow**), release tension on belt tensioning device. This will free up belt.

- Remove belt.

- Check all pulleys for damage. Check belt tensioning device for play. Replace if required.

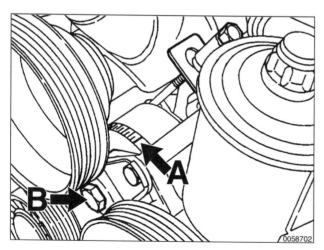

◁ Using tension adjusting screw, move belt tensioner indicator (**A**) to left-most mark (as viewed from driver seat). **B** is clamping bolt.

M103 engine belt routing

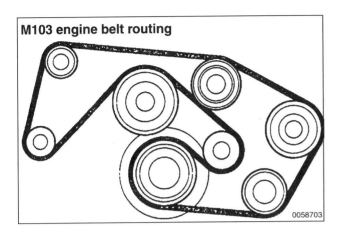

0058703

◁ Install new belt as shown in diagram.

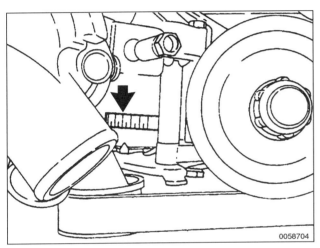

0058704

◁ Using tension adjusting screw, adjust tension pointer so it is at 7th mark on indexed tensioner (**arrow**) or left-most mark on non-indexed tensioner. Tighten clamping bolt.

Tightening torque

Belt tensioner clamping bolt . . . . 75 Nm (55 ft-lb)

– Check belt routing to make sure it is correct.

– Reinstall viscous fan clutch and fan shroud.

– Using counterholding tool 103 589 00 40 00, tighten viscous fan to fan hub.

Tightening torque

Viscous fan to fan hub. . . . . 45 Nm (33 ft-lb)

M104 engine

◁ Fan shroud for M104 engine is two-piece unit. To re-move rear portion for belt changing, remove pin (**A**) and rotate rear section (**B**) to left to remove.

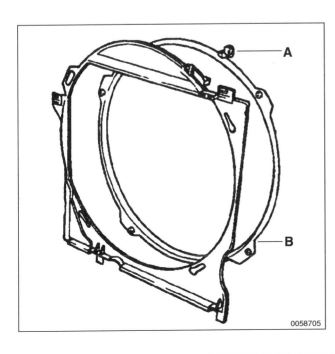

0058705

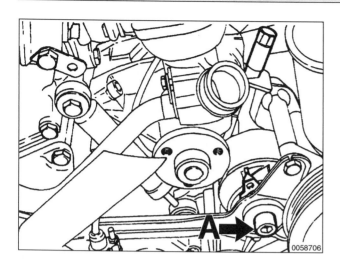

◁ Loosen clamping screw (**A**) ½ turn.

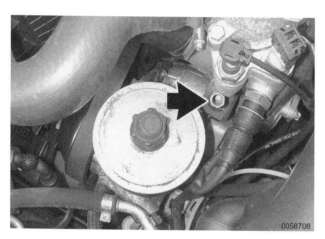

◁ Loosen tension adjuster (**arrow**) until belt can be removed.

– Check all pulleys for damage. Check belt tensioning device for play and replace if required.

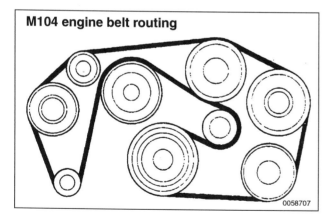

M104 engine belt routing

◁ Install new belt as shown in diagram.

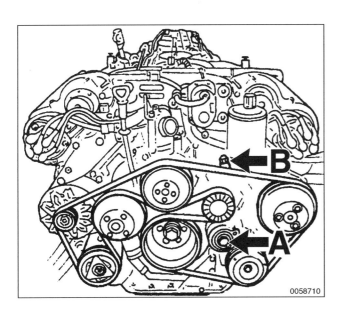

◁ Using tensioning adjustment screw, move pointer on belt tensioner to left-most position (**A**) as viewed from driver's seat. Turning tensioner clockwise, tighten until pointer aligns with right most-mark (**B**).

– Check seating of belt in all pulleys.

– Tighten clamping bolt.

Tightening torque

Belt tensioner clamping bolt . . . . 75 Nm (55 ft-lb)

– Install fan shroud in reverse order of removal.

M119 engine

– 400E and 500E fan shroud is a two piece unit consisting of upper and lower shrouds. Remove upper shroud.

◁ Loosen clamping bolt (**A**) and loosen tensioning screw (**B**) in a counterclockwise direction until tensioner is loose enough to remove belt.

– Check all pulleys for damage. Check belt tensioning device for play and replace if required.

◁ Install new belt as shown in diagram.

M119 engine belt routing

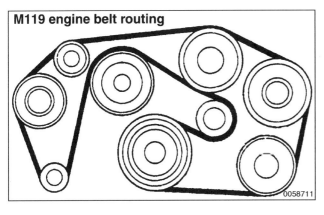

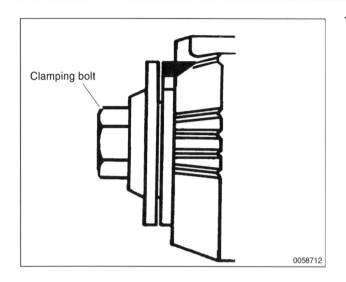

Clamping bolt

0058712

◁ Using tensioning screw, adjust belt tensioner pointer so it is pointing to right-most mark (top in picture, side view of belt tensioner).

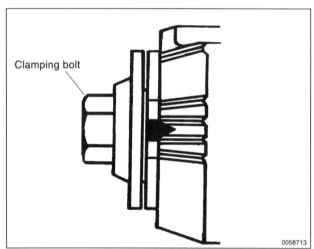

Clamping bolt

0058713

◁ Turn tensioning screw clockwise until pointer is in center position.

– Check seating of belt in all pulleys.

– Tighten clamping bolt.

Tightening torque

Belt tensioner clamping bolt . . . . 100 Nm (74 ft-lb)

– Install fan shroud in reverse order of removal.

OM602, OM603 and OM606 diesel engines

– Remove fan shroud from its mounting and place it back over fan blades.

◁ Using special tools 103 589 01 09 00 and 001 589 72 21 00, remove Allen bolt (**arrow**) in center of fan hub and remove fan clutch.

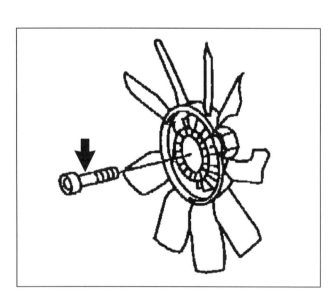

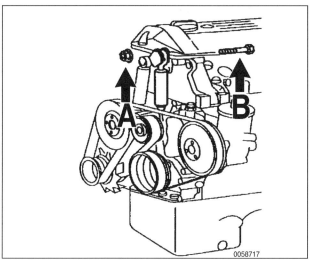

0058717

◁ Remove nut **A** from bolt **B**, then remove bolt and release tension on belt tensioner spring.

– Remove belt and check pulleys for damage. Check
belt tensioning device for play. Replace if required.

Diesel engine belt routing

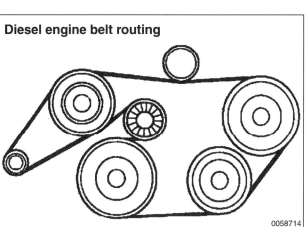

0058714

◁ Replace belt as shown in diagram.

– Reapply tension to belt tensioner spring, then reinstall
bolt and nut.

– Installation of fan clutch and fan shroud is reverse of
removal.

Spark plugs, checking and replacing (M103 6-cylinder engine)

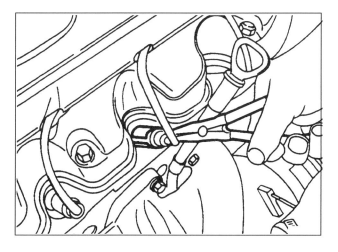

◁ Twist spark plug connector to loosen it and remove
using MB special pliers 103 589 00 37 that grab connector without damaging it.

– Blow out spark plug recesses with compressed air.

– Remove spark plugs and examine electrodes.

– Renew spark plugs if required.

– Lubricate spark plug threads with small quantity of
anti-seize grease.

– Reinstall spark plugs.

Tightening torques

Tapered seat spark plug . . . . 10 - 20 Nm (7 - 15 ft-lb)

Spark plug with gasket . . . . 25 - 30 Nm (18 - 22 ft-lb)

3

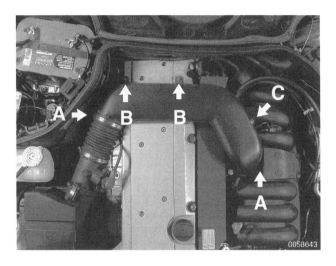

Spark plugs, checking and replacing (M104 6-cylinder engine)

◀ Remove air cleaner cross-over duct:

- Loosen hose clamps (**A**).
- Remove 10 mm nuts (**B**).
- Remove temperature sender (**C**).

◀ Remove coil pack cover:

- Remove 6 Allen bolts (**arrows**).
- Lift off cover and set aside

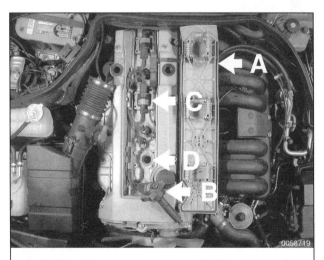

A. Coil pack cover   C. Coil pack installed
B. Coil pack removed   D. Spark plug well

◀ Pull coils and spark plug wires from cylinder head and spark plugs and lay aside.

NOTE—
Each coil pack services two spark plugs. A coil pack attaches directly to one spark plug via a connector and to the second spark plug via a short spark plug wire.

− Using compressed air, blow out spark plug recesses.

− Remove spark plugs and examine electrodes.

− Renew spark plugs if required.

− Lubricate spark plug threads with small quantity of anti-seize paste.

− Reinstall spark plugs.

Tightening torques

Tapered seat spark plug . . . . 10 - 20 Nm (7 - 15 ft-lb)

Spark plug with gasket . . . . 25 - 30 Nm (18 - 22 ft-lb)

– Installation of covers and duct is reverse of removal.

Spark plugs, checking and replacing (M119 V-8 engine)

– Remove air cleaner assembly and associated covers.

◄ Remove both spark plug valley covers (one on each side of engine). Each valley cover is secured by two screws (**arrows**).

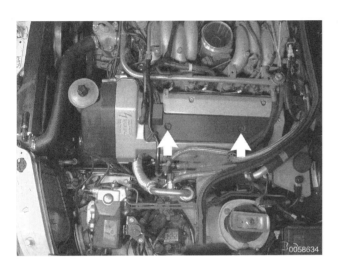

◄ Remove spark plug connectors.

– Using compressed air, blow out all spark plug recesses.

– Remove spark plugs and examine electrodes.

– Renew spark plugs if required.

– Lubricate spark plug threads with small quantity of anti-seize grease.

– Reinstall spark plugs.

Tightening torques

Tapered seat spark plug . . . . 10 - 20 Nm (7 - 15 ft-lb)

Spark plug with gasket . . . . 25 - 30 Nm (18 - 22 ft-lb)

– Installation of covers and air cleaner is reverse of removal.

Coolant / antifreeze level, checking and filling

> **WARNING—**
> *Open expansion tank / radiator cap only at coolant temperatures below 90°C (194°F).*

– Place shop towel over expansion tank / radiator cap and turn cap only to first detent to release excess pressure.

◀ Turn cap to second detent and remove cap from expansion tank / radiator.

◀ Check level and concentration of coolant mixture. Top up and / or correct mixture proportions as required.

> **CAUTION—**
> • *The antifreeze / anticorrosion fluid should not drop below 40% by volume (corresponding to antifreeze protection to -25°C / -13°F) to avoid inadequate corrosion protection.*
> • *Use only approved antifreeze. See* **Table a**.
> • *Do not use any additives in the coolant mixture.*

Coolant mixture to -37°C (-34.6°F)

Water. 50%

Antifreeze / anticorrosion fluid. 50%

Coolant level

Cold engine. . . . . up to mark on expansion tank

Warm engine. 1 cm (0.4 in) above mark on expansion tank

Coolant / antifreeze, changing

> **WARNING—**
> *Open expansion tank / radiator cap only at coolant temperatures below 90°C (194°F).*

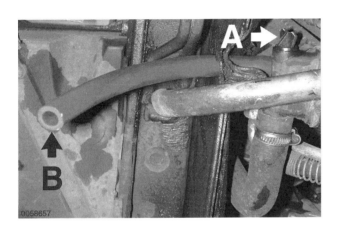

— Place shop towel over expansion tank / radiator cap and turn cap only to first detent to release excess pressure.

◁ Note location of radiator drain valve (**A**).

— Attach hose to radiator drain plug (**B**).

— Place free end of hose into appropriate container to catch drained coolant.

— Refill radiator and cooling system See **Table e** for coolant capacities.

3

Table e. Cooling system capacities in liters (US quarts)

Engine	Total cooling system capacity	Quantity of antifreeze for protection to -37°C (-35°F)	Quantity of antifreeze for protection to -45°C (-49°F)
M103, M104, OM602	9.5 (10)	4.75 (5)	5.25 (5.5)
M119	15.5 (16.4)	7.75 (8.2)	8.5 (9)
OM603	10 (10.6)	5 (5.3)	5.5 (5.8)
OM606	8 (8.5)	4 (4.2)	4.5 (4.75)

Automatic transmission fluid level, checking and filling

When checking fluid level, vehicle should be parked on level surface with engine running for at least 1 to 2 minutes. The transmission must be at operating temperature.

Fluid level varies with fluid temperature. Minimum and maximum marks on dipstick are based on normal fluid temperature of 80°C (176°F).

— To check level, first apply parking brake.

— Place gear selector lever in **P** position.

– Run engine for 1 to 2 minutes.

◁ Working at rear of engine on passenger side, open latch (**arrow**) at top of dipstick, pull out dipstick and wipe with lint-free rag. Reinsert dipstick fully with latch open. Pull dipstick back out and read level.

> **CAUTION—**
> *If fluid level is too low, the pump will audibly draw in air, causing foaming which can lead to incorrect fluid level readings. In this event, stop engine and wait at least 2 minutes for foaming to stop.*

– After reading or correcting level, close latch.

◁ With transmission at normal operating temperature, level should be at MAX mark.

> **CAUTION—**
> *If fluid level is too high, excessive agitation and overheating of fluid can force foaming fluid through breather vent. Extended operation in this condition can cause transmission damage.*

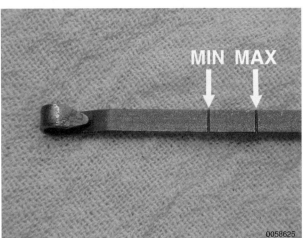

– If level requires correction, add necessary amount of fluid through funnel into dipstick tube with engine running. Distance between MIN and MAX mark on dipstick is approximately 0.3 liters (10 oz.) of transmission fluid.

– After filling fluid to specified level, move selector lever through positions **R-N-D-N-R**, pausing for a few seconds in each position, then return to **P** position. This ensures proper distribution of fluid.

– Recheck fluid and correct again if necessary.

> **CAUTION—**
> *If fluid level is too high, excess fluid must be drained or drawn off to prevent possible transmission damage.*

Level control / ASD / 4MATIC fluid, checking and filling

Level control was installed on the 300TD Turbo, 300TE and E320 station wagons, as well as the 500E sedan.

ASD is the Mercedes-Benz acronym for automatic locking differential, available as an option only on the 300D 2.5 Turbo sedan.

4MATIC was available as an option on the 300E sedan and the 300TE station wagon.

All three of the above use the same hydraulic system. See below for specification.

The hydraulic system has a fluid reservoir equipped with a cap and integral dipstick. The reservoir configuration is somewhat different between cars equipped with ASD or 4MATIC and cars without ASD or 4MATIC.

◄ To check hydraulic fluid level, remove cap with integral dipstick from reservoir.

NOTE—
  * *The fluid level should be checked with the ignition switched off.*

  * *Vehicles equipped with level control must be unloaded to obtain an accurate fluid level reading.*

— Wipe dipstick with lint-free shop towel and reinsert in reservoir.

— Remove cap / dipstick again and read level. Level should be between MIN and MAX marks on dipstick.

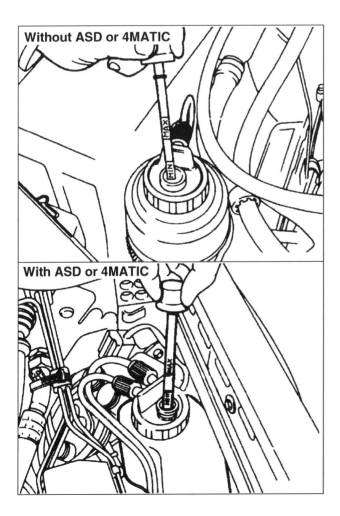

Without ASD or 4MATIC

With ASD or 4MATIC

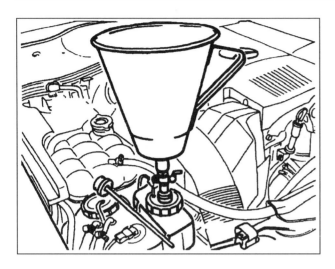

◁ If level is low, use filter funnel to add fluid.

Hydraulic fluid specification

Level control, ASD, 4MATIC fluid
recommendation . . . . MB part no. 000 989 91 03 10

Brake fluid level, checking

> *CAUTION—*
> *Use only new brake fluid from a sealed container. Never re-use brake fluid. Brake fluid is a paint solvent—avoid contact with painted surfaces.*

During its service life, boiling point of brake fluid will decrease as a result of moisture being absorbed from the atmosphere. Heat generated during heavy braking can cause water in brake fluid to boil, causing impaired braking. For this reason, replace brake fluid according to the following table.

Production date	Brake fluid change interval
Through March 1991	Once every year
From April 1991	Once every two years

Brake fluid replacement is covered earlier.

◁ Brake fluid level should be between MAX and MIN marks on brake fluid reservoir.

– Check vent opening in reservoir cap for any obstruction.

– Screw cap back on reservoir.

– If fluid is below MAX mark and brake pads are not worn, diagnose cause of fluid loss.

Power steering fluid level, checking and correcting

> **CAUTION—**
> *Maintain clean conditions when working with open power steering reservoir.*

> **NOTE—**
> *Power steering fluid level should be checked when cold—approximately 20°C (68°F).*

Check power steering fluid level in fluid reservoir:

– Park car on level ground with engine off.

– Unscrew vent cap, wing nut or knurled nut from power steering reservoir and remove cover.

◀ Check power steering fluid level. Level should be between MAX and MIN marks with fluid at approximately 20°C (68°F).

– If level is below MIN mark, add fluid to reservoir to bring level up.

Power steering fluid specification
Recommended fluid . . . . . . MB Q 46 0001 or Mobil ATF D

> **CAUTION—**
> *Do not overfill the reservoir. Pay attention to temperature marks*

– Install cover, making sure gasket seats properly. Screw on vent cap, wing nut or knurled nut (hand tighten only).

Power steering fluid and filter, changing

Mercedes-Benz service recommendations do not include changing the power steering fluid or filter. However, experience over a 30 year period has shown that fresh fluid keeps the power steering pump and gear in better condition. It is sufficient to change the fluid in the power steering reservoir every 15,000 mile maintenance service and the filter every 60,000 miles. The process is very straightforward.

3

NOTE—
There is no need to have the fluid warm for this change.

− Remove reservoir cover.

◄ Using a 10 mm deep socket, unscrew 10 mm (M6) nut that holds fluid level spacer tube to cover stud.

◄ Remove fluid level indicating spacer tube by lifting it out.

◄ Remove filter retaining spring.

◅ Using a pair of needle nose pliers, remove power steering fluid filter. Hold filter over housing for a few seconds to fully drain fluid. Place filter on clean cloth and examine for contamination. Filters are very inexpensive.

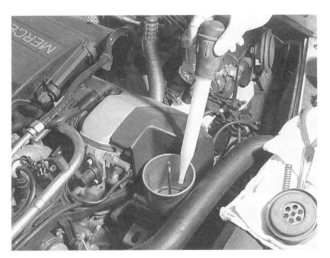

◅ Using a clean syringe, remove all fluid in reservoir.

◅ Replace filter, if required. Reassemble filter, spring and level indicating spacer tube. Hold plastic spacer down against retaining spring while tightening nut.

Tightening torque

Power steering filter retainer spring
to reservoir . . . . 10 Nm (7 ft-lb)

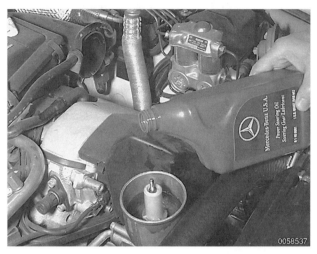

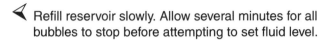

◄ Refill reservoir slowly. Allow several minutes for all bubbles to stop before attempting to set fluid level.

- Follow temperature marks on level indicating spacer tube. (Steering fluid needs room to expand when it heats up.)
- Check gasket on reservoir lid and reinstall lid.
- Screw on rubber covered stud nut hand tight.
- Start engine and run for a few minutes.
- Shut off engine, remove cover and recheck fluid level.

Windshield washer fluid level, checking and correcting

– Locate washer fluid reservoir(s). Station wagon models have a rear window wiper and washer system.

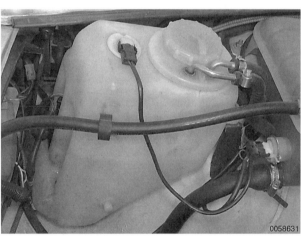

◄ All models have windshield washer tank up front in engine compartment. When headlight washer / wipers are included there is a second washer pump in tank.

Washer fluid capacity

Windshield / headlight washer tank. . . . . . .5 liters (5.3 qts)

Refrigerant charge level, checking

◄ Clean sight glass on receiver / dryer (**A**) and disconnect either wire from pressure switch (**B**).

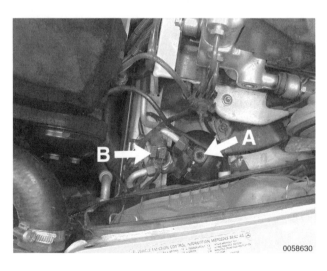

◁ Turn on A/C system with engine running and temperature selector wheel set to a low interior temperature.

> **WARNING—**
> *Never run an engine in the work area unless it is well ventilated. The exhaust should be vented to the outside. Carbon monoxide (CO) in the exhaust kills.*

– Looking at sight glass, reconnect pressure switch wire and observe refrigerant level:

• Refrigerant level should rise in a very short time and be free of bubbles or foam.

> **NOTE—**
> • *While this method gives a good indication of refrigerant charge level, it is not accurate. An accurate charge level can only be determined by an experienced air conditioning service technician using a pressure gauge set.*
>
> • *At ambient temperatures above 95°F (35°C) some bubbles will be present even though the refrigerant level is correct.*

Refrigerant capacities

R12 cars . . . . 2.4 lbs (1.1 kg)

R134a cars . . . . 2.2 lbs (1.0 kg)

Ventilation dust filter, replacing

 Pull off seal (**arrow**) between windshield and water drain up to windshield wiper arm. Fold seal around wiper arm to keep it out of the way.

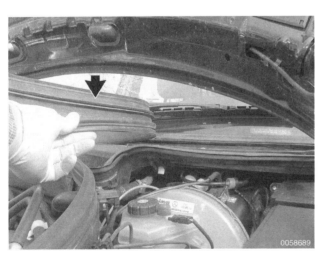

3

◁ Remove lip seal (**A**) which runs across entire cowl just under water drains (**B**) and across fresh air intake (**C**).

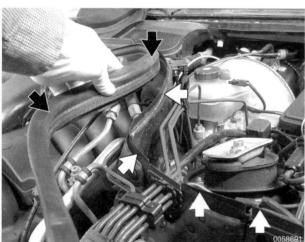

◁ Remove lip seal (**black arrows**) which runs across entire engine compartment forward of bulkhead (**white arrows**).

◁ Remove center part (**arrow**) of second plastic trim. There are 2 clips.

◁ Remove left water drain (**A**) by removing 4 screws at bottom of windshield and 2 screws in center section itself. Lift straight up exposing air filters (**B**).

◁ Remove two right-side air inlet mounting screws and lift out air inlet.

◁ Fold over clamping bracket (**arrow**). Only bracket shown will fold. The others do not.

3

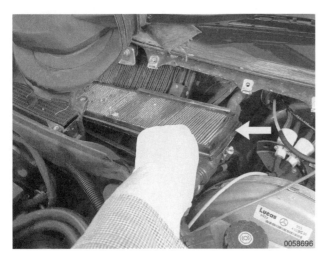

◄ Lift up dust filter (**arrow**) and pull out towards left side. If necessary, assist removal via right opening.

– Similarly, slide out second dust filter from left side.

◄ Install new filters in reverse sequence to removal of old filters. Installed new filters viewed from driver side of car should appear as shown.

NOTE—
When installing, make sure dust filters are correctly positioned in the clamps. Both dust filter halves should be securely engaged at their separation joint as shown.

◄ Installed new filters viewed from passenger side should appear as shown.

– Installation of all other parts is in reverse sequence of removal.

Diesel fuel filter, replacing

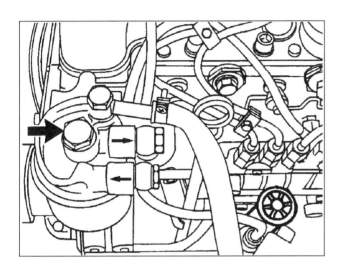

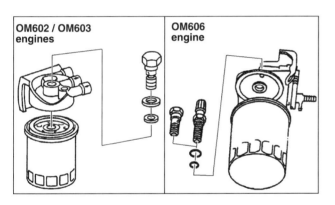

OM602 / OM603 engines | OM606 engine

> **WARNING—**
> *Fuel will be expelled when the filter is removed. Do not smoke or work near heaters or other fire hazards. Keep a fire extinguisher handy.*

> **CAUTION—**
> *Clean thoroughly around the filter connections before removing them.*

3

◄ Loosen mounting screw (**arrow**) and remove housing with filter element in downward direction (OM602 / OM603 engine shown). Hold filter in vertical position to avoid spilling fuel.

– Transfer fuel from old filter to new filter to shorten engine cranking time to fill new filter.

◄ Install new filter.

> **NOTE—**
> *Assembly varies depending on engine model. Refer to accompanying illustration.*

– Start engine. If fuel level in filter has been allowed to drop, some time will be spent cranking engine over. Once engine is started, check for leaks.

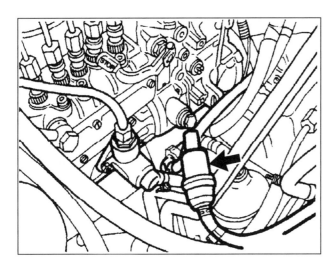

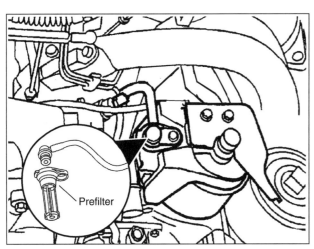

Prefilter

Diesel fuel prefilter, replacing

> **WARNING—**
> *Fuel will be expelled when the filter is removed. Do not smoke or work near heaters or other fire hazards. Keep a fire extinguisher handy.*

> **CAUTION—**
> *Clean thoroughly around the filter connections before removing them.*

◄ Remove and replace fuel prefilter (**arrow**).

> **NOTE—**
> • *OM602 / OM603 engine shown in accompanying illustration.*
>
> • *On OM602 / 603 engine, observe fuel flow direction on filter.*

◄ On OM606 engine, fuel prefilter is mounted adjacent to main fuel filter in same housing.

– After replacing filters, run engine and check for leaks.

Air cleaner element, replacing

– In very dusty conditions:
  • Use compressed air to blow out air filter perforated metal backing.
  • Use no more than 5 bar (75 psi) pressure at a distance of no less than 8 in (20 cm).
  • Blow air through reinforced side.
  • Do not wash air filter elements.
  • Make sure air filter sealing compound is in good condition.
  • Make sure rubber seals in air cleaner compartment are in good condition.

M103 engine

— Remove three 10 mm nuts that hold air cleaner to rubber support buffers.

— Lift air cleaner assembly off air intake body.

— Undo four 10 mm nuts on top of air cleaner and clips around circumference and lift off top section.

— Inspect center O-ring that seals air cleaner to air intake body. Replace air filter.

— Installation is reverse of removal.

M104 engine

◁ Undo clips (**arrows**) which hold air cleaner housing top section to bottom section and to air intake pipe.

— Remove housing top section and remove air cleaner element.

— Clean out air cleaner housing sections.

— Inspect air cleaner housing sections and replace if damaged.

3

◁ Insert new air cleaner element and note correct location of rubber seals.

M119 engine

– Remove flexible tubes connecting air cleaner to air intakes behind headlights.

– Remove forward decorative shield by pulling upward.

– Remove two 10 mm nuts at rear of air cleaner assembly.

– Lift front edge of air cleaner assembly off two mounting clips and remove assembly.

– Unsnap clips that hold upper and lower housings together on both sides.

– Remove old air filter and clean out air box.

– Inspect sealing throttle body O-ring.

– Installation is reverse of removal.

TRUNK AREA MAINTENANCE

The information under this heading describes routine maintenance done in the trunk or rear luggage area of the car. It is not necessary for the car to be raised and supported off the ground.

Spare tire pressure

– Set pressure in spare tire to highest pressure used on car. The correct tire pressures are listed on the gas filler flap.

Rear window washer fluid, checking and correcting

◅ Station wagon models are equipped with a separate rear window washer tank (**arrow**) located behind passenger side rear trim cover.

– Add specified quantity of Mercedes-Benz windshield washer concentrate. Refer to table on package for mixing ratio.

– Fill washer reservoir with water.

– Note differing concentrations for summer and winter usage.

– Alternatively, use any off-the-shelf premixed wind-shield washer fluid.

Washer fluid capacity

Rear window washer tank
(station wagon models) . . . . 2.5 liters (2.6 qts)

Convertible top hydraulic fluid, checking and filling

– Lower convertible top and retract roll bar.

◄ Remove cover from right side trunk well to gain access to fluid reservoir.

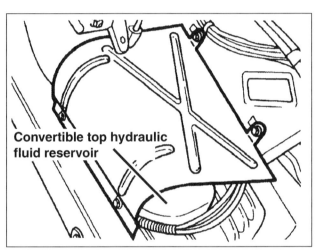

Convertible top hydraulic
fluid reservoir

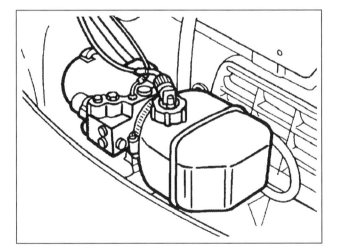

◄ Check fluid level on fluid reservoir. Fluid should be between MAX and MIN marks. Correct if necessary.

Convertible top hydraulic oil

Recommended oil . . . . MB part no. 000 989 91 03

Reservoir capacity. . . . . 1.25 liters (1.32 qts)

– Reinstall cover at right side trunk well.

Chapter 4

6-Cylinder Engines

M103
M104

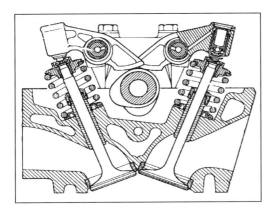

4

GENERAL

This chapter describes the 6-cylinder gasoline engines used in the E-Class from 1986 through 1995.

The M103 engine is a single overhead camshaft engine used in the early E-Class. It was available in two displacements, 2.6 liter and 3.0 liter. The M103 engine was discontinued at the end of the 1992 model year.

The M104 engine, first introduced in the 1990 300CE model, is a more powerful and technically advanced twin cam design. It went through three displacements and two engine management systems during its five years of life in the E-Class.

See **Table a** for complete 6-cylinder engine applications and specifications.

NOTE—
The engine number is stamped on the cylinder block, ahead of the right-hand engine mount.

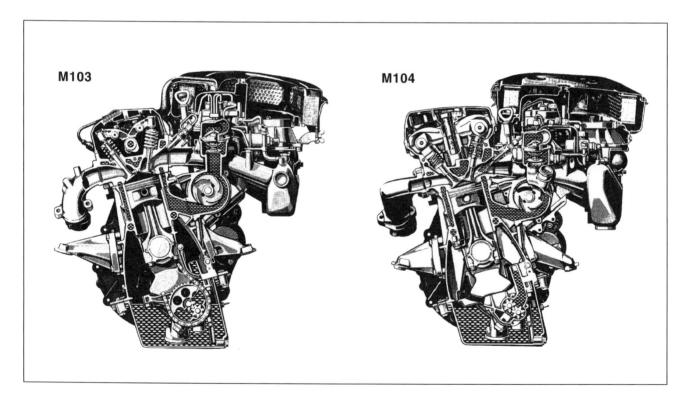

M103   M104

Table a. 6-cylinder engine technical data (US only)

Engine number	M103.940	M103.983	M103.985	M104.980	M104.942	M104.992
Year(s) & Model(s)	1987 - 1991 260E, 300E 2.6	1986 - 1992 300E, 300TE 1988 - 1989 300CE	1990 - 1992 300E 4MATIC, 300TE 4MATIC	1990 - 1992 300CE	1993 300E 2.8	1993 300E 1994 - 1995 E320 (sedan, wagon, coupe, cabriolet)
Engine management system	CIS-E (continuous injection System-Electronic)				HFM-SFI (hot film management - sequential fuel injection)	
Bore/stroke	82.9 x 80.2 mm (3.26 x 3.16 in)	88.5 x 80.2 mm (3.48 x 3.16 in)			89.9 x 73.5 mm (3.54 x 2.89 in)	89.9 x 84.0 mm (3.54 x 3.31 in)
Displacement	2,597 cc (158 cu in)	2,960 cc (181 cu in)			2,799 cc (171 cu in)	3,199 cc (195 cu in)
Compression ratio	9.2 : 1			10.0 : 1		
Firing order	1-5-3-6-2-4					
Maximum engine speed, loaded (rpm)	6,550 (1987) 6,200 (1988 on)			7,000	6,400	
Maximum engine speed, unloaded (rpm)	6,550 (1987) 6,200 (1988 on)			4,000		
Horsepower @ rpm (SAE)	158 @ 5,800	177 @ 5,700		228 @ 6,300	194 @ 5,000	217 @ 5,500
Torque (ft-lbs)@ rpm (SAE)	162 @ 4,600	188 @ 4,400		201 @ 4,600	199 @ 3,750	229 @ 3,750

Recommended fuel octane
  RON
  MON
  RON/MON
	96
	86
	91					

4

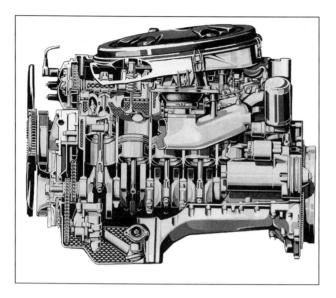

M103 ENGINE

◁ The M103 engine is evolved from the M102 4-cylinder engine in the 190 series cars. This single overhead camshaft engine is installed at a 15° angle toward the passenger side, allowing for a lower hood line.

Engine block

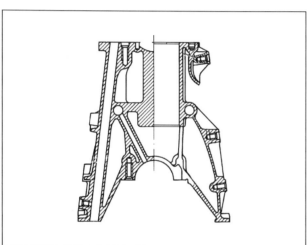

◁ The engine block is cast in gray iron. The crankshaft main bearing saddles are deeply set into the bottom of the block for rigidity and support.

There are seven main bearing saddles with caps that are bolted in place with 11 mm (0.433 in) stretch bolts. Main bearing cap bolts are tightened to 55 Nm (40 ft-lb) plus an additional 90° angle torque.

Crankshaft

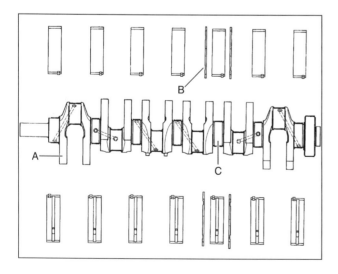

◁ The crankshaft has twelve counterweights (**A**) to minimize vibration. The bearing journals and rear main seal contact area are induction hardened. Thrust washers (**B**) control crankshaft axial clearance at the fifth main bearing journal (**C**). Both ends of the crankshaft are sealed with radial lip seals.

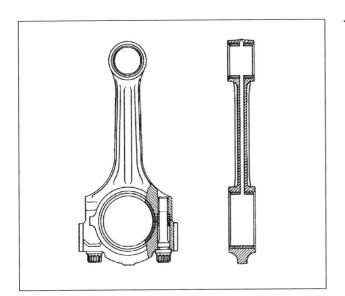

Connecting rods and pistons

◁ The connecting rods are piston guided with a drilled oil bore for wrist pin lubrication. The wrist pins are free floating. A drilled bore in the top of the connecting rod supplies pressurized oil to the underside of the piston for additional cooling. The rods are forged and balanced.

The M103 light weight pistons are lead-coated for enhanced break-in characteristics. The flat top pistons have a kidney shaped recess with two flycuts for valve clearance. The compression rings and chamfered oil control rings are chrome-plated. The tapered scraper ring is iron. The piston pin bore is offset by 1 mm (0.04 in) toward the thrust side.

4

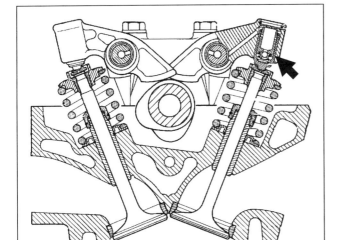

Engine timing and valvetrain

The hollow camshaft is induction hardened. Oil flows through the camshaft to the seven cam bearings through drillings and grooves. Oil is also supplied through the cam to the cam lobe splash oil tube.

◁ The rocker arms pivot on shafts mounted in the camshaft bearing caps. The cam contact area of the rocker is hardened and chrome plated.

Hydraulic valve clearance elements (**arrow**) are mounted in the rocker arms and contact the valves via a swiveling ball foot. The hydraulic elements keep the rockers in constant contact with the camshaft. This helps reduce valvetrain noise while maintaining constant lash, independent of engine temperature.

The exhaust valves are sodium filled and chrome plated. The intake valves are nitrite hardened.

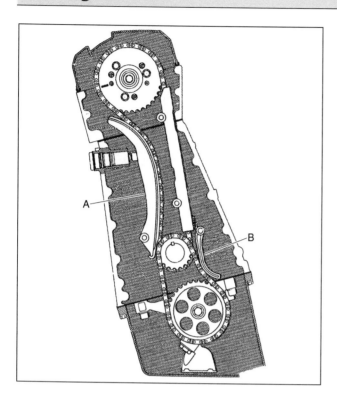

◄ The single row timing chain is tensioned by a nylon-lined aluminum rail (**A**). The oil pump is chain driven with a tensioning slipper to take up slack (**B**).

The chain tensioner is hydraulic with a non reversing detent spring and a secondary tensioning spring. The detent spring limits the backward motion of the tensioner while the secondary tensioning spring maintains chain tension when there is insufficient oil pressure.

NOTE—

On assembly, camshaft timing can be adjusted over a 6° range.

Belt tensioner

A single polyribbed belt drives the alternator, the coolant pump and all engine accessories. The belt is kept properly tensioned by the belt tensioner.

◄ The belt tensioner consists of a rubber bushing (**1**) pressed into an aluminum housing. The tensioning pulley (**4**) is pressed against the drive belt by tightening the adjusting assembly (**2**) to pretension the rubber bushing. Belt flutter is reduced via the shock absorber (**3**).

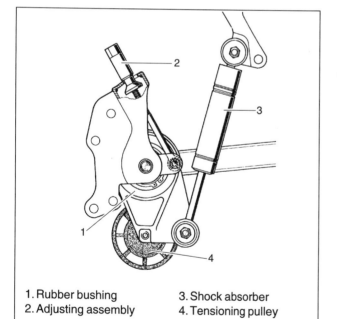

1. Rubber bushing
2. Adjusting assembly
3. Shock absorber
4. Tensioning pulley

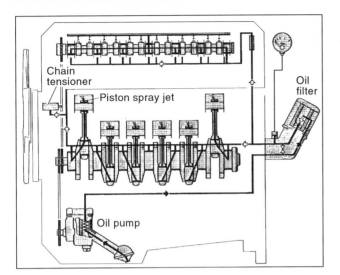

Engine lubrication

◁ The gear type oil pump is chain driven from the crankshaft. The pump is fitted with an overpressure relief valve (5 bar / 72.5 psi). This valve will open and by-pass oil around the filter if the pressure differential between the filtered and unfiltered side of the filter exceeds 2.3 bar (33.4 psi). A low oil level sensor is fitted in the oil pan.

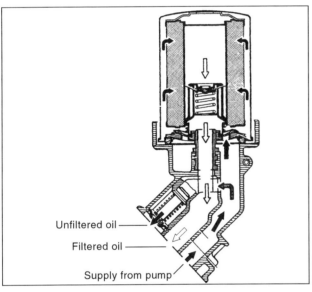

◁ Because the oil filter is installed upside down, a spring-loaded check valve prevents the oil in the filter from draining down into the oil sump when the engine is off. It also keeps oil in the filter during an oil change and allows for immediate filtered oil circulation upon start-up.

The oil filter has a 2.3 bar (33.3 psi) overpressure by-pass relief valve in the event that the filter becomes clogged or restricted.

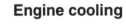

Engine cooling

A viscous fan clutch controls the radiator cooling fan speed based on operating temperature and engine speed.

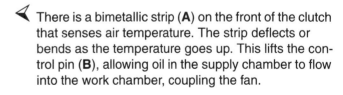

◁ There is a bimetallic strip (**A**) on the front of the clutch that senses air temperature. The strip deflects or bends as the temperature goes up. This lifts the control pin (**B**), allowing oil in the supply chamber to flow into the work chamber, coupling the fan.

When the fan is fully coupled the fan speed will increase with engine speed up to approximately 4,500 rpm, at which point the centrifugal override will disengage the fan within 3 seconds. The fan will reengage when the rpm drops below 4,500 rpm.

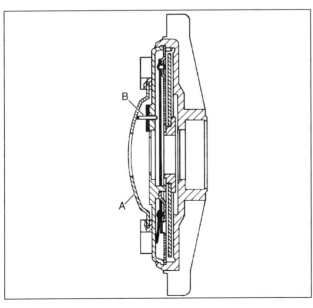

4

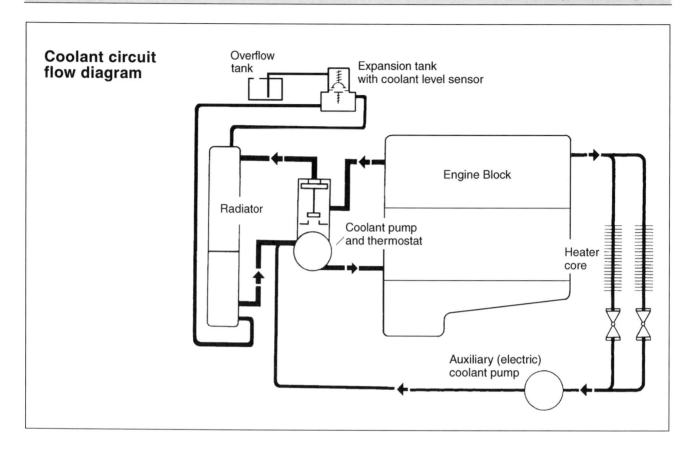

Coolant circuit flow diagram

The aluminum radiator is a cross-flow design with integral automatic transmission oil cooler. An auxiliary electric fan is mounted in front of the radiator to aid in engine and A/C system cooling.

Engine mounts

The engine is mounted through two rubber hydraulic mounts at the front and a rubber mount with rebound stop at the rear.

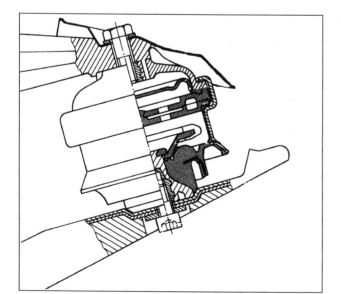

M104 ENGINE

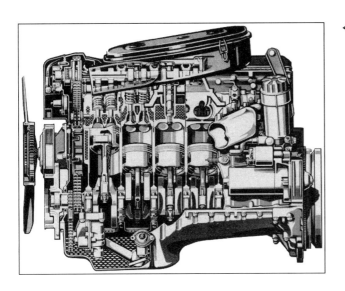

◄ The twin cam M104 engine was first introduced in the 1990 300CE coupe. This engine is used in all 300E/E320 models starting in 1993.

Engine block

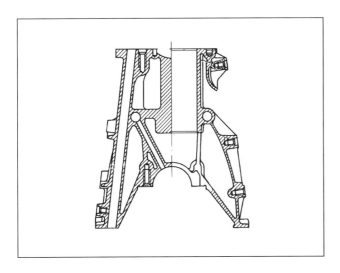

◄ The engine block is cast in gray iron. The crankshaft main bearing saddles are deeply set into the bottom of the block for rigidity and support.

There are seven main bearing saddles with caps bolted in place using 11 mm (0.433 in) stretch bolts. Main bearing caps are tightened to 55 Nm (40 ft-lb) plus an additional 90° torque angle.

Crankshaft

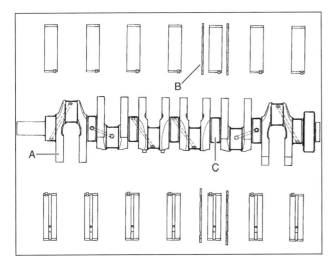

◄ The crankshaft has twelve counterweights (**A**) to minimize vibration. The bearing journals and rear main seal contact area are induction hardened. Thrust washers (**B**) control crankshaft axial clearance at the fifth main bearing journal (**C**). Both ends of the crankshaft are sealed with radial lip seals.

NOTE—

Oil grooves in thrust washers face crankshaft thrust surface during engine assembly.

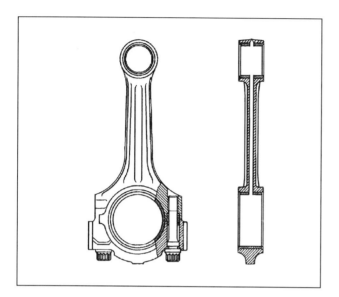

Connecting rods and pistons

◁ The connecting rods are piston guided with a drilled oil bore for wrist pin lubrication. The wrist pins are free-floating. The rods are forged and balanced. After sizing, the rods are heat treated to remove variations in concentricity.

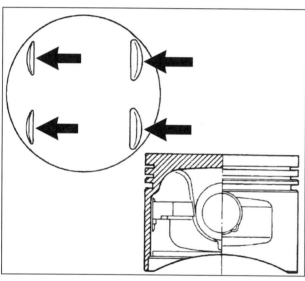

◁ Due to the high compression of the M104 engine, the pistons are strengthened in the skirt area to reduce slap and distortion. There are 4 flycuts (**arrows**) machined into each piston top for valve clearance. The piston is nickel plated across the top and at the compression ring land and groove. The piston skirt is graphite treated and the piston is cooled by oil spray jets located in the crankcase. The piston pin bore is offset by 0.4 mm (0.016 in) toward the thrust side.

The compression ring is asymmetrically barrel-faced instead of rectangular. Neither the tapered oil scraper nor the spring-loaded beveled-edge oil control ring are chrome plated.

Valves

The intake valve stem diameter is 8 mm (0.314 in) and the exhaust valve stem diameter is 9 mm (0.35 in). The exhaust valves are sodium filled and seal against hardened seats. Double opposite-wound valve springs close the valves.

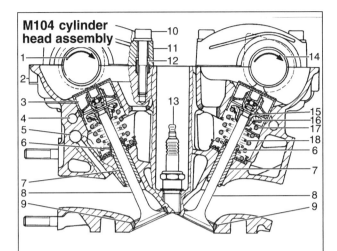

M104 cylinder head assembly

1. Exhaust camshaft
2. Cylinder head casting
3. Hydraulic valve lifter
4. Oil galley
5. Air injection duct
6. Valve stem seal
7. Valve guide
8. Valve
9. Valve seat
10. Camshaft bearing cap bolt
11. Bearing cap
12. Locating sleeve
13. Spark plug
14. Intake camshaft
15. Valve keeper
16. Upper valve spring retainer
17. Outer valve spring
18. Inner valve spring

Valvetrain

Both intake and exhaust camshafts are mounted in seven bearings. Oil flows through the camshaft to the cam bearings through drillings and grooves. The cast iron camshafts are hollow and sealed on the ends.

NOTE—
The camshafts are fragile. Keep them stress-free during removal and installation.

◀ The camshaft lobes are in constant contact with the valve ends via hydraulic valve lifters. This helps reduce valvetrain noise while maintaining constant lash, independent of engine temperature.

4

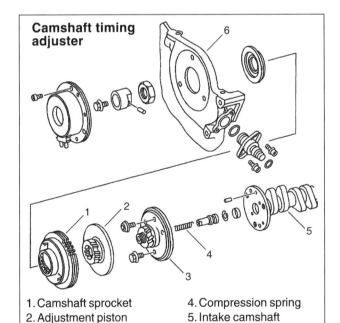

Camshaft timing adjuster

1. Camshaft sprocket
2. Adjustment piston
3. Flanged hub
4. Compression spring
5. Intake camshaft
6. Front cover

Variable valve timing

On the M104 engine, the intake camshaft is coupled to its chain drive by the camshaft timing adjuster, which changes the camshaft timing depending on engine rpm. This allows the engine to operate more efficiently over a wide range.

◀ The adjuster, controlled by the engine management system, uses a combination of a compression spring and engine oil pressure to push the adjustment piston back and forth between the flanged hub bolted to the camshaft and the camshaft sprocket. Helical gear teeth in the sprocket, the piston and the flange hub perform the mechanical engagements in each position.

The adjuster rotates the camshaft by 32° or 34° (depending on engine) between the default retarded position and the advanced position, relative to crankshaft rotation. The adjustment takes about one second to complete. See **Table b**.

NOTE—
All rpm values are engine load vs. engine rpm dependent.

Table b. Variable valve timing

Engine rpm	Camshaft position	Effect on engine
0 to 1,000-2,000	retarded	Improved idle and cylinder filling
1,000-2,000 rpm to 5,000 rpm	advanced	Increased torque, reduced fresh charge loss
Above 5,000 rpm	retarded	Later valve timing = improved volumetric efficiency
Engine off	retarded	Easy starting

Belt drive system

◄ The engine uses a single polyribbed belt to drive the coolant pump and engine accessories.

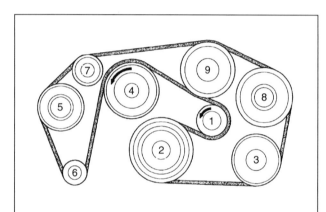

1. Tensioning pulley
2. Crankshaft
3. A/C compressor
4. Fan pulley
5. Secondary air injection pump
6. Alternator
7. Idler pulley
8. Power steering pump
9. Coolant pump

Engine lubrication

The engine is equipped with a low oil level indicator sensor in the oil pan. The oil pump shafts are polygonal in shape to locate the drive sprocket.

The oil pump is equipped with a 5 bar (72.5 psi) over-pressure relief valve. The oil filter is equipped with a 2.3 bar (33.3 psi) pressure bypass relief valve. This valve bypasses the oil filter whenever the pressure differential between the clean and dirty side of the filter exceeds 2.3 bar. This happens with a clogged oil filter or when the engine is very cold and the oil is very thick.

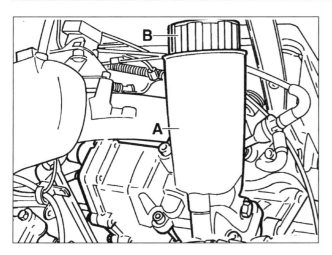

◄ A paper oil filter element (**B**) is fitted inside the oil filter housing (**A**). The housing is fitted with a check valve that opens when the filter is removed, allowing the dirty oil to flow into the oil pan. For this reason, always remove the oil filter before draining the oil pan.

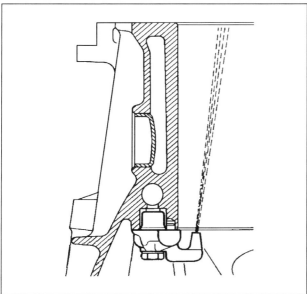

◄ Supplemental piston cooling is accomplished via spray nozzles in the crankcase. These spray nozzles shoot a stream of oil at the underside of the piston to reduce piston dome temperature by 30°C (86°F).

4

Engine cooling

The engine is equipped with a viscous fan clutch which controls the cooling fan speed based on engine speed and operating temperature.

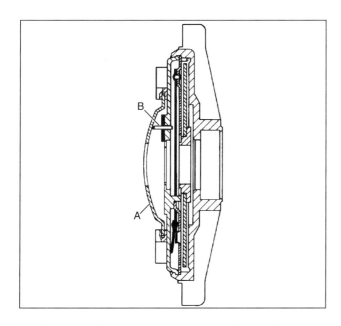

◄ There is a bimetallic strip (**A**) on the front of the clutch that senses air temperature. The strip deflects or bends as the temperature goes up. This lifts the control pin (**B**), allowing oil in the supply chamber to flow into the work chamber, coupling the fan.

When the fan is fully coupled the fan speed increases with engine speed up to approximately 4,500 rpm, at which point the centrifugal override disengages the fan within three seconds. The fan reengages when the engine rpm drops below 4,500 rpm.

The engine is equipped with an aluminum cross-flow radiator with an integral automatic transmission oil cooler. A pair of auxiliary electric cooling fans are mounted in front of the radiator/air conditioning condenser assembly. Signals from the engine coolant temperature sensor and the climate control system are used to activate the auxiliary fans.

Engine mounts

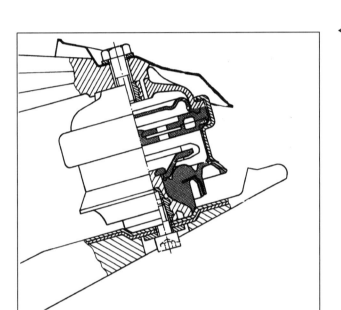

◁ The engine is mounted on two rubber hydraulic mounts at the front and a rubber mount with rebound stop at the rear. Right and left front mounts are the same part.

TIPS, MAINTENANCE, SERVICE

Head gasket leaks

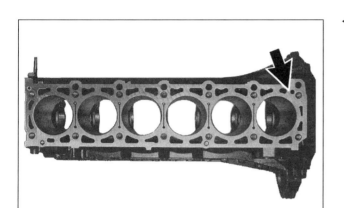

M103 and M104 are known for cylinder head gasket failure. When the gasket fails, it usually does not dump water into the combustion chamber or allow combustion pressure into the cooling system. Instead oil enters the cooling system.

At the rear of the gasket, water and oil channels pass very close to each other (**arrow**). It is here that the gasket develops a crossover between these channels. If the gasket fails in this way, oil is visible in the coolant.

Sometimes the gasket will leak oil to the outside parting line between the head and the block. Many times this leak will not leave oil puddles, as the oil only leaks when the engine is running (except for small quantities of residual oil). Because the engine is tilted 15° to the passenger side, the oil will just drip down into the airstream and leave the undercarriage with dark stains. The engine will have measurable oil loss without any sign of puddling.

If the leak is into the cooling system, then in addition to replacing the head gasket, the cooling system must be thoroughly cleaned. Without proper cleaning oil will saturate the cooling system hoses, making them soft and prone to bursting.

To clean the cooling system, use Mercedes-Benz alkaline cooling system cleaner (MB part no. 001 986 21 71). Using a 3% solution works well. Run the engine for 10 minutes before completely flushing the cleaner out of the system with clear water. The heater must be on and running to clear the oil from the heater core.

4

Camshaft bearing cap bolt, stripped threads (M103 engine)

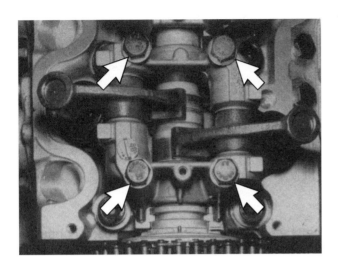

◄ In high mileage M103 engines, it is not uncommon for the cam bearing caps bolt threads (**arrows**) to strip out of the head. As the bearing caps also retain the rocker arm shafts, the engine will misfire as valve lift is eliminated by the loose camshaft bearing cap.

– Check camshaft cap bolts for looseness with wrench. (A stripped bolt will be noticeably loose.)

– Remove loose bearing cap bolts and remove cap.

– Drill damaged threads to correct tap size for insert according to repair kit manufacturer's instructions.

NOTE—
Use Heli-Coil, Time-Sert or equivalent steel insert thread repair kit.

– Clean out hole. Be careful to keep aluminum drillings out of engine.

– Install thread repair insert.

– Reinstall camshaft bearing cap(s) and bolts.

Tightening torque

Camshaft bearing cap
to cylinder head . . . . 21 Nm (16 ft-lb)

– Check remaining bolts with torque wrench to make sure none are stripped.

Valve guide clearance excessive (M103 engine)

If the cylinder head is off to replace the head gasket, be sure to check the valves and valve guides. Many M103 engines from 1986 through 1990 have been found with excessive valve guide to valve stem clearance. If clearance problems are found, overhaul the top end of the engine.

Timing chain cover leaks

The front timing covers are known to leak on both the M103 and M104 engines. When this happens, the covers must be resealed with the correct factory sealant, Mercedes-Benz part number 002 989 45 20, along with a new rubber gasket at the bottom of the cover.

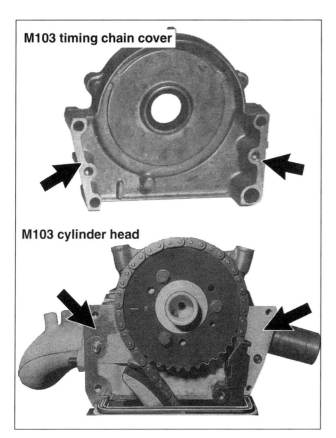

M103 timing chain cover

M103 cylinder head

◄ Shown at left are the M103 front upper timing cover (**top**) and M103 cylinder head front end (**bottom**) with the camshaft drive. When resealing, apply the sealant to all mating surfaces between the cover and the head (**arrows**).

Install a new profile gasket to the cylinder block. Once the gasket is in place, coat the top of the gasket with a thin coat of engine oil.

4

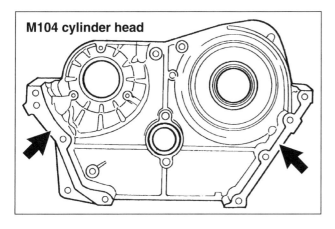

M104 cylinder head

◄ The M104 front timing cover differs from the M103 only in its configuration for twin cams. Reseal the same way as the M103, with sealant on all mating surfaces except the profile gasket channel.

NOTE—
Resealing the timing covers on the M104 engine involves significant disassembly of various components, such as ignition distributor, valve covers, or camshaft timing advance, depending on engine. For specific instructions on required procedures, refer to the factory repair information.

Oil level sensor and coolant level sensor failure

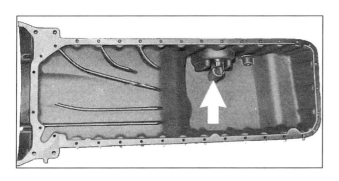

◄ The oil level sender mounted in the oil pan (**arrow**) fails with some regularity. Replacement is best done at oil change time.

The coolant level sensor mounted in the tank on the right fender is also known to fail with some frequency.

Ignition harness repairs (M104 engine)

On M104 engine, insulation of the primary ignition wiring harness to one or more of the coil packs may break down from heat, causing the signal and ground wires to touch. This shorts out the coil pack, resulting in the loss of two cylinders.

The harness is expensive to replace, but can be repaired.

— Inspect the harness carefully for the exposed wires.

— Wrap a small piece of pliable plastic (cut from an empty factory coolant bottle, for example) between the touching wires.

— Tape and shrink wrap the wires and reseal the set.

Oil changes at shorter intervals

Oil change intervals are inversely correlated to engine life; short oil change intervals results in long engine life. However, following the severe service interval (around 3,500 miles) with conventional oils and the 7,500 mile interval with synthetic oils would benefit the engine greatly.

Fuel odors (M103 Engine)

On CIS-E cars, fuel odors from the engine compartment are usually caused by a leaky electrohydraulic actuator (EHA). The EHA is mounted on the side of the CIS-E fuel distributor. Either the green O-rings between the EHA and the fuel distributor leak, or the body of the EHA itself leaks.

If the EHA is replaced, it should not be considered a bolt-on. There is a small plug on the side of the EHA and under this plug is the stop screw that sets the basic pressure for the lower chamber. The pressure measured at the lower chamber is normally 0.4 bar (5.8 psi). You will need a CIS fuel pressure gauge to measure and adjust the fuel pressure. If you reset of the EHA, the idle mixture should also be checked and adjusted. Refer to the factory repair information on making this repair.

Driveability (M103 engine)

Some M103 engines develop a slight hesitation off the line when the engine is cold. They may also cold start instantly and then die, but restart easily and then continue to run. By adjusting the fuel distributor lower chamber pressure to 0.45 bar (6.5 psi) instead of 0.4 bar (5.8 psi), both of these symptoms tend to disappear. The car also seems much livelier off the line and idles better when cold.

You are not really richening the mixture when making this adjustment. Instead the adjustment is compensating for basic wear and tear and any unmeasured air leaks that have developed over the years. You will need a CIS fuel pressure gauge to measure and adjust this the fuel pressure. If you reset the EHA, the idle mixture should also be checked and adjusted. Refer to the factory repair information on making this adjustment.

4

Chapter 5

V-8 Engine

M119

5

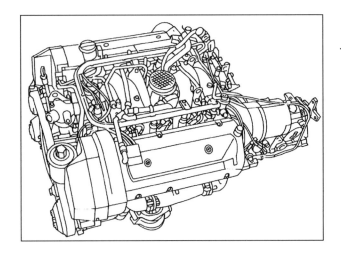

GENERAL

◄ The M119 V-8 engine uses a silicon-aluminum cylinder block, four camshafts, four valves per cylinder, adjustable intake cam timing and knock sensing technology.

The compact roof-shaped combustion chamber with center mounted spark plugs is optimized for flame travel. The combination of a short flame path, intake charge turbulence, and a high compression ratio yields optimal fuel efficiency, low exhaust emissions and high horsepower output.

Table a. V-8 engine application and technical data (US only)

Engine number	M119.974	M119.975
Year Model	1992 - 1994 500E/E500	1992 - 1995 400E/E420
Engine management system	LH-SFI (hot wire - sequential fuel injection)	
Bore/stroke	96.5 x 85.0 mm (3.79 x 3.34 in)	92.0 x 78.9 mm (3.62 x 3.10 in)
Displacement	4,973 cc (303 cu in)	4,196 cc (256 cu in)
Compression ratio	10 : 1	11 : 1
Firing order	1-5-4-8-6-3-7-2	
Max. engine speed	6,000 rpm	
Horsepower @ rpm (SAE)	315 @ 5,600	275 @ 5,700
Torque (ft-lb) @ rpm (SAE)	347 @ 3,900	295 @ 3,900
Recommended fuel octane RON MON RON/MON	95 - 98 86 90.5 - 92	

ENGINE DESCRIPTION

Engine block

◄ The engine block is cast in lightweight alloy, a combination of aluminum and silicon. The cylinders are machined into the block. No liners are used, although steel repair liners are available.

The cylinder running surfaces are treated after boring and honing. This treatment etches the aluminum so that the piston rings contact only the silicon crystals. These silicon crystals have a diameter of 0.02 - 0.05 mm (0.00078 - 0.0019 in) and provide a very wear-resistant running surface for the rings. The etched areas on the cylinder walls form pooling places for oil, providing good cylinder wall lubrication.

The block contains Heli-Coil inserts for head bolts. Both right and left outer bolts are inclined 5° to clear the block casting. The crankshaft main bearing webbing is drilled to prevent the return oil from foaming. The block is extended far below the crankshaft line, making the entire lower assembly very rigid.

Connecting rods and pistons

The connecting rods are forged and have a 4 mm (0.157 in) bore through the rod to spray oil on the underside of the pistons to cool them.

◄ The pistons are cast aluminum with iron coated over the entire running surface. The pistons have flat domes with four flycuts for the valves. Rings are chrome-plated.

The vibration damper has a new mark at 45°, which indicates the crankshaft location where the heads can be reassembled without valves and pistons touching. At this 45° position, all four camshafts can be maneuvered by hand.

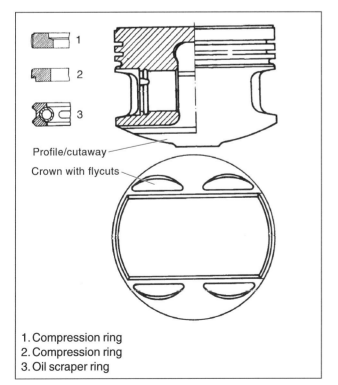

Profile/cutaway
Crown with flycuts

1. Compression ring
2. Compression ring
3. Oil scraper ring

5

Crankshaft

The crankshaft is machined and balanced with eight counterweights running in five main bearings. The main bearing caps are bolted on with four studs and the center three main bearing caps have additional side bolts.

The crankshaft is sealed front and rear with replaceable radial lip seals. The crankshaft position sensor distinguishes the two cylinder banks (cylinders 1 - 4 and cylinders 5 - 8) by magnets installed on two segments of the ring gear.

Cylinder heads

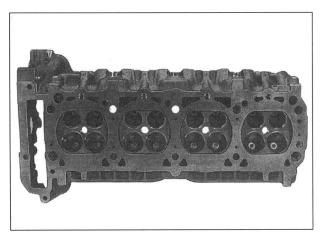

◁ The cylinder heads are aluminum with two overhead camshafts per side. The intake valves are inclined 14° and the exhaust valves are inclined 23°. Drain holes at the base of the spark plugs prevent water buildup. The valve cover uses cast-in-place spacers to control gasket crush and eliminate oil leaks.

Engine timing and valvetrain

◁ The camshafts are driven by a double-row timing chain. The chain is tensioned with a combination hydraulic / spring force tensioner.

The hydraulic lifters are treated with carbon nitrating and manganese phosphate at the contact surface. The cams themselves are hollow chilled cast iron, each supported by five bearings. Because the hollow cams are fragile, extra care must be taken when removing or installing them.

Intake valve stem diameter is 8 mm (0.314 in) while exhaust stems are 9 mm (0.354 in). Valve face diameter is 38 mm (1.496 in) for the intake and 33 mm (1.299 in) for the exhaust. The dual valve springs are wound in opposite directions and both springs ride on a rotating retainer.

Oil pan

The oil pan is two piece construction with the upper, larger section made of aluminum and the lower section of sheet metal. The interior of the upper pan contains a windage tray to control oil foaming and direct the flow of oil back into the lower sump during hard cornering.

Variable valve timing

The intake camshafts are coupled to the timing chain by a camshaft timing adjuster, which controls camshaft timing based on engine rpm. This allows the engine to operate more efficiently over a wide range.

The adjuster rotates the camshaft by 25° between the default retarded position and the advanced position, relative to crankshaft rotation. The adjustment takes about one second to complete.

◄ The adjuster, electrically controlled by the engine management system, uses a combination of a compression spring and engine oil pressure to operate the adjustment piston. Helical gear teeth in the sprocket, the piston and the flange hub enable the rotational motion. See **Table b**.

5

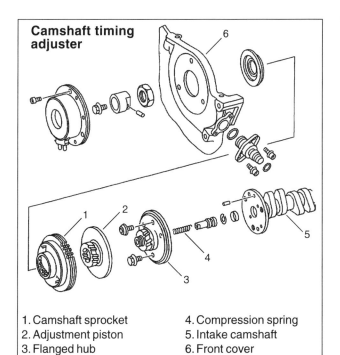

Camshaft timing adjuster

1. Camshaft sprocket
2. Adjustment piston
3. Flanged hub
4. Compression spring
5. Intake camshaft
6. Front cover

Table b. Variable valve timing

Engine rpm	Camshaft position	Effect on engine
0 - 2,000 rpm	retarded	Improved idle and cylinder filling
1,500 - 4,700 rpm	advanced	Increased torque, reduced fresh charge loss
Above 4,700 rpm	retarded	Later valve timing = improved volumetric efficiency
Engine off	retarded	Good starting

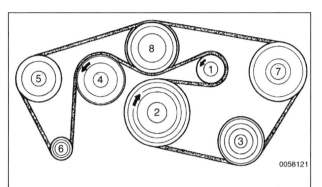

0058121

1. Belt tensioning pulley
2. Crankshaft pulley
3. A/C compressor
4. Fan pulley
5. Secondary air injection pump
6. Alternator
7. Power steering pump
8. Water pump

Drivebelt

 A single polyribbed belt is used to drive all engine accessories.

Drivebelt length

M119 engine . . . . 2,465 mm (97.05 in)

Engine lubrication

Engine oil capacity

M119 engine (includes filter) . . . . 8 liters (8.5 US qt)

The engine is equipped with a low oil level indicator sensor in the oil pan.

The oil pump is equipped with an overpressure relief valve. The oil pump shaft is polygonal in shape to locate the drive sprocket.

A paper oil filter element is fitted inside the oil filter housing . The housing is equipped with a return check valve that keeps the filter full when the engine is stopped.

Engine cooling

The radiator is constructed of aluminum and is a cross-flow design. An ATF cooler is integrated into the right tank.

The engine is equipped with a viscous fan clutch that controls the cooling fan speed based on operating temperature and engine speed .

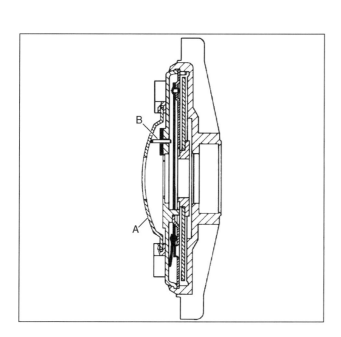

◁ A bimetallic strip (**A**) on the front of the clutch senses air temperature. The strip deflects or bends as the temperature goes up. This lifts the control pin (**B**), allowing viscous oil in the supply chamber to flow into the work chamber, coupling the fan. This thermostatic device begins to couple the fan at approximately 92° - 100°C (198° - 212°F).

When the fan is fully coupled the fan speed increases with engine speed. A centrifugal override limits the fan to 3,250 rpm at an engine speed of 4,500 rpm.

The fan shroud contains rear flaps that are drawn shut when the fan is engaged and are opened by pressure to allow flow-through air at highway speeds when the fan is uncoupled.

Two auxiliary electric fans mounted in front of the radiator t are activated at a coolant temperature of 107°C (225°F) and turned off at 100°C (212°F).

If the coolant temperature reaches 121°C (250°F) and the air conditioning is engaged, the A/C compressor will be placed in a 2 second on/off mode until the engine temperature is lowered. At coolant temperatures of 126°C (259°F) and above, the air conditioning system will be shut off until the engine cools.

Engine mounts

◁ The front engine mounts are rubber / hydraulic units. The rubber mount portion is on the bottom. The hydraulic portion contains a lower and upper chamber plus an expansion chamber for the diaphragm. Silicon based fluid is metered between the two fluid chambers to cancel engine vibration.

The rear engine support is a standard rubber mount.

5

TIPS, MAINTENANCE, SERVICE

Power steering fluid leaks

For oil leaks near the front of the engine on the driver's side, check the short hose between the power steering reservoir and the pump. This hose tends to harden from heat and develop cracks and leaks. To replace this hose, the reservoir needs to be removed.

Use only Mercedes-Benz power steering fluid in the system. ATF or aftermarket fluid can cause the power steering system to whine or groan when the engine is hot.

Timing cover oil leaks

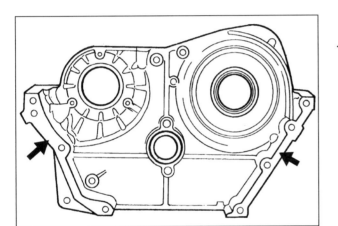

◀ Oil leaks may are common on both the right and left upper timing covers. These covers can be resealed using the factory sealant (MB p/n 002 989 45 20). Once the cover is removed and cleaned, the sealant is applied along the vertical edges (**arrows**) of the cover and along the new rubber rail under the cover.

The distributor seal, timing advance seal and water connection O-ring should be replaced any time the timing covers are removed.

Electronic Accelerator (EA) fault codes

Vehicles with ASR (traction control) may develop a problem with the Electronic Accelerator (EA). The CHECK ENGINE light illuminates and power is reduced as the engine goes into limp-home mode.

NOTE—
- *To see if your car has ASR, turn on ignition without starting engine and look in instrument cluster for an the ASR triangle with an exclamation point inside it.*

- *False codes are set in the EA control module by a defective EA actuator in the throttle housing.*

− Retrieve and record fault codes using a Mercedes-Benz compatible scan tool, such as the the Star laptop.

− Using factory repair information, replace throttle housing / EA actuator and clear all codes.

Timing chain replacement

Worn or stretched timing chains are a known problem with the M119 engines. Replacement is an involved time consuming job and requires special service tools. Timing chain replacement should be left to the experienced professional.

High engine operating temperatures

◄ Some V-8 models exhibit warm running tendencies. It is not unusual to see engine temperatures in excess of 115°C (239°F) when the outside (ambient) temperature is around 32°C (90°F).

If your engine runs hot, it is recommneded that you confirm the following:

Thermostat. Begins to open at 78° - 82°C (161° - 179°F), fully open by 94°C (201°F).

Auxiliary fans switch. Fans come on at 107°C (224°F) coolant temperature, which is usually before the belt-driven viscous coupled fan is fully coupled.

5

Viscous fan clutch. Begins to couple at airflow temperatures of 92° - 100°C (197° - 212°F). The specification for full couple is 105°C (221°F)This translates into a coolant temperature of 110° - 115°C (230° - 239°F) in the radiator.

NOTE—
Given manufacturing variances of the viscous fan units, the actual coupling temperature will vary from engine to engine.

While the factory specifies 115°C (239°F) as safe, you can trick the viscous clutch-driven fan to keep engine temperature in a lower range by modifying the fan clutch, as described below.

NOTE—
This procedure involves draining the cooling system and removing the radiator and fan shroud. Special tools are required. This procedure is best left to a qualified Mercedes-Benz repair shop.

– Remove viscous fan clutch.

◄ Remove bimetallic strip (**A**) from front of fan clutch.

— Drill small hole (**B**) through bimetallic strip and tap for M3 bolt.

— Screw M3 bolt through strip and preload strip approximately 1 mm (give strip 1 mm bow). Use lock nuts on both sides of M3 bolt to lock in position.

NOTE—

The 1 mm preload fools the clutch into full couple, while the centrifugal disconnect at 3,250 rpm still remains.

Chapter 6

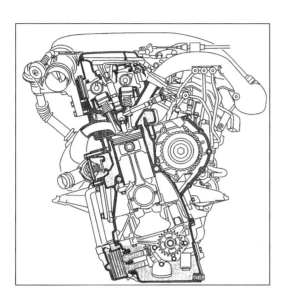

Diesel Engines

OM602
OM603
OM606

6

GENERAL

Model information and specifications for E-Class diesel engines are shown below.

Engine technical data (US only)

Engine number	OM602.962	OM603.960	OM606.910
Year Model No. of cylinders	1990 - 1993 300D 2.5 Turbo 5	1987 300D Turbo, 300TD Turbo 6	1995 E300 Diesel 6
Engine management system	EDS (electronic diesel system) with Bosch mechanical injection		
Induction system	Turbocharged		Normally aspirated
Bore / stroke	87 x 84 mm (3.42 x 3.30 in)		
Displacement	2,497 cc (152 cu in)	2,996 cc (189 cu in)	
Compression ratio	22 : 1		
Firing order	1-2-4-5-3	1-5-3-6-2-4	
Maximum engine speed, unloaded	5,150 rpm		4,800 rpm
Horsepower @ rpm (SAE)	121 @ 4,600	148 @ 4,600 Federal 143 @ 4,600 California	134 @ 5,000
Torque (ft-lb) @ rpm (SAE)	165 @ 2,400	201 @ 2,400 Federal 195 @ 2,400 California	155 @ 2,600
Recommended fuel	Diesel according to ASTM D 975 no. 1-D & 2-D		
Cooling system capacity	9 liters (9.5 US qt)	10 liters (10.6 US qt)	9 liters (9.5 US qt)

OM602 engine

◁ The 300D 2.5 Turbo models with the 5-cylinder OM602 turbodiesel engine delivered good acceleration and fuel economy with an EPA rating of 26 mpg city and 31 mpg highway. When introduced for the 1990 model year, this engine was quiet, smooth and environmentally clean.

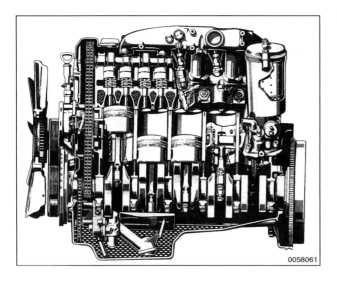

0058061

OM603 engine

◁ The 6-cylinder OM603 turbodiesel engine was sold for one model year (1987) in North America. It was specifically engineered for the E-class to deliver more horsepower, lower fuel consumption, and quieter operation as compared to its diesel predecessors. Additional benefits included reduced weight and easier serviceability.

0058060

OM606 engine

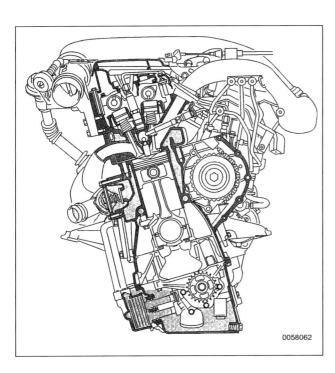

◁ The OM606 engine, offered in the last year of the E-Class, was a high-tech diesel powerplant. This normally aspirated 6-cylinder engine used state-of-the-art engine management, twin camshafts and four valves per cylinder. It was the quietest most efficient diesel E-class available.

6

0058062

ENGINE TECHNICAL

This section describes the engine components and systems on the diesel models. Many components and systems between the three engines are the same or similar. Where differences exist, they will be noted in the text.

Crankcase

OM602 engine. The cylinder bores are machined directly into the cylinder block casting. Replacement oversized pistons are available in one oversize (+0.7 mm). The crankshaft is supported with six main bearings.

OM603 / OM 606 engines. The engine block is cast in grey iron with steel cylinder liners. The crankshaft is supported with seven main bearings and the main caps are held in place with double-hex stretch bolts.

Oil pan

OM602 engine. A splash shield is installed between the crankshaft and the oil pump to prevent the crankshaft from running in the oil.

OM602 / OM603 engines. The oil pan capacity is increased by the addition of a side pan bolted to the main pan.

All diesel engines. An oil level sensor is mounted in the oil pan. The sensor can be replaced externally from below once the engine oil as been drained.

Crankcase breather system

◁ **OM602 / OM603 engines**. To insure good oil separation, blow-by gases are routed through the oil separator in the valve cover. The residual gases are then drawn into the suction side of the turbocharger and into the engine. A pressure regulator, built into the oil separator, prevents excessive crankcase vacuum. High vacuum would allow oil to be drawn into the air intake.

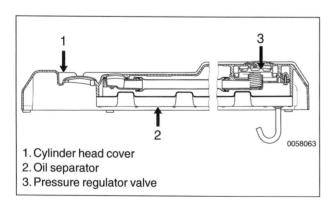

1. Cylinder head cover
2. Oil separator
3. Pressure regulator valve

0058063

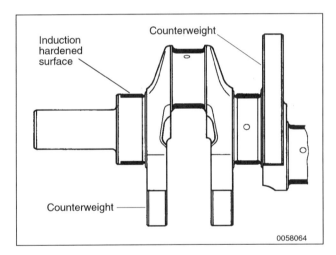

1. Valve cover
2. Ventilation manifold
3. Intake manifold
4. Pressure regulator valve
5. Ventilation hoses

◄ **OM606 engine**. The valve cover design incorporates a ventilation manifold to separate the oil from the engine blow-by gases.

Crankcase blow-by gases flow from the valve cover into a pressure regulating valve. The gases are then routed through the ventilation manifold and into the intake manifold.

Crankshaft and connecting rods

◄ **OM602 engine**. The crankshaft is equipped with ten counterweights.

OM603 / OM606 engines.The crankshaft is equipped with twelve counterweights.

All diesel engines. The running bearing surfaces and the ground radii of the bearing journals are induction hardened. The front and rear crankshaft seals are radial lip design.

The upper connecting rod bearing shells are made of different material than the lower due to higher combustion pressures. The upper and lower shells must not be interchanged during engine assembly.

◄ Free-floating piston wrist pins are splash lubricated via an oil bore or bores. Oil enters the splash oil cones from the spray jets mounted in the lower part of the engine block.

In the OM606 engine, there are two oil feed bores (**arrows**) in the connecting rods. All other engines use a single lubricating bore per rod.

6

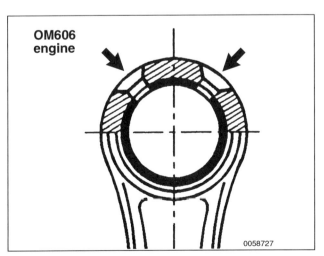

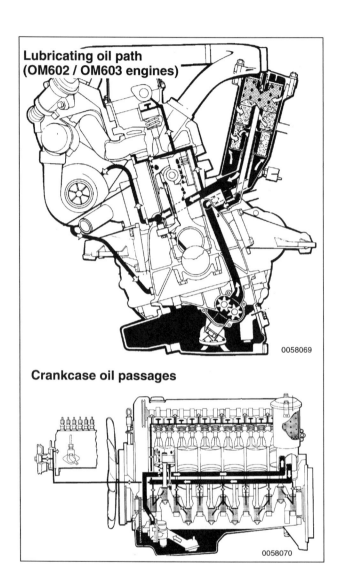

Lubricating oil path (OM602 / OM603 engines)

0058069

Crankcase oil passages

0058070

Engine lubrication and oil cooling

Engine oil capacities

Initial fill
OM602 . . . . 8.2 liters (8.6 US qt)
OM603 . . . . 9.2 liters (9.7 US qt)
OM606 . . . . 8.2 liters (8.6 US qt)

Oil change with filter
OM602 . . . . 7.0 liters (7.4 US qt)
OM603 . . . . 8.0 liters (8.5 US qt)
OM606 . . . . 7.0 liters (7.4 US qt)

OM602 / OM603 engines

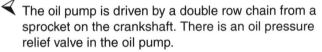 The oil pump is driven by a double row chain from a sprocket on the crankshaft. There is an oil pressure relief valve in the oil pump.

Oil pressure is measured at 80°C (176°F) and must be at least 0.5 bar (7.25 psi) at idle and at least 3 bar (43.5 psi) before 3,000 rpm.

The OM602 and OM603 engines are equipped with a thermostatically-controlled air-to-oil intercooler. At 110°C (230°F), the thermostat opens to route oil through the intercooler. The thermostat is fully open at 125°C (257°F).

The oil cooler is mounted behind the bumper in the left wheel well and protected by a louvered cover. The thermostat is located in the oil filter housing.

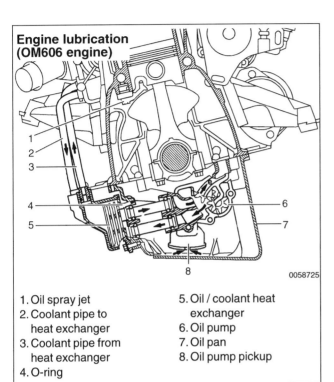

Engine lubrication (OM606 engine)

0058725

1. Oil spray jet
2. Coolant pipe to heat exchanger
3. Coolant pipe from heat exchanger
4. O-ring
5. Oil / coolant heat exchanger
6. Oil pump
7. Oil pan
8. Oil pump pickup

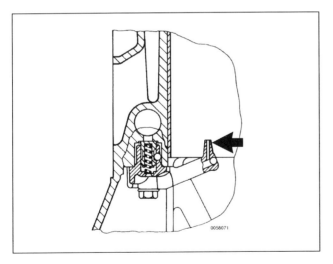

0058071

OM606 engine

The oil pump is driven by a double row chain from a sprocket on the crankshaft. There is an oil pressure relief valve built into the oil pump.

Oil pressure is measured at 80°C (176°F) and must be at least 0.5 bar (7.25 psi) at idle and at least 3 bar (43.5 psi) before 3,000 rpm.

◁ The OM606 engine uses an oil-to-coolant heat exchanger. The heat exchanger is integrated into the side of the engine oil pan.

Pressurized oil travels from the oil pump through the heat exchanger and on to the oil filter and lubrication system. There is no thermostat required. When the oil is below operating temperature of 80°C (176°F), heat is transferred from the coolant to the oil. As the oil gets hot, the heat will transfer from the oil to the coolant.

Pistons and piston rings

◁ Cylinder block mounted oil spray jets spray oil directly under each piston dome to aid in piston cooling and lubrication. The jets are located on the right side of the engine block (**arrow**) and open at 1.5 bar (21.75 psi) of oil pressure and close below 1 bar (14.5 psi).

6

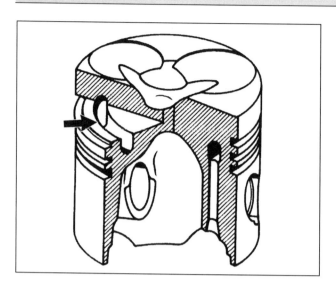

◁ **OM602 / OM603 engines**. To counter the high thermal load in the turbocharged engines, the pistons are further cooled using a cooling duct (**arrow**) in the piston. Oil is fed into the duct via the spray from the spray jet. There is a recess cut in the bottom of the piston skirt to clear the jet.

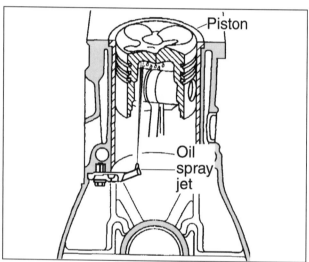

◁ **OM606 engine**. The pistons on the normally aspirated OM606 engine are cooled by oil spray from below. There is no internal cooling duct in the piston as on the turbodiesels.

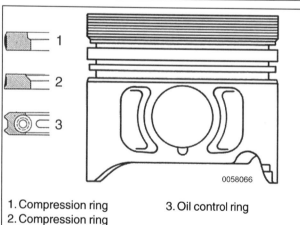

1. Compression ring   3. Oil control ring
2. Compression ring

◁ In all engines, each piston has two compression rings and one oil control ring. The piston skirt is graphite coated for good wear characteristics.

The contact face of the compression rings are plasma sprayed with molybdenum to reduce friction. The oil control ring contact surface is chrome-plated.

Cylinder head gasket

The cylinder head gasket uses stainless steel for compression sealing and a silicon bead along the perimeter for oil sealing. This style head gasket does not require a retorque after the break-in period.

Cylinder head, valvetrain and timing

 To handle the increased heat generated by the 22 : 1 compression ratio, the exhaust valves are sodium filled and chrome plated.

OM602 / OM603 engines

The exhaust valve stem seals are is made of Viton (green in color). The intake valve stem seal made of polyacrylate (black in color).

The camshaft is mounted on six bearing (OM602 engine) or seven bearings (OM603 engine) and lubricated by directed oil flow. The cam lobe profile has been designed to soften valve closing to help eliminate the typical diesel engine clatter.

Camshaft drive is via a single row timing chain with a ratchet-type chain tensioner. Valve actuation is through rocker arms containing hydraulic elements to maintain constant valve lash.

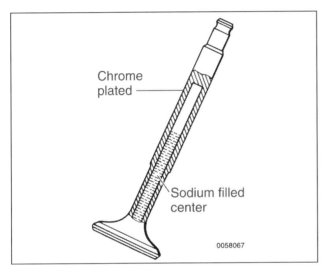

Chrome plated

Sodium filled center

0058067

6

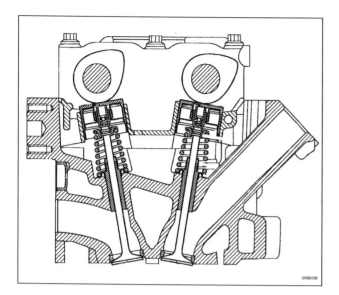

OM606 engine camshaft drive

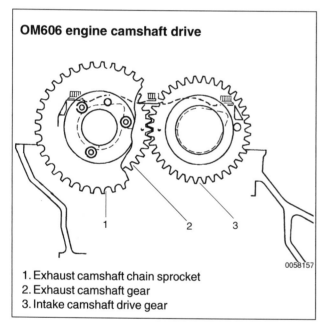

1. Exhaust camshaft chain sprocket
2. Exhaust camshaft gear
3. Intake camshaft drive gear

Belt path

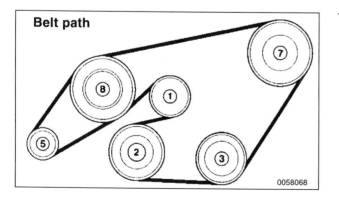

OM606 engine

◀ The OM606 cylinder head uses a cross-flow design with four valves per cylinder. Separate intake and exhaust camshafts ride in removable camshaft housings. The fuel mixing prechambers have been moved to the center of the combustion chambers.

Valves

Valve stem dia. . . . . 6 mm (0.236 in)
Valve head dia.
intake. . . . . 29 mm (1.142 in)
exhaust . . . . 26 mm (1.024 in)

Valve springs are progressive and tapered. The benefit is less mass for the camshafts to move. This is especially beneficial at high engine speeds.

The double overhead camshafts are held in a camshaft housing bolted to the cylinder head. The camshafts are hollow chilled iron castings, with end plugs for oiling purposes. Camshafts ride in seven bearings each. The camshafts are delicate and care must be exercised when removing and installing them.

◀ The exhaust camshaft is driven via a double row timing chain and the intake camshaft is gear-driven off the exhaust camshaft.

Drivebelt

◀ All of the accessories on the engine are driven by a single polyribbed belt. The belt tensioner keeps uniform tension on the belt at all engine speeds. Both the tensioner pulley and the tensioner itself are equipped with double row ball bearings.

Drivebelt length

OM602 engine. . . . . 2,100 mm (82.68 in)

OM603 engine. . . . . 2,145 mm (84.45 in)

OM606 engine. . . . . 2,140 mm (84.25 in)

Engine cooling

The engine is fitted with a viscous clutch for the fan. The fan is fully coupled at 90° - 95°C (194° - 203°F). The maximum fan speed is 3,300 rpm, also controlled by the viscous clutch. The fan has nine blades and is 460 mm (18.1 in) in diameter.

The radiator is a cross-flow design with turbulence plates and an internal transmission cooler in the right side header tank. The cooling system requires a pressure release cap marked 1.4 bar (20.3 psi).

OM603 engine. The coolant drain block is a hollow bolt, which allows a hose to be slipped over it for mess-free coolant draining.

OM606 engine. To prevent corrosion of engine aluminum parts, the coolant expansion tank has a supply of a silicate chemical installed from the factory. This is one-time only additive that is released into the coolant.

Cooling system capacity

OM602 engine	9 liters (9.5 US qt)
OM603 engine	10 liters (10.6 US qt)
OM606 engine	9 liters (9.5 US qt)

6

Engine mounts

The front engine mounts are rubber / hydraulic. The hydraulic portion contains a lower, an upper chamber, and an expansion chamber for the diaphragm. Silicon based fluid is shuttled between the upper and lower chambers to cancel out engine vibration.

The rear engine support is a standard rubber mount.

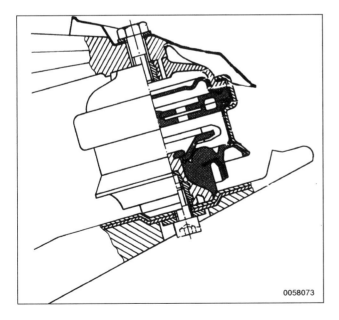

0058073

TIPS, MAINTENANCE, SERVICE

Trap oxidizer (OM603 engine)

The OM603 engine was originally equipped with a trap oxidizer (**arrow**) as part of the exhaust system. The trap oxidizer was used to control particulate emissions. The trap units disintegrated in short order and pieces of the ceramic internals fell into the turbocharger and the engine. This caused major engine damage. Mercedes-Benz redesigned the trap and recalled all the OM603 E-Class sedans and station wagons in for retrofitting.

The revised trap worked well, held up well, and gave the OM603 engine a noticeable increase in power.

The recall campaign replaced the entire exhaust system from the turbocharger back to the tailpipe. The old trap unit is a large diameter cylinder. The new unit is almost as small as the exhaust pipe itself.

Cylinder head and gasket failure (OM602 / OM603 engines)

Because these engines run high compression and high boost pressures, it needs to be cooled down at idle prior to shutting down. Many of these cars suffer cracked cylinder heads and blown head gaskets because the owners do not give the engine the proper 30+ second cool-down.

While the head gasket problem only requires removing the cylinder head to replace the gasket, and perhaps milling the head to flatten it, cracks are a more serious problem. The OM603 is known for cracked cylinder heads, while the OM602 primarily suffers head gasket failure.

Most of the cracked heads crack deep inside the valve guide area and repairs are almost impossible to perform. New cylinder heads are quite expensive and, due to the limited number of cars sold, there are very few used heads available.

Always give the engine an idle cool-down if it has been running at turbo boost pressure.

Turbo boost pressure

To maximize engine performance, boost pressure should be checked and adjusted regularly. The turbocharger wastegate is adjustable. When making adjustments, it is recommended to set the boost pressure a little on the high side. Refer to the factory repair information for checking and adjusting turbo boost pressure.

Turbo boost pressure

Max. boost pressure . . . . 0.95 bar (13.7 psi)

> **WARNING—**
>
> *Checking and adjusting boost pressure requires a boost gauge and must be checked by driving the car on the road. DO NOT attempt to make this test by yourself. You must have a passenger helper focused on the boost gauge while you focus on driving.*

6

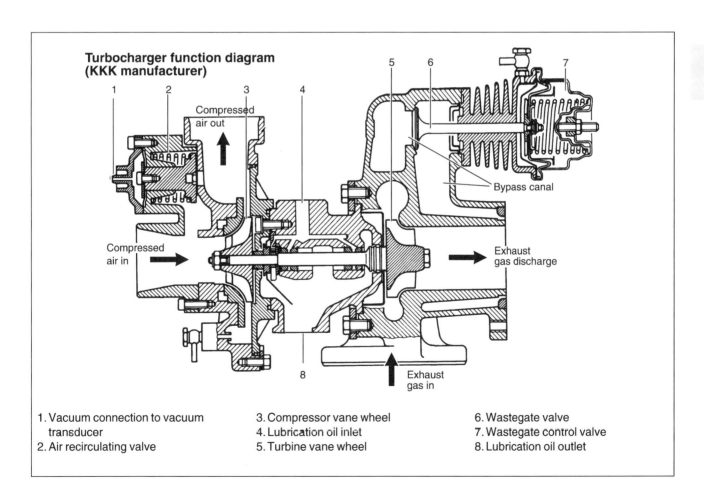

Turbocharger function diagram (KKK manufacturer)

- Compressed air out
- Compressed air in
- Compressed air out
- Exhaust gas discharge
- Exhaust gas in
- Bypass canal

1. Vacuum connection to vacuum transducer
2. Air recirculating valve
3. Compressor vane wheel
4. Lubrication oil inlet
5. Turbine vane wheel
6. Wastegate valve
7. Wastegate control valve
8. Lubrication oil outlet

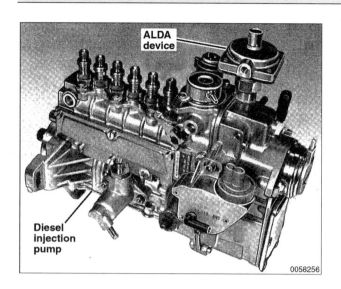

ALDA device

Diesel injection pump

0058256

◁ When power suddenly drops off for no apparent reason, check the plastic pressure line that goes from the intake manifold through the switchover valve to the ALDA barometric device. If this line becomes plugged, the ALDA will not sense boost pressure and will not richen the mixture under boost. Be sure this hose is always unobstructed.

Oil changes

As with all diesel engines, rigorous oil change frequency is the key to long life. The factory-specified change interval for normal service is 5,000 miles and severe operating conditions require 2,500 mile changes. Turbocharged diesel engines should be considered to be running under severe operating conditions all the time.

Oil change schedules and specifications are detailed in **Chapter 3**.

OM606 oil filling procedure

When refilling the OM606 engine during an oil change, directing the bottle nozzle toward the front of the motor will allow oil to quickly flow down the timing cover and into the oil pan.

The oil return from the cylinder head tends to be rather slow on this engine. You should never start the engine until all the oil has flowed into the pan.

Vacuum pump (OM602 / OM603 engines)

Diesel engines do not produce engine vacuum like gasoline engines do. Therefore, a vacuum pump is needed to supply vacuum for many systems including

• EDS (electronic diesel system)
• Brake booster
• Climate control system
• Vacuum modulator system

Vacuum pump failures are well known for both OM602 and OM603 engines. Check valve failures are common and over time and high mileage, the pump bearings wear out. If pieces of the vacuum pump drop into the engine timing housing, the timing chain can break, and destroy the engine.

When a vacuum pump becomes noisy or emits any rattling noises, the pump should be replaced immediately.

Belt tensioner

The polyribbed (serpentine) belt tensioner will wear. Once worn, it will wobble around and make noise. This wobble will elongate the mounting hole in the timing housing cover. Replace the belt tensioner as soon as it appears out of parallel with the belt run. Replacing this sooner rather than later will save the cost of removing the timing housing cover and repairing the threads.

6

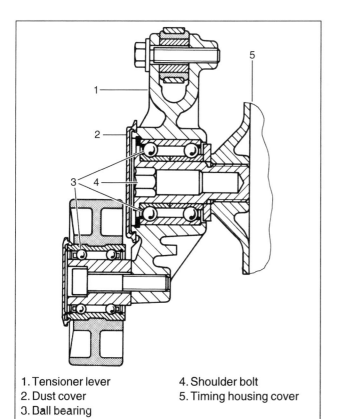

1. Tensioner lever
2. Dust cover
3. Ball bearing
4. Shoulder bolt
5. Timing housing cover

Injection line tightening

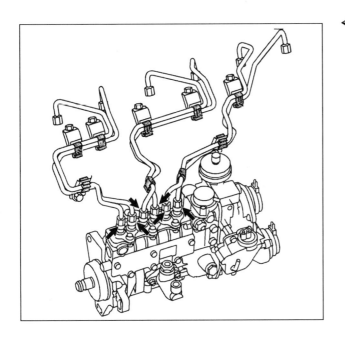

◀ Care should be taken to tighten the injection line unions and fittings to specification when removing and replacing the injection lines at the pump body. Overtorquing can result in a warped, non-functioning injection pump body.

Tightening torque

Injection line to component . . . . . . 10 - 20 Nm (7 - 14 ft-lb)

Gasket maker

> **CAUTION—**
> Never use silicon sealant (RTV) when working with engine gaskets.

Turbo engines are heavily dependent upon the oil jets under the pistons to remove the heat of combustion, especially when the engine is under high boost pressures. If this oil flow is interrupted in any way, such as with a chunk of RTV gasket material, the resulting heat buildup will quickly cause the piston to expand and seize in the bore.

Use a high quality gasket dressing such as Hylomar® and use sparingly.

Chapter 7

Fuel Injection

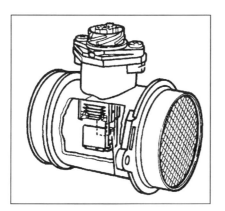

7

TABLE

GENERAL

The W124 E-Class cars are all equipped with a Bosch fuel injection system designed specifically for Mercedes-Benz cars. **Table a** lists injection system application information.

NOTE—
Engine application information is given on the endleaf of this book.

Table a. Injection system applications

Engine designation	Fuel system
M103 (2.6 liter, 3.0 liter, 6-cyl. SOHC, all years) **M104** (3.0 liter 6-cyl. DOHC, 1990 - 1992)	CIS-E (KE-III, continuous electro-mechanical fuel injection)
M119 (4.0 liter, 4.2 liter, 5.0 liter V-8, all years)	LH-SFI (hot-wire mass air flow sensor, sequential fuel injection)
M104 (2.8 liter, 3.2 liter 6-cyl. DOHC, 1993 - 1995)	HFM-SFI (hot-film mass air flow sensor, sequential fuel injection, integrated ignition)
OM602 (2.5 liter 5-cyl. SOHC turbocharged diesel, 1990 - 1993) **OM603** (3.0 liter 6-cyl. SOHC turbocharged diesel, 1987) **OM606** (3.0 liter 6-cyl DOHC normally aspirated, 1995)	Electronic Diesel System (EDS)

The fuel system has three main functions:

• Deliver fuel to engine
• Admit filtered air to engine
• Mix fuel and air in precise proportions and deliver mixture to cylinders as a combustible vapor

The fuel injection system injects atomized fuel into the intake air stream under pressure. This method of active fuel metering means that the fuel mixture entering the engine can be controlled more precisely and used more efficiently, yielding improved driveability, fuel economy, and performance.

FUEL SUPPLY (GASOLINE MODELS)

The fuel supply system is basically the same for all three gasoline fuel injection systems. On most models, two electric fuel pumps, mounted externally under the car, supply filtered fuel under pressure to the fuel injection system.

NOTE—

• *1986 and 1987 cars were equipped with a single fuel pump, while all later cars used the dual pump setup (as shown below). The pump assembly is mounted in the right rear underside of the car. A protective, aerodynamic cover hides the components.*

• *On 1988 300TE models, the second fuel pump is mounted above the final drive, closer to the fuel tank.*

• *Fuel flows directly around the electric fuel pump motor internal elements, but there is no danger of explosion because there is never an ignitable mixture in the pump.*

Electric fuel pump

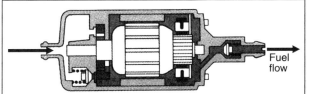

◄ The fuel pump(s) is designed to deliver more fuel than the maximum requirement of the engine. Excess fuel flows back to the fuel tank via the diaphragm fuel pressure regulator.

◄ The fuel supply system consists of one or two roller cell type pumps (**A**), the fuel filter (**B**), and a fuel accumulator.

During starting, the pump runs as long as the ignition key is held in START position. The pump continues to run when the engine has started (ignition speed signal is present). A safety circuit will stop the pump if the ignition is ON but the engine has stopped turning (for instance, in case of an accident).

Fuel pump relay

CIS-E fuel pump relay

◄ The voltage for the fuel pump(s) is supplied by the fuel pump relay (**arrow**). When the ignition key is turned on, the relay runs the fuel pump(s) for about one second. Once the starter is actuated and a speed (tachometer) signal is present, the pump will continue to run. The fuel pump relay also contains the engine speed (rev) limiter.

The maximum speed of the engine is governed by the speed signal of the ignition system. When the preset redline speed is reached, the fuel pump voltage is pulsed.

7

The fuel pump relay also powers the cold start valve (CIS-E cars only). The cold start valve supplies supplemental fuel during cold starts (up to 8 seconds, depending on engine temperature) Once the engine is running, the cold start valve does not operate.

NOTE—

From model year 1990, the fuel pump relay is combined with the air conditioning compressor control module (KLIMA). The new unit, called the engine systems control module (MAS), controls:
-Fuel pump
-Air conditioner compressor
-Oxygen sensor heating
-Secondary air injection
-6,450 rpm limiter.

Fuel Filter

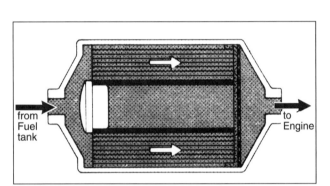

◁ The fuel filter is mounted next to the fuel pump and downstream from it. The filter contains a fine paper element with a damper installed on the inlet side to reduce fuel noises.

Fuel accumulator (CIS-E cars only)

The accumulator functions to maintain residual pressure in the fuel system after the engine has been switched off. This results in faster restarts, particularly when the engine is hot. The fuel accumulator also reduces the pulsation noise of the electric fuel pump.

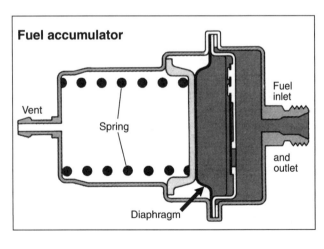

Fuel accumulator

Vent

Spring

Diaphragm

Fuel inlet

and outlet

 ◁ During fuel pump operation the accumulator chamber is filled with fuel. This causes the diaphragm to move back against the force of the spring until it reaches the stops in the spring chamber. The diaphragm remains in this position as long as the engine is running.

When the engine is switched off and the fuel pump stops, the spring loaded diaphragm deflects to maintain the line pressure at about 2 bar (30 psi). The spring chamber is vented into the fuel pump suction line in case the diaphragm ruptures.

NOTE—

The accumulator should maintain 2 bar (30 psi) of pressure for at least 30 minutes. This helps prevent vapor lock caused by fuel vaporization and easy restarts. If experiencing hard starting when the engine is hot, check the fuel system residual pressure with the engine off.

FUEL SUPPLY (DIESEL MODELS)

Diesel fuel supply is via a simple mechanical pump on the side of the diesel injection pump in the engine compartment.

For the sake of engine longevity, always maintain cleanliness in the diesel fuel system by periodically replacing the fuel filter. See **Chapter 3**.

BOSCH CIS-E (KE-III)

CIS-E control module

0058272

 The Bosch CIS-E fuel injection system, also known as KE-III, is a mechanical injection system with electronic control. The CIS-E system is a further development of the basic CIS mechanical injection system that dates back to the mid-1970s. The main difference between the CIS and the CIS-E system is that the latter is equipped with an electrohydraulic actuator (EHA) in place of the warm-up regulator. Fuel delivery volume is regulated by an electronic control module; hence the addition of 'E' to the designation.

The basic mechanical function of the system is simple in principle. Fuel is drawn out of the fuel tank and supplied to the CIS-E fuel distributor under pressure. The system pressure is held constant by a pressure regulator. Based on the amount of air drawn past the air flow sensor plate, the injectors continuously spray a fine atomized fuel charge into the intake ports. When the intake valves open, the air-fuel mixture is drawn into the cylinders.

Electronic controls are used for mixture adaption and idle speed control for varying engine operating conditions. The individual components of the fuel supply system are described below.

Fuel injectors

 The mechanical fuel injectors are precision spray nozzles. Above a minimum pressure, the injector nozzles open and continuously deliver atomized fuel into the engine intake ports. The injectors are held in place in the intake manifold runners by thick rubber O-rings.

The fuel is atomized by the oscillation of the injector's needle valve. The injectors vibrate audibly when fuel is flowing through them. When the engine is switched off, the injectors close tightly so that no fuel drips into the intake ports.

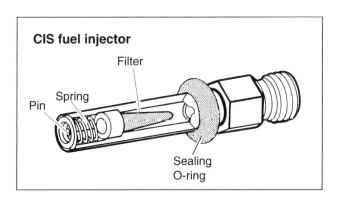

CIS fuel injector

Filter

Spring

Pin

Sealing
O-ring

7

CIS-E fuel injection

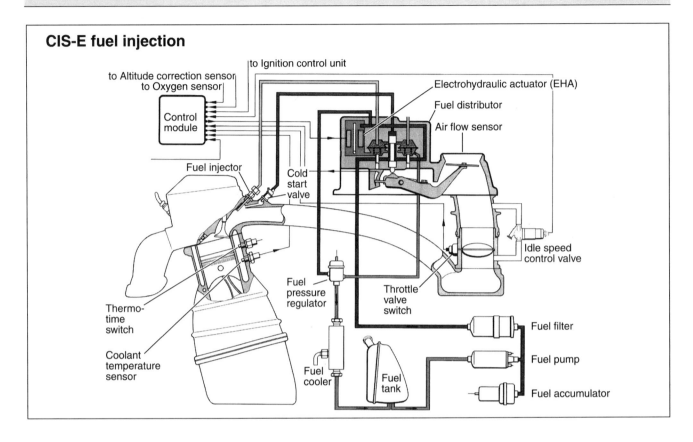

Fuel pressure regulator

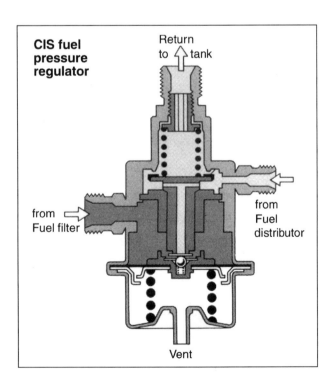

◄ The fuel pressure regulator maintains 5.4 bar (78 psi) of fuel pressure when the engine is running. This pressure is not adjustable. The normal operating range for the regulator is 5.3 - 5.5 bar (77 - 79 psi).

System pressure directly affects the quantity of fuel injected and must be accurately maintained. The pressure regulator also compensates for variations in supply pressure from the fuel pump during periods of rapid load change. The pressure is regulated by a spring loaded diaphragm and excess fuel is returned to the fuel tank. The pressure regulator contains a check valve that works in conjunction with the accumulator to maintain system pressure when the engine is turned off.

Throttle valve

◀ The throttle valve controls the amount of air entering the engine. The throttle valve switch signals the CIS-E control module when the throttle is fully closed (idle) or wide open.

Fuel distributor

◀ The mixture control unit contains the downdraft air flow sensor assembly, the electrohydraulic actuator (EHA), and the fuel distributor.

Based on the measured air and engine operating conditions, the fuel distributor meters fuel continuously to all cylinders at once. As the air flow sensor plate is pulled down, fuel passes from the fuel distributor through steel pipes to the injection nozzles.

◀ The circular air-flow sensor plate is positioned in the intake duct so that all air entering the engine flows past it. The plate is attached to a lever that pivots, allowing the plate to move up and down. Intake air flowing through the housing pushes the sensor plate down.

Air measurement is turned into an injection quantity by the control plunger in the center of the fuel distributor. The plunger rests on the end of the air-flow sensor lever. It rises when the sensor plate falls and falls when the plate rises. When air flow into the engine increases and lowers the air-flow sensor plate, the rise of the plunger increases fuel flow to the fuel injectors proportionally.

7

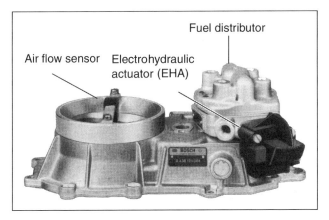

CIS-E mixture control unit

Fuel flow
1. to Fuel pressure regulator
2. to Fuel injector
3. to Cold start valve
4. from Fuel pump
5. Fuel return

Components
6. Control plunger
7. Upper chamber
8. Diaphragm
9. Lower chamber
10. Mixture adjusting screw
11. Air-flow sensor plate
12. Electrohydraulic actuator (EHA)
13. Fuel distributor
14. Air-flow sensor housing

Electrohydraulic actuator (EHA)

The EHA, mounted to the side of the fuel distributor, constantly fine tunes the air-fuel mixture to compensate for warm-up enrichment, emission control demands, and all other varying engine operating conditions.

◄ The CIS-E control system adjusts the basic air-fuel mixture by varying the control current to the electrohydraulic actuator (EHA). Altering the current to the EHA changes the pressure drop at the control plunger, directly affecting the volume of fuel flowing to each injector.

The current supplied to the EHA is determined by the CIS-E control module. To determine how much current to apply, the control module depends on inputs from various engine sensors. These inputs include engine speed, engine temperature, throttle position and air flow sensor plate position among others. Control is very accurate and fast.

NOTE—
The control module has a built in logic circuit that monitors sensor inputs. If a sensor suddenly goes out of range (no signal or false signal from the coolant temperature sensor, for example) the control module will compare the new reading to the last stored reading in its memory, recognize the implausible signal and revert to a fixed operating mode.

Electronic idle speed control

◄ Idle speed is electronically controlled via the idle speed air valve, which maintains idle speed by bypassing varying amounts of air around the closed throttle valve.

When the throttle is in rest position, a programmed nominal speed (rpm) in the CIS-E control module is continuously compared to the engine's actual speed. If the actual speed varies from the programmed speed, the duty cycle signal to the valve is changed to maintain the desired engine speed.

CIS-E fuel distributor and EHA

Injector fuel

Actuator fuel

Diaphragm

Control unit connector

Distributor

EHA

Actuator fuel

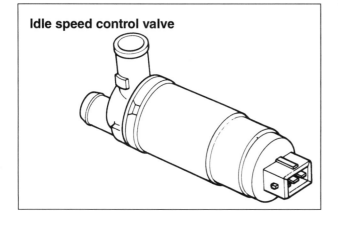

Idle speed control valve

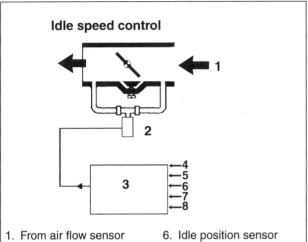

Idle speed control

1. From air flow sensor
2. Idle speed control valve
3. CIS-E control module
4. Engine speed sensor
5. Engine temp. sensor
6. Idle position sensor
7. A/C on input
8. Shift lever position switch

◁ The CIS-E control module uses the following inputs to regulate idle speed:

• Engine speed (ignition terminal TD)
• Coolant temperature (engine coolant temp. sensor)
• Closed throttle position (throttle valve switch, idle contact)
• Automatic transmission position (shift lever position switch)
• A/C compressor cut-in (A/C relay)

Cold start valve

◁ The cold start valve provides supplemental fuel to the engine during cold starting. The valve is operated via the fuel pump relay. If the engine temperature is below a specified temperature, the valve will operate for up to 8 seconds when the starter is actuated. The relay calculates the length of spray time based on engine temperature.

7

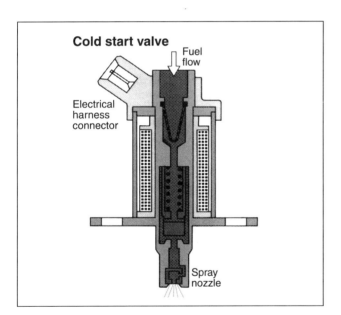

Cold start valve

Fuel flow

Electrical harness connector

Spray nozzle

Altitude compensation

The altitude sensor provides the control module with a voltage signal indicating altitude above sea level. It supplies information about sea level, 1,000 and 2,000 meters (3,000 and 6,000 feet) to the control module so the mixture may be leaned out to compensate for the lack of oxygen and cylinder filling at higher altitudes.

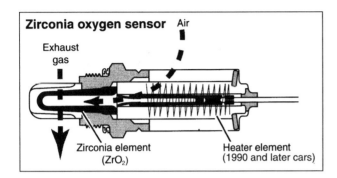

Zirconia oxygen sensor Air

Exhaust gas

Zirconia element (ZrO₂)

Heater element (1990 and later cars)

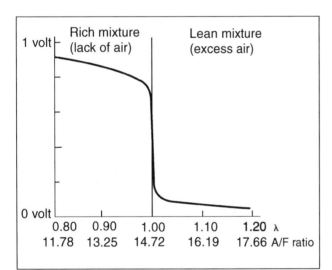

1 volt

Rich mixture (lack of air)

Lean mixture (excess air)

0 volt

0.80	0.90	1.00	1.10	1.20	λ
11.78	13.25	14.72	16.19	17.66	A/F ratio

Oxygen sensor

◄ The oxygen sensor adapts the air-fuel mixture by sending a varying voltage signal to the CIS-E control module. The zirconia (ZrO₂) oxygen sensor, fully warmed up, generates 0.1 - 0.9 volt fluctuating current in response to oxygen content in the exhaust gas. Fuel mixture is electronically regulated based on the voltage output of the sensor.

Oxygen sensor output is unreliable when cold. Starting with 1990 models, an oxygen sensor designed with a built-in heating element comes up to operating temperature quickly.

◄ A high concentration of oxygen in the exhaust gas indicates a lean mixture and a low oxygen content indicates a rich mixture. The signal from the oxygen sensor is used by the CIS-E control module to influence engine performance and driveability.

NOTE—

- *The signal from the oxygen sensor is ignored by the CIS-E control module until the sensor reaches operating temperature. Therefore, when troubleshooting cold engine driveability problems, the oxygen sensor can be ruled out as a cause.*

- *For 1990 the CIS-E control module is equipped with on-board diagnostics with resident memory. Other new control features incorporated into the control module are:*
  -Transmission shift point delay
  -Exhaust gas recirculation control
  -Charcoal canister purge control
  -Data exchange with the EZL ignition module.

ELECTRONIC FUEL INJECTION (LH AND HFM)

◄ 1993 and later M104 (twin-cam 6-cylinder) engines and the M119 (V-8) engines use Bosch pulsed injection systems with air mass measurement. Two different systems (LH and HFM) are used on the W124 cars, as listed in **Table a** given earlier.

The main difference between LH and HFM is that the latter combines the fuel injection function with the ignition function in a single control module.

Pulsed systems meter fuel to the engine by electronically controlling the amount of time that the injectors are open. The main components of the pulsed sys-

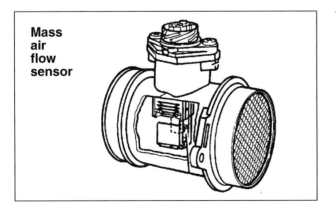

Mass air flow sensor

Bosch LH (hot-wire) fuel injection

Fuel injector

Fuel pressure regulator

Coolant temperature sensor

Electronic throttle control

Mass air flow sensor

Oxygen sensor

Engine control module (ECM)

Fuel filter

Fuel pump

Fuel tank

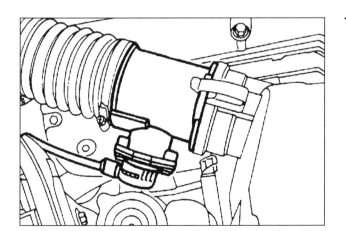

tems are the mass air flow sensor, the electronic control module and the electromagnetic injectors.

◁ **Air measurement.** The hot-wire and hot-film mass air flow sensors are both 'thermal' load sensors. They are installed between the air filter and the throttle valve where they monitor the mass of the air being drawn into the engine.

An electrically heated element (wire or film) is mounted in the air stream where it is cooled by the flow of incoming air. A control circuit modulates the current necessary to maintain the temperature differential between the wire or film and the intake air at a constant level. It is the current needed to maintain this differential that indicates the mass of the intake air to the control module.

7

Hot wire mass air flow sensor

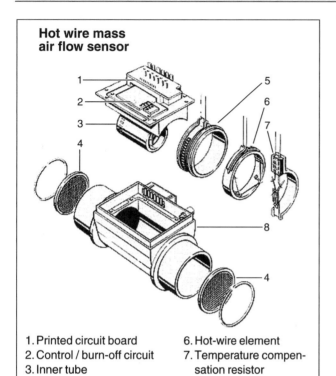

1. Printed circuit board
2. Control / burn-off circuit
3. Inner tube
4. Guard
5. Precision resistor
6. Hot-wire element
7. Temperature compen-
   sation resistor
8. Housing

◀ The mass air flow sensor (hot wire or hot film) has no moving parts, translating into mechanical simplification and the speed benefits of electronics.

Because the output signal can change if the surface of the hot wire becomes dirty or contaminated, the wire is briefly heated to a high "burn-off" temperature every time the engine is switched off. Burn-off is not required for the hot-film sensor.

Electric fuel injector

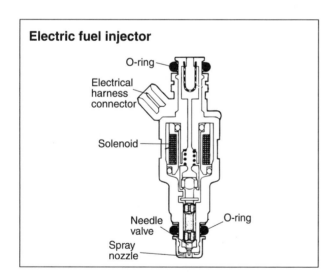

O-ring
Electrical harness connector
Solenoid
Needle valve
Spray nozzle
O-ring

◀ **Fuel metering.** The engine control module (ECM) meters fuel by changing the opening time (pulse width) of the fuel injectors. To ensure that injector pulse width is the only factor that determines fuel metering, accurate fuel pressure is maintained by a fuel pressure regulator. The injectors are mounted to a common fuel supply called the fuel rail.

A coolant temperature sensor signals engine temperature for mixture adaption. An exhaust oxygen sensor signals information about combustion efficiency for control of the air-fuel mixture.

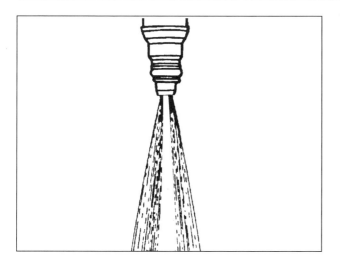

◄ On engines with four valves per cylinder, the flow from the injector is divided into two separate streams, one for the backside of each intake valve.

Idle speed. LH and HFM fuel injection in the Mercedes-Benz is designed with no provision for idle adjustment. Idle speed is controlled electronically.

NOTE—
The integration of idle speed control, cruise control, and throttle actuation is further detailed in the section **Throttle Control Systems** *in* **Chapter 11***.*

Knock (detonation) control. Knock sensors monitor and control ignition knock through the engine control module (ECM). A knock sensor functions like a microphone and is able to convert mechanical vibration (knock) into electrical signals. The control module is programmed to react to frequencies that are characteristic of engine knock and varies the ignition timing point accordingly.

Engines with LH and HFM fuel injection are equipped with two knock sensors.

The LH and HFM injection systems feature on-board diagnostics (OBD) and adaptive technology. Fuel system adaption compensates for conditions such as engine wear and unmeasured intake air and is designed to maintain driveability as the engine ages.

ELECTRONIC DIESEL SYSTEM (EDS)

Three different diesel engines were installed in E-Class cars through the production run, as shown in the following table.

Table b. Diesel engine applications

Year, model	No. cyl.	Engine number	Chassis number
1987, 300D Turbo 1987, 300TD Turbo	6	OM603	124.133 124.193
1990 - 1993, 300D 2.5 Turbo	5	OM602	124.128
1995, E300 Diesel	6	OM606	124.131

7

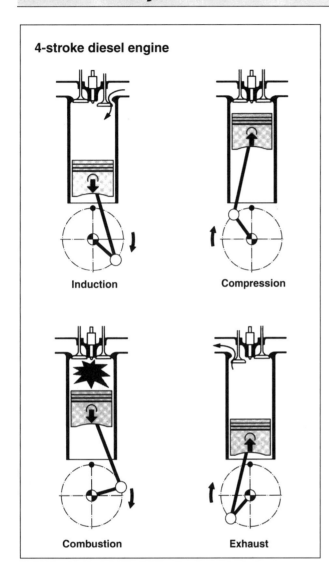

4-stroke diesel engine

Induction   Compression

Combustion   Exhaust

◀ The four-stroke diesel engines installed in E-Class cars utilize the sequence induction-compression-combustion-exhaust familiar from gasoline-powered 4-stroke engines. However, instead of using an electric spark to ignite the fuel-air mixture, the heat produced by high compression in the diesel cylinder (typically around 22: 1 in the E-Class) triggers combustion. Diesel engine design allows each cylinder to fill up with air during the intake stroke. The air is then compressed. At the top of the compression stroke just the correct amount of fuel is injected into the cylinder at just the correct time. The compressed (hot) air immediately ignites the fuel.

Diesel fuel contains more carbon atoms in longer chains than gasoline (typical gasoline = C_9H_{20}, while typical diesel fuel = $C_{14}H_{30}$). On average, 1 gallon of gasoline contains approx. 132×10^6 joules (125,000 BTU) of energy, while 1 gallon of diesel contains approx. 155×10^6 joules (147,000 BTU) of energy. It also takes less refining to produce diesel fuel. The combination of higher efficiency from high compression combustion and a fuel with higher inherent energy content, which is cheaper to produce, makes diesel engine technology an attractive alternative to gasoline-powered internal combustion engines.

Once underway, a traditional diesel engine can run indefinitely with no electrical input. When starting a cold diesel, however, electrical glow-plugs are used to preheat the combustion chambers for a few seconds and facilitate combustion. See **Chapter 11**.

EDS for OM603 engine

The OM603 diesel engine, introduced in 1987, marked the beginning of tighter emission control systems for passenger car diesel engines. Smog regulations, particularly in California, were beginning to strangle diesel sales. 1987 E-Class diesel cars with Electronic Diesel System (EDS) passed emissions requirements for all fifty states.

The EDS control module is capable of:

• Idle speed adjustment
• EGR control
• Recirculating air control to the trap oxidizer
• Diagnostic monitoring

Electronic Diesel System (EDS)
OM603 engine

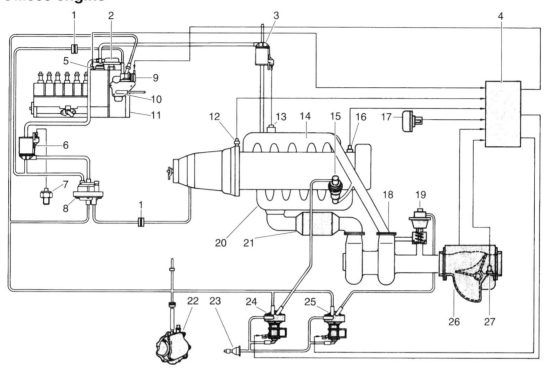

1. Vacuum damper
2. Aneroid compensator (ALDA device)
3. Engine overload protection switchover valve
4. EDS control unit
5. Fuel rack position sensor
6. Transmission vacuum switchover
   valve
7. 50° Temperature switch
8. Vacuum amplifier
9. Idle actuator

10. Vacuum control valve
11. Diesel injection pump
12. Crankshaft speed sensor
13. Engine overload protection switch
    (1.2 bar)
14. Intake manifold
15. EGR valve
16. Coolant temperature sensor (EDS)
17. Altitude correction sensor
18. Turbocharger
19. Air recirculating valve

20. Exhaust manifold
21. Trap oxidizer
22. Vacuum pump
23. Filter
24. EGR Air recirculating valve
25. Air recirculating valve vacuum trans-
    ducer
26. Air flow sensor (EDS)
27. Intake air temperature sensor

7

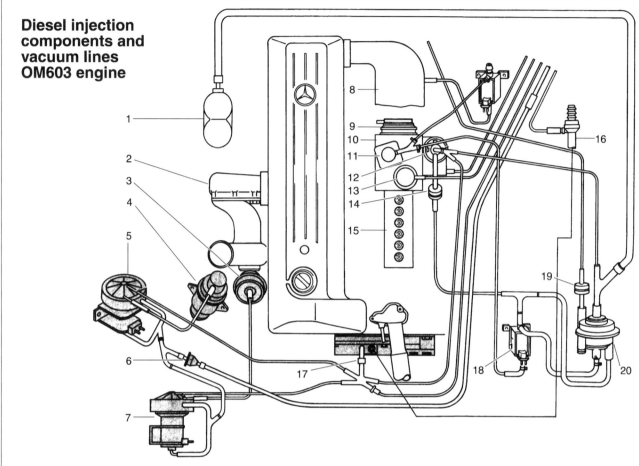

Diesel injection components and vacuum lines OM603 engine

1. Vacuum reservoir (under left front wheel housing trim)
2. Turbocharger
3. Air recirculating valve
4. EGR valve
5. EGR valve vacuum transducer
6. Filter
7. Air recirculating valve vacuum transducer
8. Intake manifold
9. Idle speed control
10. Governor
11. Aneroid compensator (Alda device)
12. Vacuum control valve
13. Vacuum shut-off
14. Vacuum damper
15. Diesel injection pump
16. Brake booster check-valve
17. Filter
18. Vacuum amplifier switchover valve, automatic transmission
19. Vacuum damper
20. Vacuum amplifier

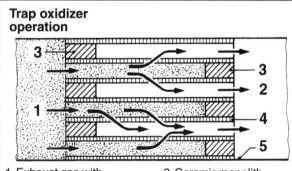

Trap oxidizer operation

1. Exhaust gas with particulates
2. Filtered exhaust gas
3. Ceramic monolith
4. Porous cell walls
5. Steel cylinder

The 1987 300D Turbo and 300TD Turbo were equipped with a trap oxidizer, located between the exhaust manifold and the turbocharger. The trap oxidizer is a self-regenerating filter of ceramic monolith construction housed in a steel cylinder. The surface area of the monolith is electroplated with silver alloy.

The trap oxidizer works by forcing the exhaust gas through porous cell walls. Exhaust particles are held back in the porous structure and are then oxidized by the high exhaust gas temperatures. The oxidation is facilitated by the silver alloy layer. The particles are almost totally converted to carbon dioxide (CO_2).

The trap oxidizer is able to regenerate and clean itself out at exhaust gas temperatures above 360°C (680°F). If the exhaust temperature is above 580°C (1076°F) for a prolonged period, the filter will regenerate completely.

The normal operating back pressure from the trap oxidizer is around 2 bar (30 psi). There is a tap on the exhaust manifold where this can be measured.

EDS for OM602 engine

EDS for the OM602 turbodiesel engine is equipped with additional inputs.

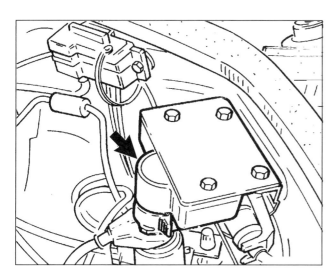

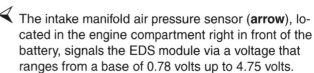
The intake manifold air pressure sensor (**arrow**), located in the engine compartment right in front of the battery, signals the EDS module via a voltage that ranges from a base of 0.78 volts up to 4.75 volts.

7

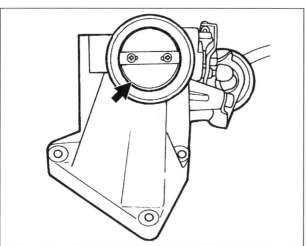

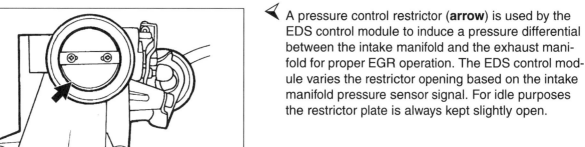
A pressure control restrictor (**arrow**) is used by the EDS control module to induce a pressure differential between the intake manifold and the exhaust manifold for proper EGR operation. The EDS control module varies the restrictor opening based on the intake manifold pressure sensor signal. For idle purposes the restrictor plate is always kept slightly open.

Electronic Diesel System (EDS) components, OM606 engine

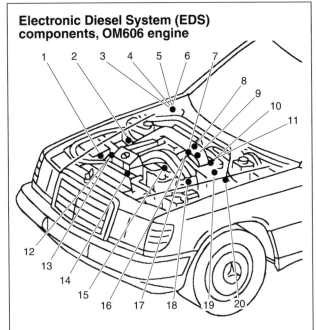

1. BARO sensor
2. EGR valve
   Pressure control valve
3. Engine harness connector (12-pole)
4. Data link connector
5. Over-voltage protection relay
6. ISC module
   EGR/resonance intake manifold control module
7. Engine coolant temperature sensors (ISC, preglow system)
8. Engine coolant temperature sensor
9. Resonance valve components
10. A/C compressor cut-out / EGR microswitch
11. ISC electromagnetic actuator
12. Vacuum amplifier
13. EGR switchover valve
    Pressure control flap switchover valve
14. Vacuum pump
15. Vacuum element "STOP"
16. Vacuum control valve
17. Modulator pressure vacuum element
18. Crankshaft speed sensor

EDS for OM606 engine

◁ The OM606, installed in 1995 E-Class diesel cars, is a normally aspirated, 4-valve per cylinder 6-cylinder engine. It is equipped with a mechanically governed in-line fuel injection pump, exhaust gas recirculation (EGR) and an oxidation catalytic converter.

Refer to the accompanying illustration for component locations. Note the following components and features in the OM606 engine fuel system:

Fuel filter with shut-off valve. Fuel prefilter and shut-off valve are installed in upper part of fuel filter. Shut-off valve replaces emergency stop lever on fuel injection pump.

Fuel preheater. Engine coolant heat exchanger installed in cylinder head preheats diesel fuel to insure trouble-free operation with winter diesel fuel to -25°C (-13°F).

Idle speed control (ISC). ISC module controls engine idle, detects and stores Diagnostic Trouble Codes (DTCs) for later retrieval.

Resonance intake manifold. Two resonance flaps in intake manifold make it possible to vary manifold runner length. Three different lengths are available, making it possible to obtain good torque in lower rpm range as well as good performance in mid and upper rpm range.

Emission controls. Exhaust gas recirculation (EGR) and intake manifold air pressure control system result in reduction of nitrogen oxides (NO_x) and of particulate matter.

Oxidation catalytic converter. Exhaust gases flowing through the catalytic converter are further oxidized: carbon monoxide (CO) to carbon dioxide (CO_2) and hydrocarbons to carbon dioxide and water (H_2O). This process also reduces particulate matter emissions, as hydrocarbons in the carbon soot are oxidized.

BARO sensor. The BARO sensor deactivates the pressure control flap at approximately 2,000 meters (6,100 ft).

TIPS, MAINTENANCE, SERVICE

Engine control module (ECM), replacing

The engine control module (ECM) in LH-SFI and HFM-SFI systems is designed to detect and store vehicle-specific information: Transmission type, Federal or California version, Electronic Accelerator (EA) or Idle Speed Control (ISC), presence or absence of ASR, etc. Adaptation factors such as throttle valve angle and fuel trim are also stored in the module.

To install a different module, use the Mercedes-Benz hand-held tester, STAR laptop or equivalent diagnostic scan tool to clear previously stored information and to reenter module codes.

Diesel fuel filter, replacing

When changing the diesel fuel filter, pour the fuel out of the old filter into the new filter. This will decrease the time that is needed to crank the engine to prime the fuel system.

Fuel filter replacement procedure is in **Chapter 3**.

Trap oxidizer reengineered

 The 1987 300D Turbo and 300TD Turbo were equipped with a particulate combustion device called a trap oxidizer, located between the exhaust manifold and the turbocharger. After some time in service, the device broke apart internally, shedding pieces of ceramic into the engine and the turbocharger. Mercedes-Benz reengineered the oxidizer and instituted a recall campaign for free replacement with the new design. The newer trap oxidizer is much smaller, about the diameter of the exhaust pipe itself. The replacement unit gives the engine better breathing characteristics and allows it to make more horsepower.

7

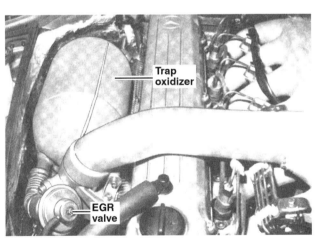

Trap oxidizer

EGR valve

Chapter 8

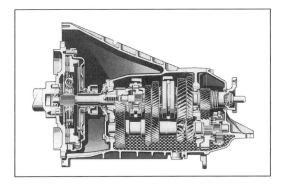

Transmissions

8

GENERAL

This chapter describes the transmissions used in the E-Class. There is one manual transmission and two automatic transmission versions used.

MANUAL TRANSMISSION

A 5-speed manual transmission was available in the 300E from 1986 to 1988, and in the 260E from 1987 to 1988. The 5-speed was a no cost option but fewer than three hundred were sold.

Clutch

The clutch disc, made of asbestos-free material, measures 240 mm (9.44 in) in diameter. The pressure plate maintains a contact force ranging from 6,300 to 7,000 Nm (4,646 to 5,162 ft-lb). The master cylinder piston diameter is 19.05 mm (0.750 in) and the slave cylinder piston is 23.81 mm (0.937 in).

Gearbox

The 5-speed counter-shaft type transmission has an overdrive fifth gear. All forward gears are synchronized. **Table a** shows the gear ratios.

Table a. Manual transmission gear ratios

Gear	Ratio	Number of gear teeth (mainshaft/ countershaft)
Countershaft constant	1.567	47/30
1st gear	3.856	32/13
2nd gear	2.183	39/28
3rd gear	1.376	41/36
4th gear	1.000	direct
5th gear	0.799	26/51
reverse	4.218	35/13

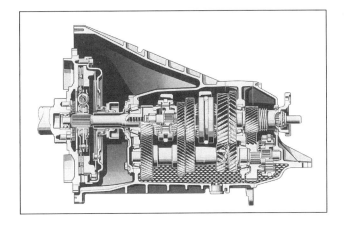

Transmission construction

◁ The transmission case and all of the covers are made of light aluminum alloy with the clutch housing forming an integral part of the gear box case. Fifth gear is located in the rear transmission cover.

The transmission is aligned to the engine using dowel pins which are seated into the transmission housing and have matching machined bores on the engine block.

The manual transmission holds 1.5 L (1.58 qt) of automatic transmission fluid (ATF). The transmission front cover is sealed with Loctite® 573 anaerobic sealant instead of a gasket.

8

AUTOMATIC TRANSMISSION

Several different versions of the 722.3 and 722.4 series transmission were installed in the E-Class over its ten year production run. **Table b** shows the installed versions for the US.

Table b. Automatic transmission applications

Model	Chassis Number	Transmission Number
260E, 300E 2.6	124.026	722.429
300E 2.8	124.028	722.433
300E	124.030	722.358
E320	124.032	722.369
400E, E420	124.034	722.354 > 09/92 10/92 > 722.355
500E, E500	124.036	722.365
300CE	124.050	722.358
300CE	124.051	722.359
E320 Coupe	124.052	722.369
E320 Cabriolet	124.066	722.369
300TE	124.090	722.358
E320 Wagon	124.092	722.369
300D 2.5 Turbo	124.128	722.418
E300 Diesel	124.131	722.435
300D Turbo	124.133	722.357
300TD Turbo	124.193	722.357
300E 4MATIC	124.230	722.342
300TE 4MATIC	124.290	722.342

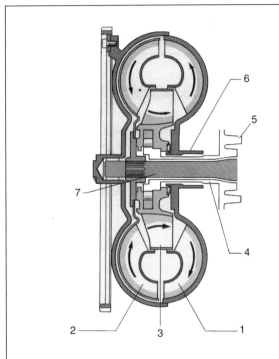

1. Pump wheel
2. Turbine wheel
3. Guide wheel
4. Transmission front cover
5. Primary pump drive flange
6. Torque converter housing
7. Input shaft

Torque converter

 The torque converter includes the following components:

- The pump wheel, also called the primary wheel, is bolted directly to the output of the engine through the flex plate, which is bolted to the crankshaft with three pairs of bolts spaced at 120° intervals around the flex plate.
- The turbine or secondary wheel is connected to the input shaft.
- The guide wheel, also known as the stator, is mounted on the free-wheeling unit that is connected to the stator shaft.
- The primary pump drive flange fits into and drives the primary (front) pump.

The torque converter holds more than half of the total fluid supply in the transmission. As the engine turns, the pump wheel spins. The turbine blades on the pump wheel force the transmission fluid to flow through the turbine wheel. The blade design on the turbine wheel causes the turbine wheel to start turning in the same direction as the pump wheel. The fluid then flows off the turbine wheel through the vanes of the guide wheel.

The guide wheel is locked in the direction opposite to the direction of rotation of the engine. The force of the fluid coming off of the guide wheel adds to the force of the engine driving the pump wheel.

The sum of the engine torque and the additional torque provided by the guide wheel is equal to the torque of the turbine wheel applied into the transmission. The ratio of the output torque to the drive-off torque (torque multiplication) within the converter is 1.8 - 2.0 : 1.

8

◁ Power flows through the torque converter as follows:

As the turbine wheel speed increases, it changes the angle of attack of the fluid coming off it and going through the guide wheel, causing the speed of the guide wheel to constantly change in relation to the turbine wheel.

As the guide wheel speed increases, the fluid flow starts moving off the flat surface of the blade and onto the backside of the blade, causing the guide wheel to rotate in the same direction as the pump and turbine wheels.

As the different wheel rotations approach the same speed, the torque multiplication approaches a value of 1. As the torque converter reaches its normal operating state, its speed is 0.87 - 0.9 of engine speed. At this point the torque converter acts as a fluid clutch with a maximum lock up efficiency of 98%.

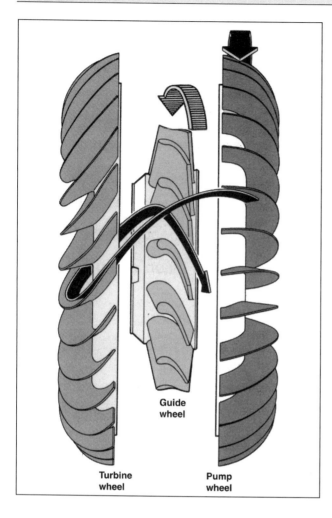

Guide
wheel

Turbine
wheel

Pump
wheel

Transmission construction

◁ The transmission housing and bell housing are made of aluminum alloy as a one piece casting. The single piece construction makes the transmission housing very rigid. Additional internal strengthening comes from the fluid distribution plate of the valve body which is cast as part of the transmission housing.

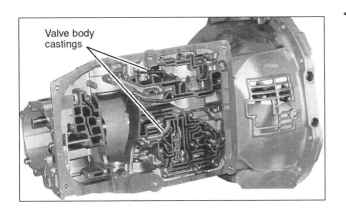

Valve body castings

The upper valve body passageways are cast into the transmission body.

The front cover, which holds the front pump and the stator shaft, is made of aluminum alloy. The K1 clutch is mounted on the backside of this unit on an extension of the stator shaft. The transmission has two planetary gear sets along the power transmission line.

Fluid pumps

There are two fluid pumps within the transmission housing. The front or primary pump supplies the entire transmission hydraulic system with fluid pressure. It is driven by the engine through the torque converter.

A secondary pump located at the rear of the transmission will operate only with the engine stopped and after the car has come to a complete stop (loss of pressure in closure valve). This pump allows the car to be tow- or push-started. The secondary pump is driven by the transmission input shaft, which drives a worm gear that turns the shaft of the centrifugal governor.

Shift valve

The shift valve housing or valve body is the hydraulic control center for the transmission. It has two layers, bolted together, which join the fluid distribution plate in the bottom of the transmission housing. All operating pressures and transmission gear changes are controlled within the shift valve housing and are modulated by external inputs from the throttle position cable.

Throttle position cable and engine vacuum modulator

The throttle position cable goes to the throttle linkage and indicates demand while the vacuum modulator detects engine vacuum and indicates load.

On gasoline powered engines, the throttle cable is connected to the control pressure control valve via a pivot lever inside the transmission. The vacuum modulator directly controls the modulator pressure control valve. These two systems determine when and how hard shifts will occur.

8

Diesel engined cars do not have a throttle position cable and shift only via the vacuum modulator. To control transmission shifting, the vacuum control valve on the injection pump regulates vacuum to the vacuum modulator.

Planetary gears

◁ A pair of planetary gear sets are used in the transmission drivetrain to vary the drive ratios. By stopping and locking some of the parts within the planetary gear set, different gear ratios are available without resorting to sliding or aligning parts. A simple planetary gear set is shown at left.

1. Internal gear   3. Sun gear
2. Planetary gear   4. Planetary gear carrier

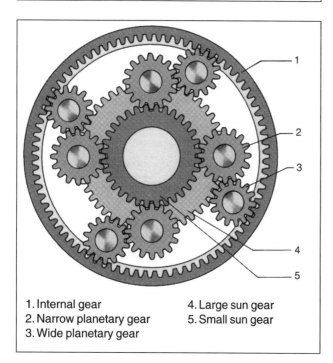

1. Internal gear   4. Large sun gear
2. Narrow planetary gear   5. Small sun gear
3. Wide planetary gear

◁ The more complex *Ravigneaux* planetary gear set is a compound gear set that has within it two simple gear sets. This provides two gear ratios from one planetary set.

◁ Using a band to grab the outside of the sun gear will stop the sun gear and drive the planet gears.

◁ By locking a clutch pack (shown at left) on the inside of the gear set, the sun gear can be forced to rotate. Combinations of inner and outer locking give the ratios that are available from the transmission.

◁ The clutch pack contains both friction discs and metal discs inside the pack.

8

Gear and clutch combinations

The various combinations that make up the transmission gearing are shown in **Table c**.

Table c. Gear / clutch combinations

Gear	Power transmission	Hydraulically actuated units	Gear ratio
1st	Both planetary gear sets	Brake band B2	3.6 : 1
2nd	Both planetary gear sets	Brake band B1 Brake band B2	2.41 : 1
3rd	Rear simple planetary gear set	Clutch K1 Brake band B2	1.44 : 1
4th	No planetary gear sets	Clutch K1 Clutch K2	1 : 1
reverse	Both planetary gear sets	Disc brake B3 Free-wheeling unit locked via clutch K2	5.14 : 1

TIPS, MAINTENANCE, SERVICE

Fluid condition

The color and odor of the transmission fluid are key indicators of internal transmission condition. Look for clear and bright red fluid with no visible dirt or small particles on the dipstick. Sniff the fluid to make sure it has a fresh clean smell with no burnt odor.

If there is any odor from the transmission fluid, drain the fluid in the pan and remove the pan. Examine the inside of the transmission for metal or clutch materials gathered in the pan or coating the inner surfaces of the transmission.

Service history

Check the transmission service history. A properly serviced automatic will list 30,000 miles between transmission fluid and filter changes. If the car was used in severe service, then the fluid change interval is 15,000 miles with a filter every 30,000.

Major problems

The major problem with these transmissions are:

- Fluid leaks from the front pump area
- Wear on the B3 brake pack friction discs
- Broken B2 operating piston (very slight possibility)

Diesels and vacuum system

Since engine vacuum is what determines automatic transmission shifting, it is very important that the vacuum system is leak free. Any loss of vacuum in the circuit will indicate a higher load to the transmission than actually exists. As the vacuum goes down, shift pressures increase to cause the transmission to shift hard, especially when coasting to a stop. If your transmission has developed hard shifting the first thing to do is test the integrity of the vacuum system.

Repairing fluid leaks

Transmission fluid may leak under the car right at the area where the engine joins the transmission housing. This is more than likely a bad front pump seal. This leak would be consistent and occur each time the engine is shut down after the car is driven. If the leak starts small and gradually increases, it is almost certainly the pump seal. This requires removing the transmission and replacing the input seal, the pump O-ring and the pump gasket.

It takes approximately 6 to 9 hours for transmission removal and 2 hours to reseal the front end of the transmission. If you must replace the front pump seals make sure to have the engine rear main seal done at the same time. It should only cost an additional half-hour of labor time to pull the drive plate and install a new seal.

It is advisable to try and live with the leak as long as possible due to the cost of repair. If the seal starts to really leak there is no choice, but if you can wait it is much better to overhaul the entire transmission when you have it out.

Overhauling one of the 722.3 or 722.4 transmissions is really a matter of replacing all of the seals and O-rings in the transmission along with replacing the friction discs. It is not common to find mechanical problems in these transmissions.

8

If the car is parked for a week or more, the fluid in the torque converter may drain back into the transmission housing itself and start to overfill the transmission, causing excess fluid to run out of the front input seal. This type of leak can start suddenly with a parked car and leave a fairly large puddle immediately. Just top up the fluid level, as there is nothing wrong.

Transmission slipping

If the transmission slips between gears (the engine revs up when changing gears) there is a very good possibility that the friction discs are worn out in brake pack B3.

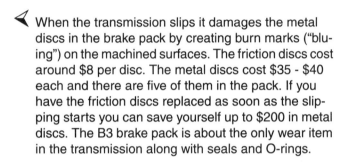

◁ When the transmission slips it damages the metal discs in the brake pack by creating burn marks ("bluing") on the machined surfaces. The friction discs cost around $8 per disc. The metal discs cost $35 - $40 each and there are five of them in the pack. If you have the friction discs replaced as soon as the slipping starts you can save yourself up to $200 in metal discs. The B3 brake pack is about the only wear item in the transmission along with seals and O-rings.

Burn marks

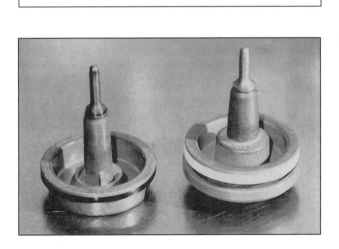

◁ Some of the previous versions of this transmission experienced B2 piston failure. The failure rate for the E-Class version is extremely low. If a B2 piston should break, the transmission will lose all forward gears because the B2 piston engages the B2 band in 1st, 2nd and 3rd gears.

Transmission control

All of the E-Class automatic transmissions from 1986 through 1991 start in second gear when the gear selector lever is in **D** or **3**. If the selector lever is pulled back into the **2** position the car will start in first gear. To obtain a first gear start with the lever in position **D** or **3** it is necessary to press the gas pedal to the kick-down switch and this makes for very uncomfortable driving as you are in a maximum acceleration condition. To be able to use first gear without resorting to the rapid acceleration of the kick-down position you can use the gear selector lever and manually control the transmission.

When you are stopped, pull the selector lever back into the **2** position which will force the transmission to start in first gear. As you accelerate you can force the **1 - 2** shift by moving the gear lever from position **2** up to position **3**. As soon as the car starts the shift into second gear, pull the selector lever back into position **2**. This will not cause the car to downshift to 1st gear, but rather hold 2nd gear until you wish to shift to 3rd by moving the lever up to **3**. This technique gives you almost total manual control of the transmission.

While some of the valve bodies from 1989 through 1991 can be modified to have a first gear start every time, some of the early 1989 models cannot. None of the 1986 to 1988 valve bodies can be modified. The first gear start technique described above does not add any wear to the transmission and in fact, reduces wear on the engine because the load on the engine of starting the car from a stop in second gear is much higher than starting in first gear. If you have a 1986 to 1989 model, you might try getting a later version valve body from a scrap yard, or you can order it from Mercedes-Benz although they are a bit pricey at around $700.

Information resources

Any good automatic transmission repair manual, obtainable from your local lending library, will explain transmission function.

You can also purchase sheets of microfiche from Mercedes-Benz publications at 800-367-6372 (800-FOR-MERC).

8

Table d shows transmission numbers applicable to the E-Class from 1986 through 1995, referenced to Mercedes-Benz microfiche sheets.

Table d. Automatic transmission service information

Fiche title	ID number	Date
Function description of automatic transmissions 722.3/4/5	07 102 2159 01	04/91
Automatic transmissions 722.3/4/5/6 Complaints, causes and remedies	1238	2/96
Automatic transmission 722.3 up to 08/88	07 102 2155 05	04/89
Automatic transmission 722.3 part I 09/88 on	Z1 2157 04 01	06/96
Automatic transmission 722.3 part II 09/88 on	Z1 2161 01 01	09/96
Automatic transmission 722.4 up to 09/89	07 102 2156 05	04/90
Automatic transmission 722.4 10/89 on	Z1 2160 04 01	06/96

Chapter 9

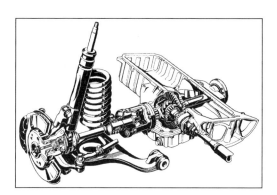

Suspension, Brakes, Steering

9

GENERAL

This chapter describes the E-Class suspension, brakes and steering. Also included are descriptions of the driveline and the electronically-controlled traction control systems.

SUSPENSION

Front suspension

◁ The front suspension consists of a lower control arm, damper strut, and suspension spring. The strut bolts to the steering knuckle in three places and the strut upper rubber mount serves as the mounting point. A polyurethane stop sleeve on top of the strut rod limits suspension travel.

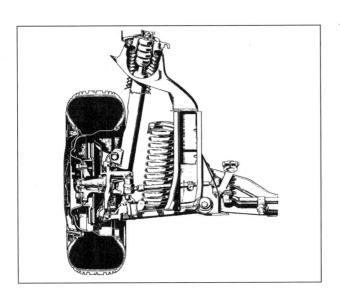

◁ The damper strut is an evolution of the dual-tube gas filled shock absorber, although there is no longer a piston separating the two chambers. The inner tube is the working chamber, which contains the piston rod with the working piston. The outer tube, called the outer chamber, is ⅔ filled with oil. The outer chamber provides a reservoir for oil loss from the working chamber and provides for expansion of the working oil when the strut gets hot.

1. Piston rod
2. Damper strut outer tube
3. Working piston
4. Working cylinder
5. Outer (reservoir) tube
6. Bottom valve

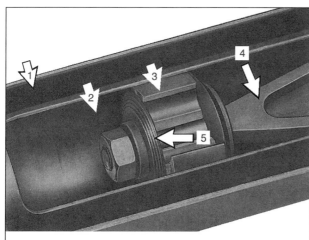

1. Outer chamber
2. Working chamber
3. Piston

4. Piston rod
5. Main shock valve (leaf type)

◁ Gas pressure acts on the oil column in the outer chamber to reduce foaming. This gas pressure also helps to control small movements of the strut. The two chambers are separated by a valve that limits oil flow during strut compression and allows oil back into the working chamber during rebound.

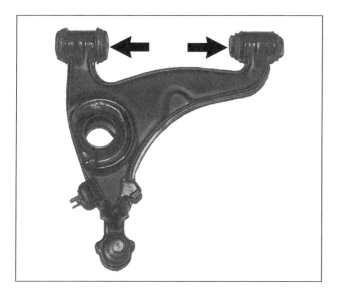

◁ The lower control arm is mounted to the suspension through replaceable rubber bushings (**arrows**). Both camber and caster are adjustable by eccentric bolts at the inner pivot points.

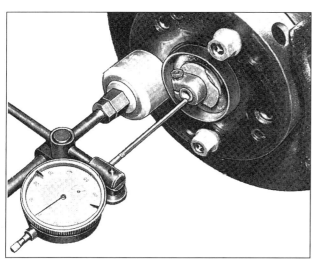

◁ The wheel bearing is preloaded during installation and is set using a dial indicator. Bearing play is 0.01 - 0.02 mm (0.0004 - 0.0008 in).

9

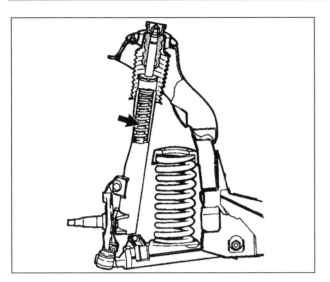

◁ The 500E is fitted with a modified front suspension. The front damper strut has an compression limiting spring (**arrow**) inside the strut housing for added support while cornering. Along with large damper strut mounts, the 500E uses stiffer springs, stiffer dampers, stiffer sway bar mounts, and a crossbrace at the rear of the control arms for support during braking.

On all models except the 500E, the front sway bars are 26.5 mm (1.04 in). The bar diameter on the 500E is 28 mm (1.10 in).

NOTE—
On cars with the optional sportline package, a different steering pitman arm is used as lowering the car alters the steering geometry.

Rear suspension

◁ The rear axle is a multi-link, fully independent suspension system. The wheel carrier is held in place and guided by five independent links. The spring link has an aerodynamic plastic cover and helps protect against road gravel.

This five link setup eliminates most rear end dive when accelerating hard. Straight ahead driving is very relaxed because the rear end is not experiencing small toe-in changes or track width changes as the springs compress.

The rear camber specifications are slightly negative and remain that way regardless of load. This improves the feel and handling of the car.

The entire rear subframe (axle carrier) is suspended from the frame floor with four replaceable subframe bushings. The bushings vary in hardness depending on model. Replacement bushings should be ordered by chassis number (VIN).

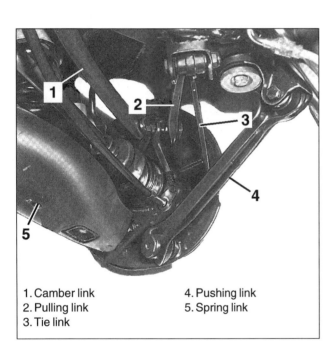

1. Camber link	4. Pushing link
2. Pulling link	5. Spring link
3. Tie link	

◁ The final drive (differential) mounts to the rear subframe through three rubber bushings (**arrows**), two at the rear and one at the front. These rubber bushings isolate the interior of the car from final drive vibration and noise.

The first modifications to the rear suspension came with the 1987 station wagon. With an increased load capacity, the entire rear subframe and some of the suspension links were reinforced.

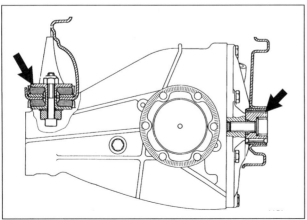

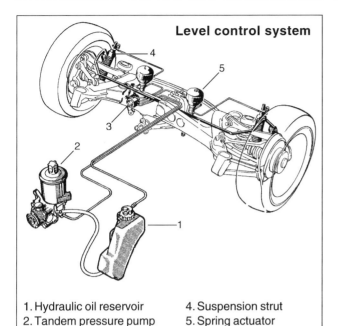

Level control system

1. Hydraulic oil reservoir
2. Tandem pressure pump
3. Level valve
4. Suspension strut
5. Spring actuator

Level control
(station wagon and 500E)

◁ Level control is a hydropneumatic system installed on the rear axle of the station wagons and the 500E sedan. It automatically adjusts and maintains the rear ride height based on vehicle loading.

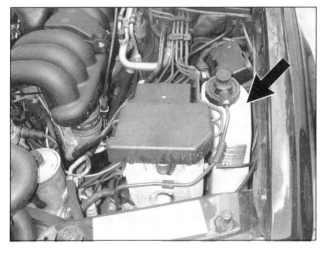

◁ The hydraulic oil reservoir (**arrow**) on the station wagon is located on the driver's side of the engine compartment. On the 500E it is on the passenger side.

Hydraulic fluid capacity

System capacity . . . . 3.5 liters (3.7 US qt)

Reservoir capacity (car at curb weight)
MAX mark . . . . 1.2 liters (1.26 US qt)
MIN mark (unloaded car) . . . . 1 liter (1.05 US qt)

9

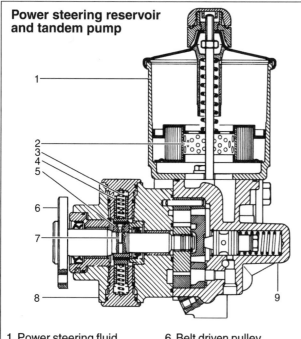

**Power steering reservoir
and tandem pump**

1. Power steering fluid
2. Power steering filter
3. Spring
4. Piston
5. Eccentric
6. Belt driven pulley
7. Shear pin
8. Level control pump
9. Power steering pump

◄ The tandem pressure pump is a combination power steering and level control pump. The pump maintains different pressures in each system with separate hydraulic oil reservoirs for each.

If there is ever an overload on the level control side of the pump, a shear pin will shear and allow the power steering pump to continue operating.

Hydraulic oil recommendation

Level control . . . . .hydraulic oil
(MB part no. 000 989 91 03)

Steering fluid . . . . Mercedes-Benz
power steering fluid (MB part no. Q 1 46 0001)

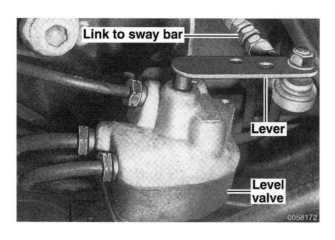

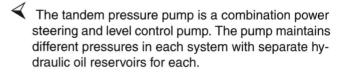

◄ The level valve is mounted at the rear suspension and connects to the sway bar via a link rod. As the ride height changes, the lever is moved either up or down allowing hydraulic fluid pressure to act on the struts and maintain the ride height.

When the car is at the preset ride height, the valve is closed and doesn't allow any fluid flow. If the car is loaded and the rear drops, the lever moves into the fill position and hydraulic fluid is pumped into the struts, raising the car until the lever is moved back into the closed position.

If the car is unloaded and the rear end rises, the lever will move to the outflow position and the car will settle to the predetermined ride height. The base ride height is adjustable by changing the length of the link.

◁ While the rear struts look like shock absorbers they are more like hydraulic cylinders found on construction equipment. The struts are very long-lived and leaks are usually at the fluid hoses or fittings. Rarely do the struts themselves need to be replaced.

◁ The strut (**arrow**) mounts between the frame floor and the lower spring link.

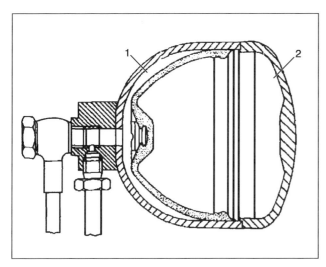

◁ The spring actuators are mounted through the frame floor and are accessed through the luggage compartment.

Each actuator contains a diaphragm in the middle. On one side of the diaphragm (**2**) is nitrogen gas under pressure and the other side (**1**) is open to level control hydraulic fluid in the strut.

Because hydraulic oil is not compressible, when the wheel bounces there must be a way to allow the fluid to flow out and back into the strut as the wheel comes back into position. The spring actuator allows this motion to occur rapidly without disturbing the height setting. These spring actuators are, in effect, the shock absorbers.

9

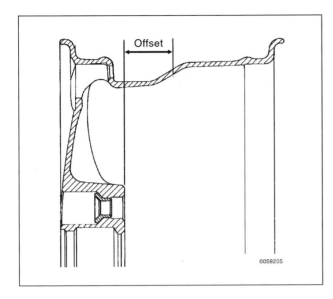

0058205

Wheels and alignment

◁ E-Class cars are fitted with light alloy wheels, 6.5 x 15 inches with a 49 mm (1.9 in) offset. 1986 and 1987 wheels were forged. From 1988 the wheels were cast.

The original tires were VR rated 195/65-15. The only exceptions to this tire size was the Sportline version carrying 7 x 15 wheels with 205/60-15 VR tires and the 500E with 8 x 16 wheels and 225/55-16 VR tires.

In 1994 the wheel offset was changed to 44 mm (1.7 in) and the tires were down rated to HR. The cars were electronically limited to 130 mph based on these H rated tires.

When setting front end alignment, a spreader bar must be used when adjusting the toe. This is a spring loaded bar that forces the front wheels apart with 90 - 110 Nm (66 - 81 ft-lb) of force. The use of a spreader bar allows the alignment to duplicate driving conditions by preloading the rubber bushings in the suspension. The use of a spreader bar is the only way to get an accurate front end alignment.

◁ To correct rear toe, offset rubber bushings can be installed in the tie link. The offset of 1.45 mm (0.057 in) will correct up to 8' of toe.

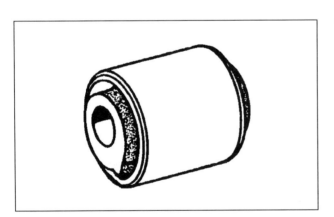

BRAKES

The brakes are four-wheel disc with floating or fixed calipers in front and fixed calipers in the rear. All calipers are iron except the fixed front calipers on the 500E, which are constructed of light weight alloy.

For the 300E from 1986 until 1993 in all versions, the calipers were single piston floating calipers. Starting in 1994 these were changed to 4-piston fixed calipers. Both the 400E and 500E had 4-piston fixed calipers from the beginning.

Table a. Brake pads and brake disc technical data (mm / in)

Model	Model number	Front brakes			Rear brakes		
		Pad thickness	Disc thickness	Disc diameter	Pad thickness	Disc thickness	Disc diameter
260E, 300E 2.6	124.026	19.3/0.76	22/0.87	284/11.18	15.5/0.61	9/0.35	
300E 2.8	124.028						
300E	124.030						
E320	124.032	16.0/0.63	25/0.98	294/11.57			
400E, E420	124.034	17.5/0.69	22/0.87	295/11.61		24/0.94	
500E	124.036	17.5/0.69	28/1.1	300/11.81	16.0/0.63		
300CE	124.050	19.3/0.76	22/0.87	284/11.18		9/0.35	
300CE Cabrio	124.051	17.5/0.69					
E320 Coupe	124.052	16.0/0.63	25/0.98	294/11.57			278/10.9
E320 Cabrio	124.066	16.0/0.63					
300TE	124.090	19.3/0.76	22/0.87	284/11.18			
E320 Wagon	124.092	16.0/0.63	25/0.98	294/11.57		20/0.79	
300D 2.5 Turbo	124.128	19.3/0.76	22/0.87	284/11.18	15.5/0.61	9/0.35	
E300 Diesel	124.131						
300D Turbo	124.133						
300TD Turbo	124.193						
300E 4MATIC	124.230						
300TE 4MATIC	124.290						

9

Brake master cylinder

The brake master cylinder on all models is made of light alloy. The master cylinder for all 5- and 6-cylinder models has a $^{15}/_{16}$ inch bore for the primary circuits and ¾ inch for the secondary circuit. The 400E and 500E have a 1 inch bore for the primary and a ¾ inch bore for the secondary circuit.

In the 500E as February of 1993 the ABS system added a lateral force sensor and a revised tandem master cylinder. These modifications changed the brake force apportionment between the front and rear brakes to transfer more braking power to the front wheels under certain high lateral force conditions, such as in hard cornering.

ABS

ABS is the German acronym for *Antiblockier System* (Anti-Block System).

The 3-channel ABS system consists of the ABS electronic control module, the ABS hydraulic unit and 2 inductive type front wheel speed sensors and a differential speed sensor.

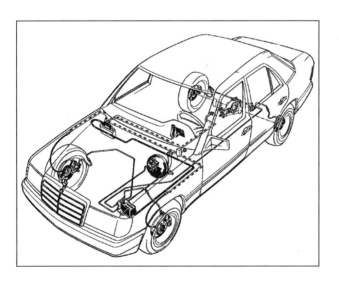

◄ The electronic control module processes the electrical inputs from the wheel speed sensors and signals the switching solenoid valves integrated in the hydraulic unit if intervention is required. The entire system is protected by an over-voltage relay.

If a fault is detected in the system, the ABS is turned off and the ABS indicator lamp illuminates.

NOTE—
A later development of the ABS system, ABS / ASR, incorporates traction control and is equipped with 4 wheel speed sensors (4-channel ABS), one at each wheel. ABS / ASR is described later in this chapter.

During ABS intervention, the electronic control module signals the solenoid valves to decrease or maintain the line pressure at the individual brake calipers to prevent wheel lockup.

The ABS control cycle

If a wheel shows a tendency toward locking because of low traction, the speed sensor will recognize this deceleration as wheel slip. The fluid pressure in that circuit will then be held at the current level no matter how hard the brake pedal is applied.

If that wheel speed is still incorrect, the outlet valve in the solenoid pack is opened to lower the pressure in that circuit and release the brake. The brake fluid is returned to the master cylinder reservoir by a return pump.

STEERING

The power steering gear has automatic free-play compensation, making it unnecessary to manually adjust steering free-play.

 Power steering pumps are made by Vickers or ZF and the pumps are interchangeable as replacement parts. The system pressure relief valve (maximum working pressure) is set at 110 - 115 bar (1,595 - 1,667 psi). An oil cooler tube for the power steering is installed in front of the radiator.

9

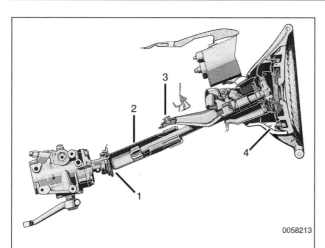

1. Predetermined buckling point in column
2. Sliding column joint
3. Jacket tube break-away point
4. Energy absorbing hub in steering wheel

◀ In the event of an accident, the energy absorbing steering wheel stays attached to the column, while the column collapses into itself, eliminating any rearward movement.

A rubber joint connects the top half of the column to the bottom half. The bottom half slides over the top half. The jacket for the column has crush points where it will bend according to design. The upper column is designed to unhook itself from its mounting point under the dash and move forward.

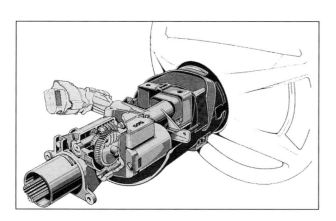

◀ The power-adjustable steering column is standard equipment. The range of adjustment is 60 mm (2.3 in) fore and aft. Steering wheel position is stored in the seat memory control module.

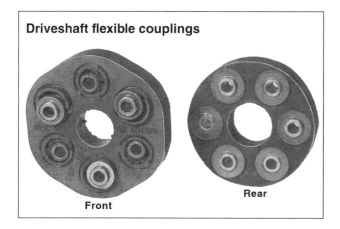

Driveshaft flexible couplings

Front

Rear

DRIVELINE

Propeller shaft

◁ The propeller shaft is a hollow tube design with flexible couplings at both ends and a center U-joint with a support bearing. Rubber couplings on the front and rear of the propeller shaft cushion acceleration and deceleration rotational forces.

Rear differential

Table b shows rear axle ratios and differential oil capacities.

Table b. Rear axle ratios and capacities (US only, automatic transmission)

Model	Model number	Axle ratio (:1)	oil capacity (liters/ US qts)
260E, 300E 2.6	124.026	3.27	1.1 / 1.16
300E 2.8	124.028	3.06	1.3 / 1.37
300E	124.030	3.07	1.1 / 1.16
E320	124.032	2.65	1.3 / 1.37
400E, E420	124.034	2.24	1.3 / 1.37
500E	124.036	2.82	1.3 / 1.37
300CE	124.050	3.07	1.1 / 1.16
300CE Cabriolet	124.051	3.06	1.3 / 1.37
E320 Coupe	124.052	2.65	1.3 / 1.37
E320 Cabriolet	124.066	2.65	1.3 / 1.37
300TE	124.090	2.87	1.1 / 1.16
E320 Wagon	124.092	2.65	1.3 / 1.37
300D 2.5 Turbo	124.128	2.65	1.1 / 1.16
E300 Diesel	124.131	2.87	1.1 / 1.16
300D Turbo	124.133	2.65	1.1 / 1.16
300TD Turbo	124.193	3.07	1.1 / 1.16
300E 4MATIC	124.230	3.07	1.1 / 1.16
300TE 4MATIC	124.290	3.27	1.1 / 1.16

9

TRACTION CONTROL SYSTEMS

ASR traction system

Beginning in model year 1991, ASR (automatic slip control) was available as an option on the gasoline models. While ABS prevents wheel lockup during braking, ASR prevents wheel spin during acceleration and vastly improved traction when starting off.

The ASR system uses the ABS components with the addition of an electronic throttle control system known as Electronic Accelerator (EA), a modified ABS / ASR hydraulic unit and ABS / ASR electronic control module.

The ASR control module receives and processes speed signals from each of the four wheel speed sensors. Two methods of control are employed to stop the wheels from spinning. ASR intervenes by applying the brakes (brake torque control) or reducing engine power via the electronic throttle (drive torque control).

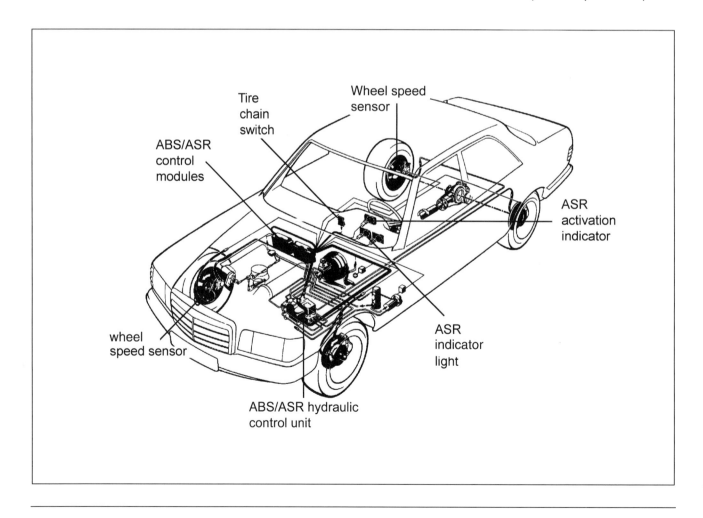

There are three distinct modes of ASR operation:

- **Under 25 mph, one drive wheel spinning:** The brake torque circuit activates by applying the brake to the spinning wheel.
- **Over 25 mph or with both drive wheels spinning:** The drive torque control circuit activates via the electronic throttle system to reduce engine power output.
- **If the drive torque control circuit doesn't stop the spinning drive wheels:** The brake torque control circuit will activate and apply the brakes to the spinning drive wheels.

Brake torque control

If the brake torque control is activated, the brake will be applied on the spinning wheel to slow the wheel until it is within the programmed range. With the brake activated on the spinning wheel, the wheel with traction is free to transmit optimal torque. In effect, ASR operates as a locking differential. A solenoid valve in the ABS / ASR hydraulic unit modulates the pressure at brake caliper.

Drive torque control

If brake torque control is not able to control wheel slippage, the ABS/ASR control module signals the drive torque control circuit to close the throttle plate. No matter what position the driver has the throttle in, the control circuit will override the driver. Once the spinning wheel is back under control, the brake torque control circuit will take precedence.

In situations where tire chains are fitted or the car must be rocked out of a low traction situation, the ASR system allows more wheel spin with the snow chain switch pushed in. When the switch is activated, an LED in the switch will light indicating the reduced ASR support. This function is limited to speeds below 25 mph.

NOTE—
It is a good idea to test out systems like ASR and ABS under controlled conditions to know how the car will react in emergencies.

9

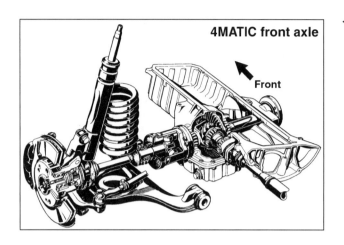

4MATIC front axle

Front

4MATIC

4MATIC is an all wheel drive system that automatically engages the front drive wheels when traction conditions warrant it. 4MATIC normally is in rear wheel drive mode and feels much like any other rear wheel drive Mercedes-Benz

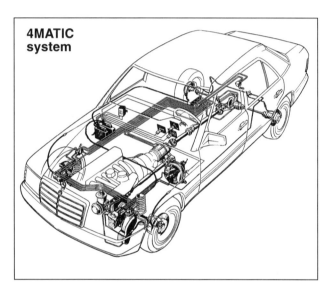

4MATIC system

If at any time the 4MATIC control module detects a speed differential between either of the two front wheels and the rear wheels, it transfer power to the front axle. Once engaged, the system works going forward and backward, accelerating and braking.

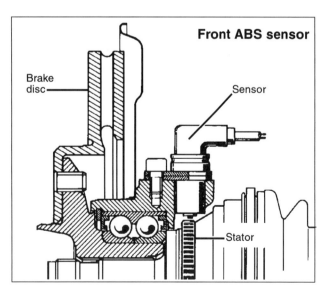

Front ABS sensor

Brake disc

Sensor

Stator

The 4MATIC control module receives input signals about wheel speed, road speed, steering angle, acceleration and brake actuation. These signals come from the wheel speed sensors (ABS sensors), the steering angle sensor, the throttle position sensor, and the stop light switch.

Based on the signals received by the 4MATIC control module, the 4MATIC system is engaged in one of three steps.

- **Step 1** shifts from normal rear wheel drive to all wheel drive with a 35 : 65 (F / R) torque ratio split.
- **Step 2** locks the center differential in the transfer case, distributing power 50 : 50 (F / R).
- **Step 3** locks front to rear and side to side, locking all four wheels together.

The 4MATIC system allows for small differences in speed between the front and rear wheels. When the car speed is over 2 mph but under 62 mph, the allowable differential is 1.2 mph. When this differential is exceeded, the system engages (Step 2). If the slip differential doesn't diminish, the system will engage Step 3 as long as car speed is below 22 mph. Step 3 will never engage over 22 mph.

When starting off, if slip is detected, the system will automatically go right to Step 3 and turn on the 4MATIC light in the instrument cluster. If the initial start fails and slip continues (the control module detects a start and the car does not exceed 3 mph within ½ second), Step 3 will remain engaged. In other words, the system will not wait for slip to develop, but assumes it will develop.

The 4MATIC warning lamp will stay lit for ½ second after the system returns to normal rear wheel drive.

In normal driving, at every start from a stop, the system will engages Step 1 up to 12 mph without the 4MATIC lamp lighting. Once vehicle movement is detected, the differential locks will be disengaged as the car accelerates through 6 mph.

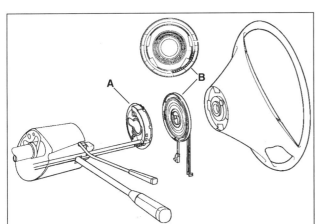

The steering angle sensor at the steering wheel consists of a sensor (**A**) and a wiper contact with magnets (**B**). The angle sensor along with the speed sensors at each front wheel allow the 4MATIC system to determine if the front end of the car is sliding.

If any of the steps are engaged frequently in a short period of time, the control module will extend the engagement period for each of the stages. This helps to avoid excessive cycling of the system.

At 3.1 mph and above, the system will revert to normal rear wheel drive when it receives a signal from the brake light switch that the brakes have been activated. By disengaging the 4MATIC system, the ABS system regains full control of the brakes. The 4MATIC system remains engaged while braking at speeds below 3.1 mph.

9

TIPS, MAINTENANCE, SERVICE

Suspension bushings

Wear and tear of suspension rubber bushings has a dramatic effect on the car's handling. Over time and distance these rubber bushings will deteriorate. Replacing worn bushings will restore the car to its new feel.

Inspect the control arm bushings at the front and the subframe mounts at the rear, the differential mounts and all of the bushings in the rear suspension links. If the bushings show signs of cracking or falling apart or even if they look off-center, they should be replaced

Wheel bearings

The grease capacity for each front hub is 65 g (2.3 oz): 15 g (0.53 oz) in the grease cap and 50 g (1.76 oz) in the bearing hub. Wheel bearing grease is provided in a 150 g container.

NOTE—
E-Class cars from 1988 use the green high temperature wheel bearing grease. Do not mix with the older tan colored grease from the 1987 and earlier cars.

The rear wheel bearings on the sedan are fairly easy to replace for a DIYer, although some special tools are required. The station wagon requires the wheel carrier be removed from the car and the bearings pressed out using a hydraulic press. Review the appropriate removal and installation procedure in the Mercedes-Benz service information prior to starting any work.

4MATIC system shut-off

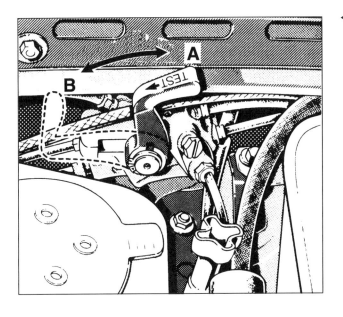

A service valve located on the passenger side front fender well can be used to shut off the 4MATIC system. This is handy if the system develops leaks or if the electronics malfunction. Using this valve can prevent possible damage to the system and you can leave it disengaged until repair work can be done. The valve will normally be in position **A**. If anything malfunctions, move the lever to position **B**. The car can still be driven in normal rear drive mode.

9

Chapter 10

Body

10

BODY EXTERIOR

Corrosion protection

For corrosion protection Mercedes-Benz uses zinc plating (galvanization) to protect many of the body panels. The engine hood, doors, sunroof, trunk lid and fuel filler flap are all galvanized. If the paint is chipped down through the primer and into the galvanized layer, the zinc will electrically migrate across the bare metal and cover it.

All of the welded seams on the car are treated with a special sealing compound that can be reabsorbed into weld material in case of repair work.

Primer

The first layer of primer that goes over the zinc coating is applied electrostatically with a complete dip of the entire bare chassis. The chassis is given a negative charge and the primer is given a positive charge so the primer is electrically bonded to the chassis. After the primary dip there is extensive PVC (polyvinyl chloride plastic) seam sealing all over the chassis.

Painted trim

From 1986 until 1989 the detachable trim parts were painted in *galinit gray*. This included the front and rear polycarbonate bumpers, the outside rearview mirror covers and all of the aluminum trim strips around the front and rear windshields, the roof and the doors. The polypropylene front and rear bumper strips were painted dark gray.

0058356

Side panels

◄ In the 1988 300CE coupe, the dual side protective trim strips were replaced with wide side panels. The bumpers and side trim panels were all painted the same color.

Table a. 300CE trim / side panel colors

Trim code	Trim name
7176	Shell gray
7177	Stratus gray
8477	Chinchilla
5944	Frigate blue

This wide trim style was extended to all E-Class models from 1990. The side panels and front and rear bumpers were accented with stainless steel and color coordinated. The outside mirror covers were painted body color. The front fender lips had their openings flared outward 60° to assist with fitting larger, wider tires. This look stayed with the car until the end of production in 1995.

1990 changes

Many exterior paint and trim colors, both standard and metallic, became available in 1990.

Table b. 1990 paint colors (single-stage)

Color code	Color name	Trim code	Trim color
9040	Black	7700	Alto gray
9147	Arctic white	7177	Stratus gray
3540	Signal red	3521	Navara red
1623	Light ivory	1631	Safari beige
1651	Pueblo beige	7176	Shell gray
7751	Ascot gray	7177	Stratus gray
6815	Agate green	6211	Kiwi green
5900	Deep blue	5301	Andor blue
5904	Midnight blue	5309	Rio blue

10

Table c. 1990 paint colors (metallic)

Color code	Color name	Trim code	Trim color
7122	Pearl gray	7700	Alto gray
7172	Anthracite gray	7176	Shell gray
9199	Pearl black	7700	Alto gray
6254	Dark green	6211	Kiwi green
6261	Sea foam green	6211	Kiwi green
5355	Diamond blue	5301	Andor blue
8432	Bison brown	8477	Chinchilla
8441	Desert taupe	8477	Chinchilla
3512	Garnet red	3521	Navarra red
3587	Cabernet red	3521	Navarra red
9702	Smoke silver	7176	Shell gray
5929	Nautical blue	5301	Andor blue

Along with the other changes in 1990, the *galinit gray* painted trim was changed to an anodized hematite (close to gun metal black).

1994 changes

 In 1994 there were more changes in the body style. Previous model runs had always maintained the body style from the first day of production to the last. The E-Class was the first line to have styling changes during a model run.

0058034

The contour of the hood was changed. The Mercedes-Benz star was moved off its traditional position on top of the grill and moved back onto the hood. The grill shape was changed along with the headlight shape. European style headlights became standard equipment.

Table d. 1994 paint colors (new)

Color code	Color name
3582	Imperial red
6269	Brilliant emerald
9149	Polar white

Table e. 1994 paint colors (discontinued)

Color code	Color name
1623	Light ivory
3512	Garnet red
3568	Signal red
3587	Cabernet red
5929	Nautical blue
8441	Desert taupe
9147	Arctic white

1995 changes

For the 1995 model year there were further changes to the color lineup. Mercedes-Benz USA decided to limit the number of colors available and dropped several from the lineup. The 1995 model year had four solid (single-stage) colors and eight metallic colors.

Table f. 1995 paint colors (single stage)

Color code	Color name	Trim code	Trim color
3582	Imperial red	3582	Imperial red
5904	Midnight blue	5904	Midnight blue
9040	Black	7700	Alto gray
9149	Polar white	7201	Marble gray

10

Table g. 1995 Paint colors (metallics)

Color code	Color name	Trim code	Trim color
3512	Garnet red	3512	Garnet red
5366	Azure blue	5366	Azure blue
6249	Spruce green	6249	Spruce green
6269	Brilliant emerald	6269	Brilliant emerald
7721	Moonstone gray	7721	Moonstone gray
9199	Black pearl	7700	Alto gray
9702	Smoke silver	7176	Shell gray
9744	Brilliant silver	7181	Atlas gray

Chassis structure

The chassis of the sedan was built with safety, aerodynamics and fuel efficiency as major considerations. The basic sedan body shell remained mostly unchanged through the 10 year production run. There were modifications to the basic body shell for both the coupe, the cabriolet and the V-8 powered cars.

V-8 chassis

The V-8 powered cars had increased track width and larger exhaust systems. Modifications for V-8 installation included the front end, the front and rear wheel housings, the fire wall, the transmission tunnel, the main floor, the rear floor and various other supports. The 500E (124.036) had front and rear fenders widened in the wheel arch area.

Coupe chassis

The coupe was strengthened to make up for the lack of a B-pillar connection with the roof. The coupe drip rails which extend from the windshield to the back window as well as all the other trim around the windshield and rear window are anodized with a dark color almost like gunmetal black. There are installation points on the drip rail for a screw-on roof rack system.

Cabriolet chassis

◁ The cabriolet had to be further reinforced to make up for the lack of a roof connection. The frame floor, the A- and B-pillar structures, the windshield frame and the soft top storage compartment were heavily reinforced. There are also diagonal struts at the front and rear of the frame floor. There are vibration dampers on the left front strut tower top, within the windshield frame top section and in both side trunk wells. The factory claims to have used over 1,000 different sheet metal pieces in making the cabriolet.

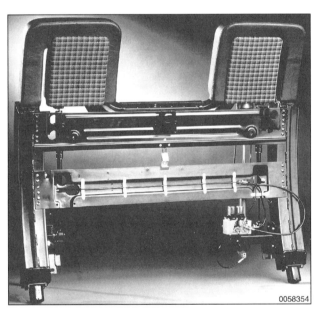

◁ The cabriolet is also equipped with a roll bar system incorporated into the rear headrests. It is activated hydraulically.

◁ The roll bar (**arrow**) pops up instantly in case of a roll over.

The convertible top has a safety glass rear window with a defroster and is well insulated against noise. The cabriolet is also equipped with a wind screen that eliminates a large percentage of passenger compartment wind with the windows up. The wind screen will not work with the rear seats occupied.

The top mechanism is a sophisticated microprocessor controlled unit, consisting of a master hydraulic unit, solenoid valves, valve blocks, microswitches and locks. When servicing a malfunctioning top, be sure the servicing technician is well trained in cabriolet tops.

10

INTERIOR

Colors

At the time of introduction, the 300E was available in seven interiror colors, while the coupe had 8 colors options. The top of the instrument panel was available in five colors and the headliner in three colors.

Table h. 300E interior colors

Upholstery color	Instrument panel color	Headliner color
Black	Black	Gray
Blue	Blue	Gray
Dark green	Dark green	Cream beige
Palomino	Dark brown	Palomino
Cream beige	Dark brown	Cream beige
Burgundy	Black	Cream beige
Gray	Dark gray	Gray

Table i. Coupe interior colors

Upholstery color	Instrument panel color	Headliner color
Black	Black	Gray
Blue	Blue	Gray
Gray	Dark Gray	Gray
Palomino	Dark brown	Palomino
Brasil (dark brown)	Brasil	Palomino
Stone pine green	Stone pine green	Creme beige
Creme beige	Dark brown	Creme beige
Burgundy	Black	Creme beige

Wood trim

All of station wagons and 300 series sedans (including the 260E) were trimmed with zebrano wood, named from its resemblance to zebra stripes.

The coupes, cabriolets, 400E and 500E were trimmed in burl walnut.

From 1986 through 1989 the wood trim was limited to the center console.

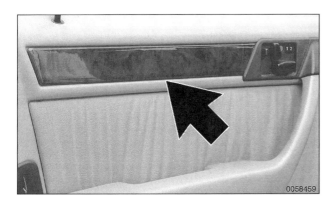

Starting in 1990, a matching (zebrano or burl walnut) 32 mm wide wood strip was installed along the width of the dash and a piece was added to each of the door panels (**arrow**).

Upholstery

The standard upholstery in 1986 was M-B Tex with leather and velour being options. Most cars were ordered with leather and it became the standard upholstery as of 1988. The door panel center portion is M-B Tex if the car has either leather or M-B Tex interior. With velour seating the door panel inset is also velour.

Storage

Front seats are separated with a console containing a small parcel area. On later models where the passenger side airbag eliminated the glove compartment, the area between the seats has a small glove compartment with a sliding wooden tambour lid. Additional storage is provided in the lift-up arm rest.

As of 1990, a small gas-charged damper provided assisted glove compartment closing.

Seats

Coupe and cabriolet seat backs are locked in the upright position via a vacuum operated system. The system is actuated once the once the door is closed and the engine is running. There is a push-button on the side of the seat back to overide the lock system in case of an electrical malfunction.

Optional orthopedic seats contain an inflatable, three-chambered, adjustable lumbar support that can be moved up and down inside the seat back. The adjustment wheel is located by the seat belt latch. Later versions of the orthopedic backrest had four air chambers (three with leather upholstery).

10

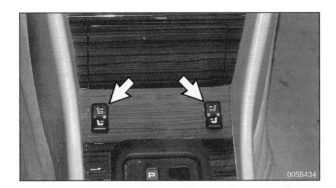

◄ Heated front seats were optional throughout the model run. The seat heater control buttons (**arrow**) with two different heat settings are on the center console ahead of the shifter.

The standard sedan is equipped with two semibucket bench seats in the rear.

◄ The two rear semibucket seats have their own headrests mounted on the parcel shelf. The driver can lower the headrests using a switch on the center console controlling a vacuum release.

A pull-down armrest is provided for the rear seats, located between the seats.

The four outboard seats are equipped with retractor shoulder belts. The front pair are part of the supplemental restraint system (SRS). There is a lap belt for use by the third passenger in the rear. Coupes and convertibles are equipped with a seat belt presenter or extender. The seat belt is presented when the door is closed and the ignition is switched on. If the seat belt is not latched within thirty seconds it is withdrawn. The presenter retracts instantly when the seat belt is buckled.

In coupes, cabriolets and sedans equipped with the Sportline option, the rear seat is only for two passengers, with a storage console sporting a wooden tambour door between the two seats. The two seats have much more of a bucket shape than the standard sedan, which accommodates an occasional third passenger. The front seats in the Sportline option have much more side support for cornering than the standard sedan seats because of larger side bolsters on the seat back and seat bottom. Sportline leather was only available in five colors; creme beige, black, blue, dark brown and gray.

◄ The station wagon seating is different in that the rear seat is divided $1/3$ and $2/3$ for varying cargo requirements. The seat backs fold down to allow long cargo to be carried in the car. Either or both side seat backs can be folded. To increase the amount of cargo room the rear seat cushions can be removed. The station wagon was also available with a third rear facing seat which folds into storage compartments in the floor. There are two shoulder harnesses available for third seat passengers.

Several seating changes were made in the 1990 model year. The velour upholstery was made softer and the fluting wider. The leather interior was done with a softer tanning process yielding much more pliable seating. The pleating was also done loosely and the fluting was changed from lengthwise to crosswise. Side support was increased using larger side bolsters. The spring frame and cushion were also improved.

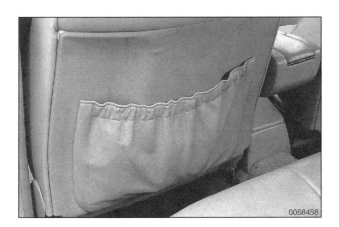

◁ At introduction in 1986, the front seat backs had a handy net storage compartment. With the 1990 model year the nets gave way to expanding storage pockets which were in the same material as the seating, M-B Tex, leather or velour.

1990 also changed the composition of the rear seat cushions from springs and pads to premolded, contoured foam. The rear seat backs and cushions are more strongly contoured and bolstered for cornering support. Seat belt buckles are stored in recesses in the molded backrest cushion (except for the station wagon, due to the folding seats). The upper mounting point for the rear seat belts is articulated for more comfort while wearing the belt.

BODY AND CHASSIS REPAIR

◁ If you purchased your E-Class used, one of the most important parts of the pre-purchase inspection was the body damage evaluation. Was the car ever in an accident? Has it been repaired, and what is the quality of the repair work? Many drivers feel that if a Mercedes-Benz is in an accident, the car should be disposed of and replaced as soon as it is fixed. However, Mercedes-Benz cars are actually very repairable if the body shop uses the correct equipment.

10

Choosing a shop

Choosing a body shop is much harder than choosing a mechanical repair shop. The quality of work done during metal repair completely depends upon the skill of the individual doing the work. Unlike mechanical repair work, where a problem is either fixed or not, body work quality is measured by degrees. With metal work and fitting new body parts, you need the skill of a craftsman.

Frame repair

◁ The quality of the body shop and skill level of the body repair technician is tested when the chassis is involved. If the frame is bent, it has to be straightened or replaced. Front frame members can be replaced, but realigning the frame requires the use of a frame rack and the correct set of jigs for the model of car being worked on.

A dedicated frame rack looks like a set of railroad rails set in a smooth and level floor. There are also portable versions that sit on wheels. The rack is a system with frame jigs which allows the repairer to reshape the frame back to original.

Unlike universal frame racks where the identification points are computer generated, the dedicated rack system mounts the car at specific points such as the steering gear bolt holes, the suspension location points or shock absorber location points. Specific chassis points must match the jig at a number of spots, and if the frame is not in the correct alignment, it must be pulled back into place.

A good body shop will argue with your insurance company about the cost of straightening the frame. The frame jigs rent by the day, so the faster the work is done, the lower the insurance company's cost. Unfortunately, frame steel does not like to be pulled directly back into place. It much prefers to be moved slowly over several days. A really good shop will then allow the frame to relax and move back toward its accident position before pulling on it again. If your car needs frame work, discuss this with your insurance adjuster and your body shop.

The best frame rack systems are those approved by Mercedes-Benz; the Celette system and the Applied Power/Blackhawk system. Jigs are preset for each chassis, so there is no guesswork. The newest frame racks look like a drive-on lift that just sits a few feet above the floor.

◁ The car is anchored at the specified anchoring spots and large arms are available to hook chain and portable hydraulic equipment to do the pulling. The newer racks are computerized and have all of the facts and figures built in. They also output a chart showing where the car started and where it ended up, like current wheel alignment equipment.

A dedicated system takes longer to use but allows the most accurate frame work.

Critical to your safety is the elimination of wrinkles in the frame. Wrinkles can happen as a result of the accident or the straightening process, and if they are not completely removed, the frame will lack structural integrity. The frame rail is supposed to absorb crash energy. Your safety may depend on the quality of the work.

Painting

◁ Today most body shops use a single paint system from one manufacturer. If the body shop stays within the system and does not try to cut costs by buying cheaper prep materials which are not part of the system, the paint will be acceptable.

The shop's paint mixing bank, supplied by the paint manufacturer, contains the tints. The shop will also have information on microfiche telling them how to mix their paint to the correct color, based on the car manufacturer's paint code. This microfiche also tells the shop how to adjust the paint for age and fade.

After the technician mixes the paint, he or she should spray a test piece, usually a fresh clean piece of sheet metal that is correctly prepared. When the piece is completely dry, it is held up to the car to see if the match works. Modern paint systems can get a very good match, even with adjustments for fade.

In the early paint banks, paint was measured by volume in a beaker. Now it is weighed, and the accuracy is astounding. The correct amount of thinner is added to the correct amount of paint, by weight. It all comes out correctly.

It is important that your favorite body shop uses all of the correct materials within their paint system. Only when the shop uses the metal prep, primers, color coats, and clear coats from the same paint manufacturer and the same system will that manufacturer stand behind the paint warranty.

10

Refinishing

When the plastic cladding components require painting there are specific products made by Mercedes-Benz that should be used:

- Metallic base paint for plastic components, MB part no. 002 986 04 37
- Clear top coat, MB part no. 001 986 45 37
- Hardener, MB part no. 001 986 82 37 or 001 986 83 37.

Other painting materials may not be as long-lasting as the original paint.

All of the correct instructions for refinishing Mercedes-Benz automobiles will be found in the "Refinishing Manual models 1963 on" which can be ordered from Mercedes-Benz publications at 800-FOR-MERC.

Chapter 11

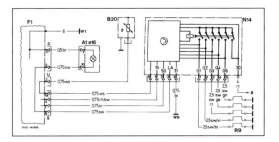

Electrical System

11

GENERAL

This chapter gives an overview of the electrical system, including fuse, relay and control module locations, ignition system and glow system descriptions, and brief coverage of the cruise control and climate control systems.

E-Class electrical systems

During the production run of the W124 E-Class, the vehicle electrical system became increasingly complex. Many systems became interconnected and interdependent. As a result, the wiring harnesses became so large and complex that new engineering solutions were desperately needed.

One solution was the use of specialized, vehicle compatible serial bus systems, or the Controller Area Network (CAN). It was first used in 1993 models.

Compared to a conventional wiring harness, the multiplex bus considerably reduces the number of wires, pins and couplers. This also enables more flexibility in wire routing and placement.

FUSES, RELAYS, MODULES

Fuse, relay, and control module locations vary depending on model year. To confirm proper identification, it is recommended that you always refer to Mercedes-Benz electrical repair information for model year specific information.

> **CAUTION—**
>
> • *Replace fuses with those of the same rating. Installing a fuse with higher rating can lead to circuit failure and may also start a fire.*
>
> • *Relay and fuse positions are subject to change and may vary from car to car. If questions arise, an authorized Mercedes-Benz dealer is the best source for the most accurate and up-to-date information.*
>
> • *A good way to verify a relay position is to compare the wiring colors at the relay socket to the colors indicated on wiring diagrams.*
>
> • *Always switch the ignition off and remove the negative (–) battery cable before removing any electrical components.*
>
> • *Prior to disconnecting the battery, read the battery disconnection cautions given at the front of this manual.*
>
> • *On cars equipped with anti-theft radio, make sure you know the correct radio activation code before disconnecting the battery or removing the radio.*
>
> • *Connect and disconnect ignition system wires, multiple connectors and ignition test equipment leads only while the ignition is switched off.*
>
> • *Only use a high quality digital multimeter for electrical tests.*

Fuse panel

◄ The majority of vehicle electrical system fuses are mounted in the fuse / relay panel located in the left rear of the engine compartment. Unclip the cover and lift open to access the fuses.

The fuse panel contains 8, 16 and 25 ampere fuses.

Fuse colors and ratings

White	8A
Red	16A
Blue	25A

Engine compartment fuse / relay panel

Relays

Fuses

11

Fuse positions

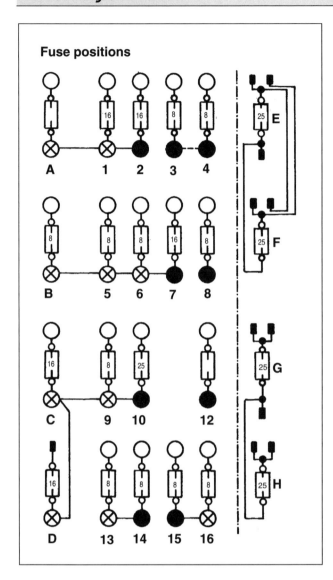

◁ Fuse positions are given in **Table a** and **Table b**.

Table a. 1986 - 1992 fuse assignments

Fuse	Rating	Protected circuit
1	16	cigar lighter folding head restraints glove compartment light radio rear window defroster switch
2	16	window regulators headlight cleaning circuit relay headlight flashers wiper / washers system comfort circuit
3	8	headlight cleaning unit instrument and switch illumination license plate light parking / taillight, right warning buzzer
4	8	front and rear foglights
5	8	bulb monitor module cruise control front dome light instrument cluster stop light tachometer
6	8	horns outside temperature gauge turn signal lights
7	16	air conditioning compressor automatic transmission electrics auxiliary coolant pump auxiliary fan relay terminal 86 back-up lights climate control system heater valve windshield washer jets heater system
8	8	left parking / taillight
9	8	clock comfort circuit relay terminal 86 diagnostic socket terminal 6 dome light, front hazard warning system radio vanity mirror light
10	25	heated rear window
11	8	alarm system
12	8	alarm system
13	8	low beam, left
14	8	low beam, right
15	8	high beam, left
16	8	high beam, right
A	8	sunroof

Table a. 1986 - 1992 fuse assignments

Fuse	Rating	Protected circuit
B	8	outside mirror adjustment and heating rear roller shade
C	16	antenna power central locking system dome light, rear door courtesy lights reading lights trunk light
D		not used
E	25	adjustment memory (front seat and steering wheel)
F	25	seat adjustment, front
G	25	window regulators, front
H	25	window regulators, rear

Table b. 1993 - 1995 fuse / relay panel fuses

Fuse	Rating	Protected circuit
1	16	backrest adjuster central locking system cigar lighter convenience module glove box light head rests, rear seat heater control module radio rear window defroster rear window roll up sunshade rear window wiper / washer system seat belt extender control module (Cabriolet) sunroof
2	16	convenience features headlight washer / wiper system seat adjustment window regulators windshield washer / wiper system

11

Fuse positions

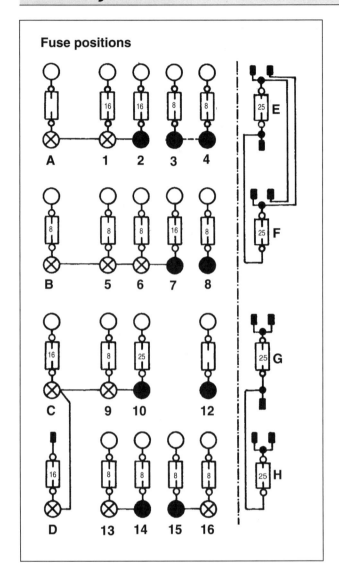

Table b. 1993 - 1995 fuse / relay panel fuses

Fuse	Rating	Protected circuit
3	8	cigar lighter illumination control switch illumination convertible top switch headrests, rear front seat adjustment and memory headlight washer / wiper seat heater control module instrument cluster lights license plate light outside rear view mirror adjust/heat radio illumination roll bar switch rear backrest / headrests right parking / tail / side lighting seat belt warning module seat heater switch sunroof warning buzzer
4	8	foglights
5	8	brake light switch convertible top cruise control daytime running lights (Canada) dome light, front exterior bulb failure module inductive speed sensor instrument cluster roll bar control bulb roll bar switch seat belt warning module tachometer warning module
6	8	ABS warning light alternator charge indicator light fanfare horns glow plug relay ignition coils injectors instrument cluster over-voltage protection relay module rollbar starter switch temperature gauge, outside three way catalyst malfunction control module

Table b. 1993 - 1995 fuse / relay panel fuses

Fuse	Rating	Protected circuit
7	16	A/C compressor clutch A/C monovalve and duovalve adjustable camshaft timing solenoid air pump clutch air pump switchover valve automatic transmission electrics auxiliary coolant pump auxiliary fan relay backup light blower motor bypass valve climate control system control / function indicator light for ASD / ASR / 4-Matic data link connector terminal 16 EGR switchover valve 2 fuel tank vent valve windshield washer nozzle heater windshield washer system, heated HFM-SFI (fuel injection) control module kickdown cutout relay kickdown solenoid valve oxygen sensor heater relay purge control valve recirculation switchover flap valve resonance intake manifold switchover valve (1995 diesel) residual engine heat utilization time-relay (not US) stationary heater control module throttle valve potentiometer upshift delay solenoid
8	8	engine compartment light parking / tail / side marker light, left
9	8	clock control elements illumination convenience feature relay diagnostic module exterior light switch illumination dome light shut off delay and reading light, front hazard warning system headrest unlocking switch, rear instrument illumination rheostat convertible top switch radio roll bar switch rear window sun shade switch seat heater switch. seat adjustment module shift lever light vanity mirror light warning buzzer contract window regulator switch
10	25	rear window defroster

11

Fuse positions

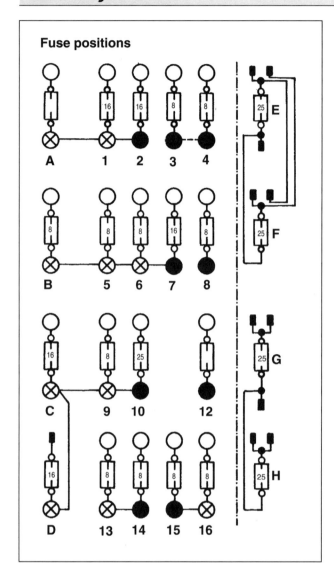

Table b. 1993 - 1995 fuse / relay panel fuses

Fuse	Rating	Protected circuit
11	8	transmission oil cooling
	15	A/C control module
12	16	A/C control module, blower motor (automatic air conditioning)
	30	blower regulator for automatic air conditioning
13	8	low beam, left
14	8	low beam, right
15	8	high beam, left
16	8	high beam, right
A	16	sunroof with pop up feature
	8	convertible top control module
B	8	alarm system
		infrared central locking control module
		rear view mirror, inside
		rear view mirrors, outside
		seat belt extender system
		seat belt warning module
C	16	alarm system
		antenna power
		backrest lock, front seat (coupe)
		CD player
		convenience features control module
		central locking control module
		dome light, rear (station wagon)
		entrance / exit light
		infrared central locking control module
		reading lights, rear
		sound system
		tailgate lock switch (station wagon)
		trunk light (except station wagon)
D	16	auxiliary fan preresistor
E	25	front seat adjustment (backrest, headrest, memory)
F	25	front seat adjustment (forward / backward)

Additional fuses

A number of fuses outside the main fuse / relay panel protect additional circuits in the vehicle.

Table c. 1993 - 1995 additional fuses

Fuse	Rating	Model	Protected circuit	Location
F1 - F4	10	V-8	Varied	Four 10 amp blade fuses fit into base relay. Same as over-voltage protection relay fuses
F10	16	Non-US cars	residual engine heat utilization time-limit	In front of fuse panel
F10	25	Non-US cars	auxiliary heater	In front of fuse panel
F15	30	All	blower motor	In front of fuse panel mounted on left shock tower
F22	16	Early 1993, all models	auxiliary fan relay module	In relay panel, position B, fuse is internal to relay and non-replaceable (replace relay)
F22	30	Late 1993 on, all models	auxiliary fan relay module	In relay panel, position B, fuse is external to relay and replaceable
F22/1	16	All	heated seats	Component compartment right side against inner fender
F22/2	8	All	cellular telephone	Right side shock tower
F24	8	Cabriolet	roll bar deployment solenoid	Right rear wheel housing next to convertible top hydraulic unit
	16	Cabriolet	roll bar control module	Fuse block in right rear wheel housing, next to convertible top hydraulic unit
F24/1	30	Cabriolet	power convertible top / roll bar hydraulic unit	Fuse block in right rear wheel housing next to convertible top hydraulic unit

Engine compartment electrical components

The rear section of the E-Class engine compartment, insulated by a bulkhead from the engine, is called the component compartment. The engine compartment electrical components are called out in the accompanying photographs.

◀ 6-cylinder cars:

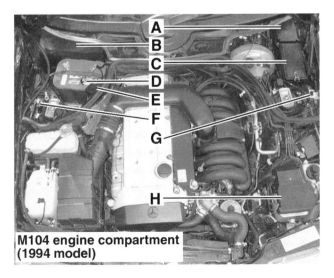

M104 engine compartment (1994 model)

A. Main relay panel

B. Module locations

C. Main fuse panel

D. Battery

E. Diagnostic plug

F. Cell phone fuse

G. Blower motor fuse

H. ABS / ASR hydraulic unit

11

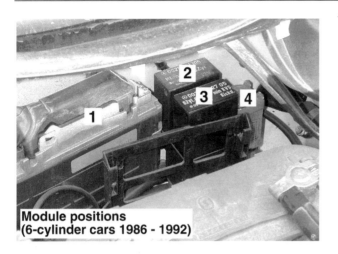

**Module positions
(6-cylinder cars 1986 - 1992)**

◄ 6-cylinder cars (1986 - 1992): Control modules located at right rear of engine in component compartment under cover:

1. CIS-E
2. KLIMA (air conditioning)
3. Fuel pump / kickdown
4. Over-voltage protection relay

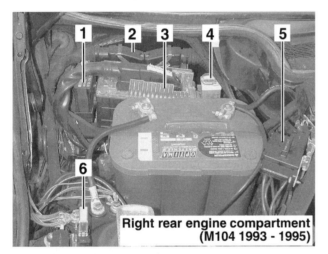

**Right rear engine compartment
(M104 1993 - 1995)**

◄ 6-cylinder cars (1993 - 1995): Electrical components in component compartment at right rear of engine compartment:

1. Engine systems control module (MAS)
2. HFM-SFI control module
3. ABS / ASR control module
4. Over-voltage protection relay
5. Diagnostic socket
6. Cell phone fuse

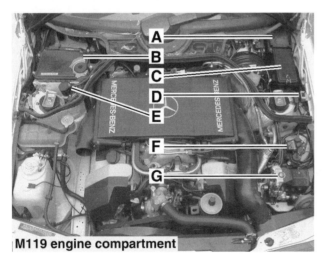

M119 engine compartment

◄ V-8 cars:

A. Main relay panel
B. Module box
C. Main fuse panel
D. Blower motor fuse
E. Diagnostic socket (38-pin connector for MB hand held tester or STAR laptop)
F. EZL / AKR control module (ignition system)
G. ABS or ABS / ASR hydraulic unit

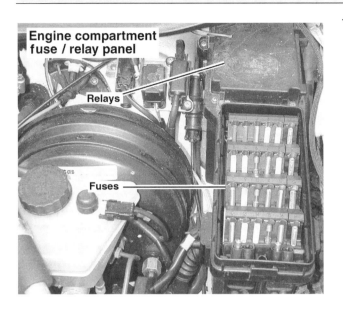

Engine compartment fuse / relay panel

Relays

Fuses

◀ The engine compartment fuse / relay panel is constructed with fuses at the front and relays at the rear under a cover. All relays are plug in type.

Relays and modules

◀ In addition to the relays in the engine compartment main fuse / relay panel, other modules and relays are to be found in a variety of locations throughout the vehicle. See **Table h** and **Table i**.

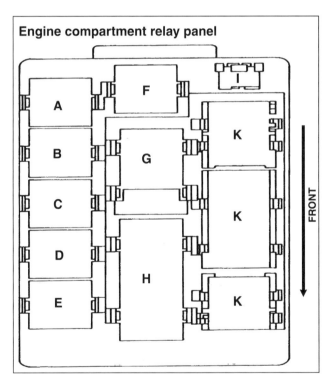

Engine compartment relay panel

I

A

F

B

G

K

C

K

D

H

E

K

FRONT

Table h. Relays and modules 1986 - 1992

Component	Model	Location
4MATIC control module	4MATIC	Component compartment right side, forward of ABS module
4MATIC function test relay	4MATIC	Front passenger footwell under footrest
A/C compressor control module	From 1990 (gas models)	*see* Engine systems control module (MAS)
A/C control module (KLIMA)	All diesel, gas up to 1989	Component compartment right side, behind battery
ABS control module	6-cyl. gas and diesel	Component compartment right side, behind battery
ABS or ABS/ASR control module	V-8	Component compartment right side, in module box
Air injection relay	All	Relay panel, position E
Alarm control module	All	Front passenger footwell under footrest
ASD control module (traction)	Diesel with ASD	Component compartment right side, behind battery
Anti-theft alarm control module		*see* Convenience control module
Auxiliary fan preresistor relay	All	Relay panel position B
Auxiliary fan relay	All	Relay panel position C
Base relay (replaces over-voltage protection relay)	V-8	Component compartment right side, in module box
Blower motor auxiliary fuse holder	All	Component compartment left side
Central locking module		*see* Convenience control module
CIS-E control module	6-cylinder gasoline	Component compartment right side, behind battery
Combination relay (turn signal / hazard, heated rear window, wiper motor)	All	Relay panel position H
Component compartment	All	Rear of engine compartment (behind bulkhead)
Convenience control module (anti-theft alarm, A/C, central locking, window regulator, sunroof)	1990 - 1992	Under left rear seat
Convenience relay	All	Relay panel position F
Cruise control / engine overload protection relay	All	Component compartment right side, near over-voltage protection relay
Cruise control amplifier module (Tempomat)	All	Behind left lower dashboard
Daytime running light control module	Canada only	Front passenger footwell under footrest
Diagnostic module	1990 California	Front passenger footwell under footrest
Diagnostic socket	All	Component compartment right side
EDS engine control module	Diesel	Component compartment right side, behind battery
Elec. Accelerator (EA) / cruise control/idle speed control module	V-8 with ASR (traction)	Component compartment right side, in module box
Engine control module (combined fuel injection, fuel pump relay, A/C compressor control)	1990 - 1992 gasoline	Component compartment right side, behind battery

Table h. Relays and modules 1986 - 1992

Component	Model	Location
Exterior bulb monitoring module	All	Relay panel position K
First gear start relay	1990 - 1992 6-cylinder gasoline	Relay panel position G
Front seat control module, left/right	All	Under left / right front seat
Front seat headrest adjustment relay, left / right	All	Under left / right front seat
Front seat heater control module	All	Under left rear seat
Front seat heater relay, left/right	All	Beneath carpeting forward of left / right front seat
Fuel pump power relays	All gasoline	Under right rear seat
Fuel pump relay	1986-1989 gasoline	Component compartment right side, behind battery
Fuel pump relay	1990-1992 gasoline	*see* Engine systems control module (MAS)
Glow plug relay	Diesel	Engine compartment on left fender
Headlight washer relay	All	Relay panel position D
Heated seats auxiliary fuse holder	All	Engine compartment left rear
Ignition control module (EZL or EZL / AKR)	All gasoline	Engine compartment on left fender
Intermittent wiper timer relay		*see* Rear window intermittent wiper timer
KLIMA relay		*see* A/C compressor control module (KLIMA)
LH-SFI fuel injection control module	V-8	Component compartment right side, in module box
Module box	V-8	Component compartment right side
Over-voltage protection relay	6-cylinder	Component compartment right side, behind battery
Power seat relay	All	Relay panel position A
Power window relay	All	Relay panel position F
Rear window wiper timer	Station wagon	Left corner of tailgate behind panel
Seatbelt warning relay	All	Driver footwell
Sunroof module		*see* Convenience control module
Supplemental restraint system (SRS) control module	All	Top of transmission tunnel behind console
Telephone, terminal 30 auxiliary fuse holder	All	In engine compartment, next to fuse panel
Transmission upshift delay relay	1990-1992 gasoline	Right of component compartment near over-voltage protection relay
Warning module (seat belts / key / lights)	All	Behind right side of instrument cluster
Window regulator module		*see* Convenience control module

11

Table i. Relays and modules 1993 - 1995

Component	Model	Location
A/C compressor control module	6-cyl., gasoline or diesel	Component compartment right side, behind battery
A/C compressor control module	V-8	Component compartment right side, in module box
A/C control panel	All	Center consol
ABS or ABS/ASR control module	6-cylinder	Component compartment right side, behind battery
ABS or ABS/ASR control module	V-8	Component compartment right side, in module box
Alarm module	Cabriolet	Behind convertible top hydraulic unit in trunk
Alarm module	All exc. Cabriolet	Front passenger footwell under footrest
ASD control module	Diesel	Component compartment right side, behind battery
Audio power amplifier module	All	Behind instrument cluster, lower right
Auxiliary fan preresistor relay	6-cylinder	Relay panel position B
Auxiliary fan preresistor relay	V-8	Relay panel position C
Auxiliary fan relay	V-8	Relay panel position B
Auxiliary fan relay module	6-cylinder	Relay panel position C
Auxiliary fuse holder (ATA)	6-cylinder	Relay panel position E
Base relay (replaces over-voltage protection relay)	V-8	Component compartment right side, in module box (contains four 10 amp blade fuses)
Blower motor regulator	All	Next to blower motor, under cowl panel
Combination relay (turn signal, heated rear window, hazard, wiper motor)	All	Relay panel position H
Component compartment	All	Rear of engine compartment (behind bulkhead)
Convenience control module (window regulator, sunroof)	All	Under left rear seat
Convenience relay module	All	Relay panel position F
Convertible top control module	Cabriolet	Behind right rear seat side panel
Cruise control		*see also* Electronic Accelerator entries
Cruise control / engine overload protection relay	6-cyl. gasoline, V-8	Component compartment right side, in module box
Cruise control / idle speed control module	6-cyl. gasoline	Component compartment right side, behind battery
Cruise control / idle speed control module	V-8	Component compartment right side, in module box
Cruise control amplifier module	Diesel	Behind left lower dash
Daylight running light module	Canada	Behind instrument cluster lower right
Diagnostic module	Gasoline for California	Under left side dashboard
Diagnostic socket	All	Component compartment right side
Disconnect diode (parking brake / ASR / electronic acceler.)	V-8	Relay panel position I

Table i. Relays and modules 1993 - 1995

Component	Model	Location
Electronic Accelerator / cruise control module	V-8, 6-cyl. gasoline	Component compartment right side, behind battery
Engine systems control module (MAS)	6-cyl. gasoline	Component compartment right side, behind battery
Engine systems control module (MAS)	V-8	Component compartment right side, in module box
Exterior bulb monitor module	All	Relay panel position K
First gear start relay module	6-cylinder gasoline	Relay panel position G
Front seat control module, left/right	All	Under left / right front seat
Front seat headrest adjustment relay, left / right	All	Under left / right front seat
Front seat heater control module	All	Under right front seat
Fuel pump relay	V-8, 6-cyl. gasoline	Component compartment right side, behind battery
Glow plug relay	Diesel	Engine compartment on left inner fender
Headlight washer relay module	All	Relay panel position D
HFM-SFI control module	6-cylinder gasoline	Component compartment right side, behind battery
Ignition control module (EZL, EZL / AKR)	Gasoline	Left inner fender
Infrared remote control module	All	Under rear seat, right side
Intermittent wiper timer relay		*see* Rear window intermittent wiper timer
LH-SFI control module	V-8	Component compartment right side, in module box
MAS module		*see* Engine systems control module (MAS)
Over-voltage protection relay	6-cylinder	Component compartment right side, behind battery
Power seat module	All	Relay panel position A
Rear window inter. wiper timer	Station wagon	Inside tailgate, under liner
Rollbar control module	Cabriolet	Transmission tunnel in front of consol
Seat belt / key / lights on warning module	All	Behind instrument cluster, lower right
Seat belt extender module, left / right	Coupe, Cabriolet	Behind left /right rear side panel
Seat belt warning module	Coupe	Relay panel position G
Secondary air injection relay	V-8	Relay panel position E
SRS control module	All	Transmission tunnel in front of console
Starter lock-out relay module	All	Behind instrument cluster, upper left
Sunroof module		*see* Convenience control module
Transmission upshift delay relay	6-cyl. gasoline	Component compartment right side, near over-voltage protection relay
Window regulator module		*see* Convenience control module

11

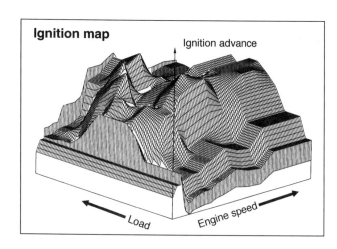

Ignition map

Ignition advance

Load

Engine speed

GASOLINE ENGINE IGNITION SYSTEMS

◄ In order to meet increasingly strict emissions standards while delivering adequate power and reliability, modern high compression engines require extremely accurate spark timing. Mercedes-Benz together with Bosch meets these requirements using microprocessor control and programmed ignition maps. Based on inputs from various sensors, the spark timing point can be accurately controlled.

E-Class ignition system applications are summarized in **Table j**.

Table j. Ignition system applications

Year	Engine	Ignition system	Injection system
1986 -1992	M103 M104	EZL basic	CIS-E
1992 -1995	M119	EZL/AKR with knock sensing	LH-SFI
1993 -1995	M104	HFM-SFI	HFM-SFI

EZL ignition system (6-cylinder engines to 1992)

◄ The EZL system uses sensors to measure crankshaft position and engine speed, engine coolant temperature, throttle position and engine load. Later versions include camshaft position, ambient air temperature and knock sensors.

The most advanced ignition system fitted to the E-Class combined the functions of spark control with fuel injection in one control unit. This system eliminated the high voltage distributor by going to multiple ignition coils. This system is called HFM-SFI (Hot Film Management-Sequential Fuel Injection) and was used on the late M104 engines.

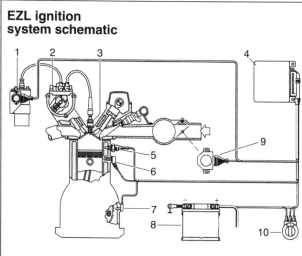

EZL ignition system schematic

1. Ignition coil
2. High-voltage ignition distributor
3. Spark plug
4. Electronic control module (ECM)
5. Coolant temperature sensor
6. Knock sensor (EZL/AKR system only)
7. Crankshaft speed and position sensors
8. Battery
9. Throttle position sensor
10. Ignition switch

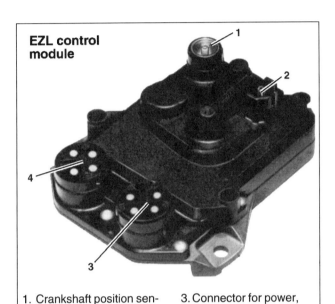

EZL control module

1. Crankshaft position sensor
2. Vacuum connection to engine intake manifold
3. Connector for power, ground and rpm signal
4. All other sensor inputs

0058735

1986 - 1989

The basic EZL system is used on gasoline engines from 1986 through the 1989 model year. The system consists of:

• EZL control module
• Ignition coil
• Crankshaft position sensor
• Engine coolant temperature sensor
• Throttle position sensor
• Ignition distributor

The EZL module contains a microprocessor preprogrammed with the ignition timing map. The microprocessor receives input from the engine sensors and computes the spark timing point.

1990 - 1992

Intake air temperature and intake manifold absolute pressure were added to the data processed by the EZL control module. These signals are taken from the fuel injection control module.

EZL / AKR ignition system (V-8 engines)

With a compression ratio of 10 : 1 to 11 : 1, the V-8 engines requires knock detection to avoid internal engine damage. The EZL system was modified for the 119 engine by adding knock sensing technology and became known as EZL / AKR (electronic ignition with anti-knock regulation).

The EZL / AKR module has dual outputs allowing it to control two ignition coils. Each coil feeds a distributor (**arrow**) mounted to the front of each cylinder head.

The dual knock sensors (one on each side of the engine block) are piezoelectric devices that pick up the mechanical vibration generated by engine knock and convert it to an electrical signal recognized by the EZL / AKR module. Having detected knock, the module retards ignition timing for a certain number of cycles, after which it gradually moves the timing back toward its original setting.

11

HFM-SFI engine management (6-cylinder engines from 1993)

The 1993-95 6-cylinder M104 engine was equipped with HFM-SFI (Hot Film Management -Sequential Fuel Injection). This advanced system combined fuel injection and ignition control in one module.

◀ HFM-SFI uses coils that are mounted on the spark plugs, doing away with the rotating high voltage distributor at the front of the engine.

This reduces the number of moving parts and reduces electromagnetic radiation, making it easier to shield sensitive control modules. Each coil pack provides spark to two spark plugs at the same time, one connected directly and the other with a short high-tension lead.

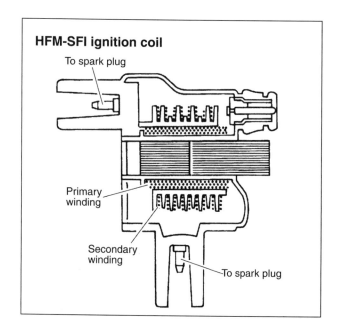

HFM-SFI ignition coil

To spark plug

Primary winding

Secondary winding

To spark plug

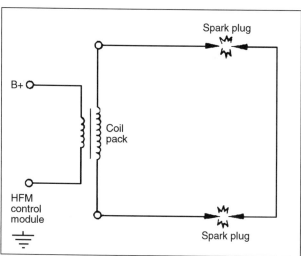

Spark plug

B+

Coil pack

HFM control module

Spark plug

◀ The voltage to the cylinder on the compression stroke is high, while the voltage to the cylinder on the exhaust stroke is low, allowing full strength spark to the igniting cylinder. The control module can recognize combustion problems by monitoring the primary current flow. If the module detects a problem with a cylinder, it can stop the fuel flow to that cylinder, preventing unburned raw fuel flowing into and overheating the catalytic converter.

The HFM-SFI system is equipped with two knock sensors. Unlike EZL / AKR technology, which retards spark timing across the engine, HFM-SFI can retard just the knocking cylinders. This keeps the ignition timing point as advanced as possible for maximum power output.

DIESEL GLOW SYSTEMS

An explanation of the diesel engine cycle is given in **Chapter 7**.

◀ The diesel combustion process is based on the heat of compression. To aid cold starting, the preglow function is used to increase the temperature of the compressed air in the cylinder. Because the glow plugs are located inside the precombustion chamber, some of the fuel hits the hot glow plugs directly and ignites. This further aids cold starts.

On OM602 and OM606 engines, the glow system was modified to help the engine run smoother just after a cold start. In these systems the glow plugs continue to heat for a period after initial ignition. This function is called after-glow.

The characteristics of the different glow systems are shown in the accompanying table.

Glow plug in precombustion chamber

1. Diesel injector
2. Glow plug
3. Precombustion chamber

Table k. Diesel engine glow system applications

Engine	Preglow duration	After-glow duration	Temp. signal used for glow duration	Circuit protection
OM603	2 - 30 seconds	None	Ambient air	80 Amp fuse in glow relay
OM602	2 - 30 seconds	Up to 60 seconds	Engine coolant temperature	Circuit breaker in glow relay
OM606	2 - 30 seconds	Up to 180 seconds	Engine coolant temperature	Circuit breaker in glow relay

◀ The glow system consists of glow plugs at each cylinder and a control relay. A glow plug has a heater element and a control element. The initial current flow to a glow plug is 30 amperes, causing it to heat immediately. As the temperature of the heater element increases, the current to the glow plug decreases to 8 - 15 amperes. The glow plug reaches approx. 900° C (1652° F) in nine seconds and a maximum of 1180° C (2156° F) within thirty seconds.

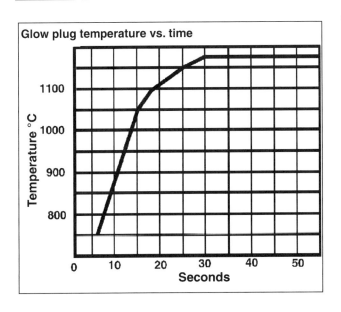

Glow plug temperature vs. time

11

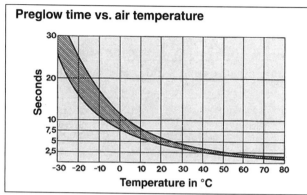

Preglow time vs. air temperature

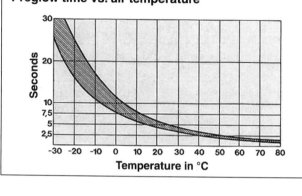

Afterglow time vs. coolant temperature

OM603 preglow system (1987)

◀ The OM603 preglow system uses a relay controller that contains an ambient air temperature sensor to determine glow time. The relay contains a safety shut-off in case of malfunction and has built-in fault diagnostics. See **Tips, Maintenance, Service** at the end of this chapter.

An 80 ampere fuse on the relay protects the preglow system.

If no attempt is made to start the engine within 20 to 25 seconds of the glow indicator light going out, the glow current is interrupted by the safety shut-off. If another attempt is made to start the engine, the glow system will switch itself back on for the length of time the starter is engaged.

OM602 glow system (1990-93)

The glow controller relay for the OM602 engine uses a self-resetting circuit breaker.

◀ An after-glow function improves smooth running during warm up. The glow plugs can continue to glow for up to 60 seconds after the engine starts.

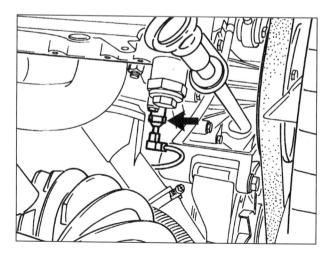

◀ The glow relay uses the engine coolant temperature sensor (**arrow**) signal to determine preglow and afterglow times.

OM606 glow system (1995)

The after-glow time was increased to 180 seconds at engine temperatures below 40° C (104° F). The glow plugs were moved to the top of the engine and are longer (120.5 mm / 4.75 in) and wider (28 mm / 1.10 in) than in previous versions.

THROTTLE CONTROL SYSTEMS

In North America, cruise control had been standard equipment on the E-Class since its introduction. Three different cruise control systems were used. See **Table I** for application information.

Table I. Cruise control applications

Year model	Engine	Fuel Injection system	Cruise control version	Functions
1986 - 1992 gasoline powered	M103 M104	CIS-E	Tempomat	Cruise control
All diesel	OM603 OM602 OM606	EDS		
1993-1995 300E, E320	M104	HFM-SFI	Electronic Accelerator (EA) (with ASR traction)	Idle speed, cruise control, drive-by-wire
			Idle Speed Control (ISC) (without ASR traction)	Idle speed, cruise control
1992-1995 400E, E420	M119	LH-SFI	Electronic Accelerator (EA) (with ASR traction)	Idle speed, cruise control, drive-by-wire
			Idle Speed Control (ISC) (without ASR traction)	Idle speed, cruise control
1992-1995 500E, E500	M119	LH-SFI	Electronic Accelerator (EA) (with ASR traction)	Idle speed, cruise control, drive-by-wire

Tempomat. The basic system was used from 1986 to 1992 in gasoline-powered cars and in diesel cars through the model run. This cruise control system used a separate electromechanical throttle actuator connected to the engine throttle linkage.

Idle Speed Control (ISC). This system uses an integrated electronic throttle actuator to control idle speed and cruise control functions.

Electronic Accelerator (EA). Models with traction control (ASR) are equipped with a drive-by-wire system. In these cars the throttle pedal is only connected to a rheostat (throttle pedal position sensor). Electronics manage all throttle functions including cruise control.

11

Cruise control (Tempomat)

The Tempomat cruise control system consists of:

• Throttle actuator
• Steering column switch (Set / Off / Accel / Decel / Resume)
• Control module
• Speed sensor (speedometer)
• Clutch pedal switch (manual transmission only)
• Brake pedal switch

When cruise control is activated (above 25 mph) by the switch on the steering column, the Tempomat control module locks in the vehicle speed. It then continuously compares the set speed with the actual vehicle road speed. The Tempomat actuator adjusts the throttle so that the actual speed matches the set speed.

Once set, speed can be increased or decreased by tapping the steering column switch in either the accelerate or decelerate direction. The speed changes by 1 kph (0.6 mph) per tap. If you tap the brake pedal, the actuator immediately disengages and a strong spring returns the throttle linkage to idle position.

After accelerating past the set speed (to pass another car, for example) the Tempomat returns the vehicle to the last set speed when the foot is removed from the throttle pedal. The speed setting is erased when the ignition is switched off.

If the set speed is exceeded by more than 4 mph (such as when going down a steep hill), the Tempomat will disengage and the throttle will return to the idle position. Once the speed differential drops below 3.5 mph, the system will reengage.

Idle Speed Control (ISC)

In the following models without traction control, the throttle is mechanically activated via throttle cable:

- 1993 and later cars with M104 engine (HFM-SFI engine management)
- 1992 and later cars with M119 engine (LH-SFI engine management)

An electronic actuator integrated in the throttle housing manages idle speed and cruise control. The actuator is controlled by the idle speed / cruise control (ISC) module.

Idle speed compensation for air conditioning compressor load is built into the ISC module. Therefore, regardless of air conditioning use, idle speed remains nearly constant.

The ISC throttle control system can hold the throttle valve at any position electrically. When the engine is first started, the throttle valve position is calculated using input from the engine coolant temperature sensor, providing for fast idle during engine warm-up. See **Table m**.

Table m. Coolant temperature vs. engine idle speed

Coolant temperature	Rpm in neutral	Rpm in gear
< 30°C (86°F)	900 - 1000	800 - 900
45°C (113°F)	750 - 850	650 - 750
60°C (140°F)	700 - 800	600 - 700
> 75°C (167°F)	650 - 750	550 - 650

11

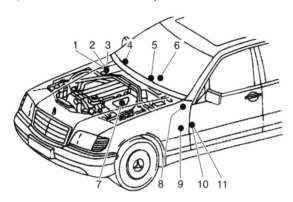

Electronic throttle control components (1992 and later models)

1. Engine control module
2. Over-voltage protection relay
3. Diagnostic connector
4. Electronic Accelerator module
   Cruise control / idle speed control module
5. Electronic speedometer
6. Cruise control switch
7. Electronic Accelerator actuator -or-
   Cruise control / idle speed control actuator
8. Diagnostic module (Calif. only)
9. Closed throttle position switch (ASR only)
10. Starter lock / back-up light switch
11. Brake light switch

Electronic Accelerator (EA)

◄ Gasoline powered cars with traction control (ASR) were fitted with the Electronic Accelerator (EA) system. This is a drive-by wire system that integrates cruise control, idle speed, and throttle intervention.

The EA system functions through the engine torque control circuit of the ABS / ASR control module. See **Chapter 9**.

> **CAUTION—**
> On ASR equipped cars, Do NOT pull on the throttle cable to raise the engine speed for any reason. If the engine speed increases via the throttle cable without the corresponding indication from the throttle pedal position indicator it will set a fault code, the CHECK ENGINE light will illuminate and the engine management system will place itself into limp-home mode. The fault code will have to be cleared with the hand held tester or the STAR laptop.

CLIMATE CONTROL

For the E-Class in North America automatic climate control was standard equipment. In other markets a manually controlled heating system was standard. Manual air conditioning and semi or fully automatic climate control systems were available as options.

◄ The automatic climate control system provides a constant temperature inside the car. Once the desired temperature is set, various sensors and air flow controllers maintain the cabin temperature. The push button system determines how and where air flow is directed. The recirculating switch (**arrow**) shuts off outside air.

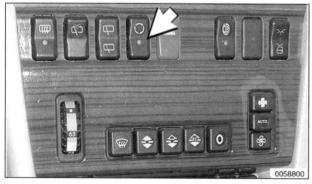

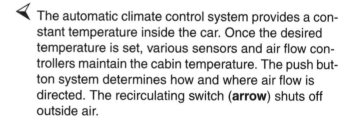

0058800

Components

The automatic climate control system consists of:

• Air conditioning system
• Engine coolant auxiliary circulating pump
• Blower motor control unit
• Heater core solenoid valve
• Fresh / recirculating air flap
• Heater system
• Heat exchanger temperature sensor
• In-car temperature sensor with aspirator
• Outside air temperature sensor
• Push button switch unit
• Hall effect speed sensor (speedometer)

Operation

The climate control panel on the center console receives input from the temperature sensors and directs the climate control activities. Heated air, air conditioned air and fresh air are all available to maintain the set temperature.

Blower speeds are infinitely variable. The blower motor control unit varies both voltage and current to the blower motor. Blower speed is regulated based on road speed. As road speed increase blower speed decreases.

TIPS, MAINTENANCE, SERVICE

EZL or EZL / AKR module, replacing

When exchanging the EZL module, pay attention to the foil covered heat conducting paste on the back. Do not remove the protective sheeting. It is there to help transfer heat.

Glow system in cold weather

As the diesel engine glow plug controller ages, the preglow light does not stay illuminated for the correct time. Experience has shown that the controller turns off the preglow light in 5 - 10 seconds. If you listen carefully you can hear the relay disengage. In cold weather, even though the glow light has extinguished, don't try to start the engine until you can hear the glow controller disengage. This added preglow time really

11

helps start a cold diesel engine. In extremely cold conditions (below 0°F / -18°C) glow the engine twice. Glow until the relay clicks off each time.

Glow system troubleshooting

If the preglow light fails to light during the dash light test, the problem may be:

- An interruption of power to terminal 30 in the glow controller
- Blown 80 ampere fuse
- Fault in preglow timer power relay
- Fault in glow plug wiring
- Fault in one or more of the glow plugs

If the glow light works in the dash light test but not when attempting to glow the system, refer to the following diagnostics table.

Table n. Glow light diagnostics

Preglow light status	Engine status	Possible cause	Repair
Off	During preglow	Either glow plug #1 or two other glow plugs defective	Check resistance of glow plug Nominal resistance: 0.5-0.7 Ω.
On	After engine has been running for 1 minute	Defective preglow relay	Replace defective relay.
On (constantly)	Engine starts normally	Glow relay is sticking in ON position	Replace defective relay.
Off (constantly)	Engine does not start or hard to start with blue / black smoke	Short circuit in glow plug #1 or any two others	Check resistance of glow plug (Nominal resistance: 0.5-0.7 Ω).
		Open circuit to glow indicator light or bad bulb Defective glow relay	Check wiring for continuity and bulb. Replace defective glow relay.

Glow plugs, testing

If glow indicator light on the instrument panel does not light or the engine is hard to start, testing the glow plugs is a good place to start.

NOTE—
Use a good digital multimeter for testing electrical components.

— Pull cover from glow plug relay.

— Remove glow plug relay harness connector.

– Connect digital multimeter common lead to ground.

– Set multimeter to ohm scale on finest resolution.

– Probe relay harness connector leads with multimeter positive lead.

– Values of 0.5 - 2.0Ω represent a good glow plug. An open circuit or a higher resistance reading indicates a weak or defective glow plug.

Glow plug size change

The glow plugs for the OM602 engine are smaller than the previous OM603. They measure 23 mm (0.91 in) in diameter instead of 27 mm (1.06 in). There is a ring groove machined around the hexagon nut used to remove and install the glow plugs.

Cruise control will not engage

If your cruise control stops operating, check the brake light bulbs and their fuse. The Tempomat unit checks for continuity in the brake light circuit and disables cruise control if the brake light circuit is faulty.

CHECK ENGINE light / limp home mode (cars equipped with ASR)

The electronic accelerator control unit is known to cause problems on 400E and 500E cars with ASR. Symptoms are loss of power and an illuminated CHECK ENGINE light illuminated. The LH-SFI control module drops the engine into limp-home mode (lower power, fixed injection map). Initially the symptoms will disappear by stopping and restarting the engine.

When this condition is present, communications and engine management fault codes are stored in the diagnostic module. In most cases, the cure is to replace the Electronic Accelerator (EA) actuator in the throttle housing.

11

Precautions for running on a chassis dynamometer (cars equipped with ASR)

If an ASR-equipped car is run on a chassis dynamometer, diagnostic trouble codes (DTCs) may be set and the engine control module may place the car into limp-home mode.

To avoid this problem:

— With ignition off, jumper sockets 6 and 1 on diagnostic plug (X11/4). This places ABS / ASR module into diagnostic mode.

NOTE—
See relay / module location table earlier in this chapter for location of diagnostic plug.

— When the dyno run is complete, remove the jumper.

NOTE—
The ASR and ABS warning lights are illuminated during this operation.

Engine control module (ECM), replacing

The engine control module (ECM) in LH-SFI and HFM-SFI systems is designed to detect and store vehicle-specific information: Transmission type, Federal or California version, Electronic Accelerator (EA) or Idle Speed Control (ISC), presence or absence of ASR, etc. Adaptation factors such as throttle valve angle and fuel trim are also held in the module.

When replacing the engine control module, the Mercedes-Benz hand-held tester, STAR laptop or equivalent diagnostic scan tool must be available to 'code' the new module codes.

Electronic Accelerator (EA) control module, replacing

Make sure ignition is off when replacing the Electronic Accelerator (EA) control module.

After installation, turn on the ignition for 90 seconds (without attempting a start) to allow synchronization of control module and EA actuator.

Inaccurate temperature tracking (automatic climate control system)

If the climate control system isn't tracking the set temperature accurately, check to make sure the center dash vents are not pointing upward, forcing cold air into the interior temperature sensor.

Automatic climate control components, extending service life

Often the driver will set the temperature wheel to one extreme or the other. Drivers have the feeling that full heat or full A/C will get the passenger compartment to the correct temperature fastest. This doesn't allow the system to work as designed.

To get the longest life from the automatic climate control system, allow the system to exercise all components. If the temperature inside the car is more than 4° away from the setting on the temperature wheel, the system will use full heat or A/C regardless.

As the interior temperature approaches the setting at the climate control panel, the automatic functions will slowly reduce blower speed. Allowing the system to work in its automatic mode, with all components functioning, will prolong the life of the system. When flap controllers and valves don't move for long periods they tend to stick in position and ruin the component.

11

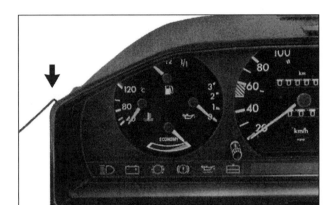

Instrument cluster, removing

◁ Pulling the instrument cluster requires a special little hook (**arrow**). This tool can be made from stiff wire.

– Push hook between cluster and dash padding just above vertical edge of cluster.

– Rotate hook until it grabs detent on edge of cluster.

– Using one hook on each side, pull uniformly on both sides until cluster is out. Initial removal of cluster will take extra pulling force.

◁ Mercedes-Benz cluster removal hook, special tool 126 589 03 33 00, costs $8 - $9.

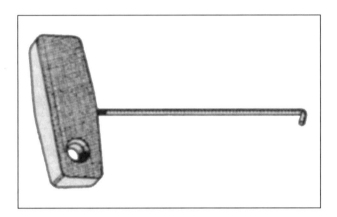

Chapter 12

Performance and Modification

12

GENERAL

While an E-Class car is not exactly a Chevy when it comes to available performance and modification equipment, there still are ways and means to accomplish the updates you would like. This chapter gives general recommendations and hints on adding and modifying equipment and accessories to your E-Class.

CHASSIS MODIFICATION

Simple suspension changes can dramatically alter the way the car handles. New matching springs, shock absorbers, and thicker sway bars are the first thing most drivers think about. While there are aftermarket companies that produce suspension components for the E-Class, there are many factory upgrades available as well.

Sway bars

Most of the E-Class cars come from the factory with spring rates fully capable of sporty driving. The issue most driver's have is with the car's large degree of body lean or roll. This makes aggressive driving uncomfortable. While it is best to deal with body lean by increasing spring rates, that stiffens the ride quite a bit.

If only the sway bars are changed, body lean is controlled, yet suspension stiffness is not increased. The only time you would realize that there are larger bars installed would be when going over a speed bump at an angle where the wheels deflect at different times.

The fact that all sway bars for the E-Class are the same shape, factory parts can be used for upgrades. See **Table a**.

Table a. Sway bar diameters

Model	Front bar (mm)	Rear bar (mm)
300E, E320 300D, TD 300TE, E320 station wagon 300CE, E320 Coupe	26.5	14.5
300E 4MATIC	26	14.5
300TE 4MATIC	27	14.5

Table a. Sway bar diameters

Model	Front bar (mm)	Rear bar (mm)
300CE Cabriolet	27.5	14.5
400E, E420	26.5	16
500E	28	18

Replacing the front sway bar takes about twenty minutes. A very easy job to do.

To replace the rear bar, disconnect the driveshaft from the differential, remove rear subframe front mounting bolts and lower the subframe. Now you can dismount and snake the old bar out and the new bar into place.

Station wagon: When changing to larger rear bar, redrill the lever arm that locates the rear height adjustment valve. You will have to use a slightly larger clamp around the larger sway bar and then drill the arm for the size of the clamp used.

Sportline package

The Sportline suspension will lower the car 23 mm (0.9 in) and increase the ride stiffness by about 20%.

Original Sportline parts can be ordered from your Mercedes-Benz dealer. Listed below are the part numbers for the complete Sportline suspension conversion.

Table b. Sportline suspension parts

Description	MB part no.
Front spring	124 321 29 04
Rear spring	124 324 28 04
Front sway bar	124 323 68 65
Front inner sway bar bushing (2 each)	124 323 45 85
Front outer sway bar bushing (2 each)	124 323 51 85
Rear sway bar	124 326 19 65
Rear sway bar bushing (2 each)	124 326 01 81
Front shock absorber	124 320 64 30
Rear shock absorber	124 320 23 31

12

Because Sportline springs are almost one inch shorter and stiffer than standard springs, the shock absorbers should also be changed to avoid moving the shocks absorber pistons out of their normal working range and ruining them. Bilstein Sport shock absorbers are a good choice with the correct valving for the lowered stiffer springs and they come with a life-time warranty.

In addition to the Sportline parts listed, there is a faster ratio steering gear identified as *steering gear 765.928*. This steering gear has a ratio of 13.28 compared to the standard ratio of 13.91.

The Sportline steering wheel is 10 mm (0.4 in) smaller in diameter than the normal sedan wheel (390 mm vs. 400 mm / 15.35 in vs. 15.75 in).

◄ The Sportline wheel / tire combination uses 205/60-15 ZR rated tires on 7" wheels. This is slightly different from the standard 195/65-15 on 6.5" wheels.

There are many aftermarket wheels available in 15" and 16" sizes. There are 7 x 15" wheels that look just like factory wheels. If you want to put as much rubber on the ground as possible try using 7.5 x 16" wheels.

AMG E360TE with Compomotive wheels

AMG E360TE with factory wheels

Brakes

E-Class brakes are very good, but one improvement you can make is fitting teflon / stainless steel brake hoses in place of the standard rubber hoses. The rubber hoses expand under pressure. The teflon / stainless braid lines will not allow any expansion, so all hydraulic force goes to the brake caliper.

There are several aftermarket companies that sell teflon / stainless braid brake lines that have DOT approval. These hoses will give the brake pedal a very firm feel that allows you excellent modulation when stopping.

ENGINE MODIFICATION

There are very few engine modifications available for E-Class cars that will allow the engine to pass US Federal emissions testing. Performance camshafts are available, but the modified camshaft will more than likely cause the engine to fail the emissions test.

Muffler

There are some rear mufflers available that claim to increase exhaust gas flow. They also make more noise than stock. They are not worth the cost or the noise. Mercedes-Benz exhaust systems flow very freely, are quiet, and last a long time.

Air filter

Free flow air filters have their proponents. However, shop experience has shown that when a free flow filters is removed for inspection, there is dirt behind the filter. The throttle plates behind a free flow filter are often covered in abrasive grime that is also being carried through the engine, causing extra wear.

EPROM chip

Reprogrammed EPROM chips have been tested by the well respected German car magazine *Auto Motor und Sport*. Their findings are that most chip changes do nothing for the engine and at times even reduce power output. While some power improvement might be noticed at full throttle where the engine management system goes into a fixed set of full power parameters, it will not be noticed at partial throttle.

Once an engine is at operating temperature, the injected fuel volume depends on oxygen sensor output. No matter what changes are made to the programming on the EPROM, the oxygen sensor will maintain the stoichiometric ratio of 14.7 : 1 (air : fuel), also known as *lambda* (λ). Any attempts to add more fuel to the mixture causes the oxygen sensor to readjust the injection system. It is only at ¾ throttle or more that the oxygen sensor is removed from the circuit during full power operation. So, while a "speed chip" may indeed improve full-throttle performance by some 15% as claimed, it does nothing at part-throttle.

ENGINE REPLACEMENT

When it comes to upgrading the power output of your Mercedes-Benz, a larger engine is usually the answer. Modifying internal components is not a simple or inexpensive task. Changing camshafts and pistons usually causes the exhaust emission levels to go outside the EPA's acceptable limit.

All of the well-known German and American tuners substitute a larger 'emissions certified' Mercedes engine to obtain additional horsepower and torque. RENNTech and their famous V-12 CLK is one example.

AMG, the famous German tuner, has been a part of the Mercedes factory since 1999. Their creations involve tweaking an existing large engine and putting it in a smaller chassis. The C-43 is one example. The 4.3 liter V-8 was tweaked from 285 to 305 hp and installed into the C-Class chassis. Because of the added horsepower, the C-43 package included brake system and suspension upgrades.

300TE to 500E

In the long run it is always cheaper to purchase a factory hot rod rather than trying to build one. When the situation doesn't allow the money to be spent all at once and you have to build your dream car slowly, the results will usually be interesting, though not necessarily equivalent.

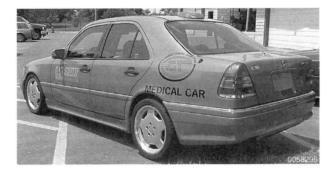

C36 engine
(side view)

C36 engine
(front view)

Here is the story of a 1988 300TE whose owner was not satisfied until it was as fast as a 500E with equivalent suspension and brakes.

◁ The replacement engine was a fortuitous find from a junkyard that contracts with MBUSA to dismantle all of their cars. The donor car was an FIA "medical car" C36 that had been used at CART PPG races until it ended up in the USA with only 18,000 very fast miles on it. This engine made 275 hp and 280 ft-lb of torque. The mission was to install this unusual C36 engine (including suspension and brakes to match) into the into the 300TE.

◁ An attempt was made to purchase the complete C36 car so that all the required parts would be available at the change-over site. Unfortunately, this was not allowed. The car was not a US-legal automobile so MBUSA insisted that it be dismantled. Some very creative exhaust work was required to enable the engine to pass California emissions requirements.

This is not an operation for the faint of heart or of funding. Here is a list of the transposed parts:

- 1995 C36 engine, control units and OBD II interface
- 1995 C36 transmission modified to accept mechanical speedometer
- 1993 E320 station wagon ABS control unit, electronic acceleration control system and cruise control system
- 1995 C36 over-voltage protection relay
- 1995 C36 fuel pump relay
- 1993 E320 station wagon fuel cooler
- 1993 E320 station wagon air conditioning manifold assembly
- 1995 C36 A/C compressor bracket assembly
- 1993 E320 station wagon air filter assembly
- 1993 E320 station wagon cruise control switch on steering
- 1995 C36 differential (2.87 : 1)
- Modified driveshaft to accept larger flange from large case differential
- 1993 E320 station wagon heater hoses

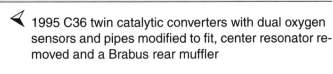 1995 C36 twin catalytic converters with dual oxygen sensors and pipes modified to fit, center resonator removed and a Brabus rear muffler

- 1992 500E light alloy brake calipers with ATE power discs and Textar front brake pads
- 1992 500E brake calipers and rotors with Textar rear pads
- Complete Mercedes-Benz Sportline suspension using Bilstein sport struts in the front (self leveling in the rear) with a 500E sway bar at the rear (larger than the Sportline unit)
- Complete European lighting with height adjusters for the headlights and relays for higher wattage bulbs along with correct wiper assemblies
- Wheels include a set of 16 x 8" from a 500E and a set of 17 x 7.5" factory wheels.
- Tires are 215/45-WR17 in the front and 225/45-17 in the rear. The wheels have an offset of 37 mm (1.46 in). This keeps them barely inside the wheel housings but they clear the huge 500E brake calipers.

Aside from the time it took to remove the M103 engine and transmission from the 1988 300TE and install the new engine and transmission, there was an additional 80 hours spent wiring in the new control units and chassis harness.

 In the modified car, front and rear Brabus spoilers were incorporated into the 300TE bodywork. The front spoilers house driving lights in a low position for good cornering illumination.

HEADLIGHT MODIFICATION

◁ Stock headlights on E-Class cars produced through the 1993 model year are less than satisfactory. The plastic light housing limits the bulb wattage to 60 watts for high beam. Installing a higher wattage bulb would generate more heat and melt the light housing, the connecting plug and the locking ring. A trick from the rally world, using both filaments at the same time for high beam, is inadvisable for the same reason.

Starting in 1994, the headlight assembly is made of metal, the same as the European unit. H4 bulbs (ranging as high as 160 watt high-beam / 100 watt low-beam in Europe) are used for these headlights.

The European headlight is also available with a vacuum motor to adjust the height of the headlight while driving. The four position dial switch is mounted next to the headlight switch on the instrument panel. It adjusts the high / low beam reflector. The procedure for installing the headlight height adjustment assembly is described later in this section.

The European light setup is a dramatic improvement over the stock US lighting and a worthwhile modification.

Besides normal hand tools, you'll need a soldering iron and homemade wire hooks to pull out the instrument cluster.

NOTE—
* *After performing this conversion, you will find the light output amazing. Using a photographic light meter, the high-beam output has been measured at four times the stock level! The low beams have better spread and output. The high beams may not look as powerful as they actually are; the foglights come on with the high beams, and their lenses splash light downward, close to the car, masking long-range improvement.*

* *Adjust the foglights high enough so that their light output pattern is additive to the high beam pattern. The 500E had foglights installed in the front spoiler and the space in the headlight assembly housed a driving light which directed light much farther ahead and beyond the high beams. These lenses can be ordered from US sources. The European headlights only come with the 300E / 400E lens pattern. I have the 500E pattern in my 400E and like them very much. My E320 station wagon is used during the winter months, so the fog lens pattern remained installed for great snow lighting.*

12

• *This headlight conversion costs about $900. Most drivers agree it is one of the premier modifications to the E-Class chassis. Doing it yourself can save on labor costs but requires about a day.*

• *If cost is no object you can maintain the headlight washer / wiper setup by installing the European version which is "plug and play" with the car's wiring harness.*

Table c. Headlight conversion parts list

Component	Manufacturer	Qty. needed	Part no.
Headlight assembly (1986 - 1989 models): **Note:** *There is a different set of headlights for the 1990 - 1993 model years. Parts retailers know about the year split.*			
Left	Hella	1	1EJ 004 440 111
Right		1	1EJ 004 440 121
12v H4 halogen 100 / 80-watt high / low-beam bulb	Osram	2	64194
12v H3 halogen 100-watt foglight bulb		2	64153
Starter booster relays	Volkswagen	2	431 951 253H
Relay holders	Hella	2	87123
Female spade connectors that clip into relay holder sockets		8	87272
6-pin electrical connector (socket)	MB	2	006 545 80 28
6-pin electrical connector (cover)		2	009 545 30 28
European headlight switch panel		1	124 60 03 65
European headlight level control vacuum switch		1	000 800 04 73
Miscellaneous supplies and connectors:			
14-gauge insulated wire		6'	
12-gauge insulated wire		6'	
10-gauge insulated wire (from battery to inline fuse holder)		6'	
40A fuse **Note:** *Use the glow-plug protection fuse holder from the diesel chassis or the rear window heater fuse holder. This makes the installation MB quality.*		1	
Vacuum tubing (hard plastic)	MB	12'	000 158 14 35
Vacuum tubing (rubber)	MB	2'	007 997 61 82
Vacuum Y or T-fitting		2	
Vacuum one-way valve		1	
Push-on terminals, butt-type wire connectors, heat-shrink tubing, grommets			

Headlights, upgrading (1993 and earlier models)

– Disconnect ground (–) cable from battery terminal.

> **WARNING—**
> *Prior to disconnecting the battery, read the battery disconnection cautions given at the front of this manual.*

– Working at front of engine compartment, disconnect electrical harness connector at each side marker assembly, release tab, and push out turn signal assembly.

> **NOTE—**
> *New side markers come with the headlights, but you must switch the original 3-pin US sockets to the Euro units, which come with 2-pin sockets. This is described later in this section.*

– Remove headlight wipers:
  • Fold wiper arms forward.
  • Undo 8 mm nuts.
  • Wiggle arms off shafts.

– Unbolt two 8 mm nuts holding metal trim below headlights, disconnect washer hose, remove trim.

◁ Undo black plastic headlight assembly fastener on sheet metal panel above each headlight.

– Undo three 8 mm bolts holding each headlight unit in place.
  • To reach inside bolt on left headlight, first remove air intake tube and snorkel.

– Remove headlight units.
  • Unplug headlight and wiper motor electrical harness connectors.

NOTE—

• *The new (Euro style) headlights require the use of a different headlight wiper / washer assembly.*

• *On a car with headlight wipers, the horizontal painted metal trim panels below the lights have holes in them. If you wish to install new style headlights but without the new wiper assembly, you can order new, primed panels without holes, MB part nos. 124 889 05 63 and 124 889 06 63. Have them painted to match, or order a can of spray paint in factory color from Tower Paint (800-779-6520 or www.towerpaint.com) and do it yourself. The spray can paint seems to be more susceptible to rock chips than properly applied body shop paint.*

• *If you choose to upgrade to the later headlight wiper / washer system, compatible with the new headlights, the costs of the additional components and the conversion is approximately $700.*

— Remove black outer housing gaskets from original headlight units.

> **CAUTION—**
> *Avoid breaking mounting tabs.*

— Install gaskets on new headlight units.

— Transfer three nut clips from old units to new.

— Attach ground wire, then slide in new headlight units.

NOTE—
Be sure the hood release cable doesn't bind.

— Line up headlight face with fender as you tighten three mounting bolts on each.

— Modify headlight harness connector and wiring as described later in this section.

◄ Before installing a new H4 bulb in headlight assembly, cut off small rounded tab on mounting flange.

> **CAUTION—**
> *Keep your fingers off the glass parts of the bulbs, and clean bulbs with alcohol solution before installation. Fingerprints have skin oil and when the bulbs first come up to operating temperature the oil will carbonize and coat the outside of the bulb, lowering the light output and reducing bulb life.*

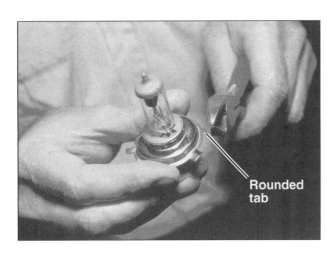

Rounded
tab

NOTE—

• *The tab on the mounting flange is meant to keep a rally wattage bulb from being installed in a normal road car.*

• *Note that the new headlight assembly has a circular vacuum servo to move the headlight reflector.*

– Reinstall air intake snorkel and flex pipe.

◄ Slide in new side marker light units and reattach electrical harness connectors to headlights and side marker lights.

NOTE—

• *The new headlight assembly requires a 6-pin harness connector instead of the original 4-pin connector. The procedure for updating the headlight harness connector is below.*

• *If you are not installing Euro headlight washers / wipers, the headlight wiper electrical connector remains unplugged, as do the headlight washer hoses.*

• *To avoid washer fluid loss, disconnect the headlight washer pump electrical connector at the fluid reservoir behind the right headlight.*

H4 harness connector, installing

– Disconnect ground (–) cable from battery terminal.

> **WARNING—**
> *Prior to disconnecting the battery, read the battery disconnection cautions given at the front of this manual.*

– Working at headlight electrical harness connector, trim back harness insulation shrink tubing.

◄ Remove cover off stock (4-pin) female headlight electrical connector and identify wires.

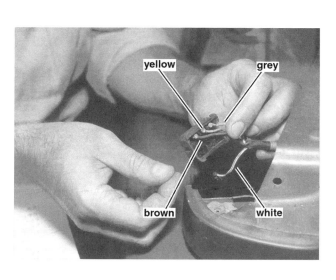

Headlight wire colors

Gray.	foglight
Yellow	low beam
White.	high beam
Brown	ground

– Slide soldered pins out of 4-pin plastic connector and install in correct locations in 6-pin connector (MB part no. 006 545 80 28).

12

NOTE—

• *Terminals on both the 4-pin and the 6-pin connector are marked with DIN-standard (European) numbers. Be sure to transfer wires to matching numbered terminals.*

• *Terminal 58 of 6-pin connector is unused. It is for the small round European running light below the main headlight bulb.*

• *In the US, the side marker light serves this purpose; that is why the side marker light connector has three pins instead of two as on European cars.*

Headlight wiring circuit, upgrading

We recommend that you rewire the new headlights so that maximum high beam illumination is attained by turning on the low beams and foglights when high beams are in use. When you modify the headlight wiring using the procedure outlined below, the foglights can be switched on or off when the low beams are on.

◄ The wiring upgrade detailed in this procedure provides the headlight bulbs with the maximum available current flow and protects the vehicle electrical system from overloads. You will use relays to power the headlight bulbs. The relays are switched on and off using the existing wiring system.

Relay holder

Relay

NOTE—

The standard high beam filament in a US H4 bulb is normally rated at 60 watts. The European rally bulb, by contrast, is rated 100 watts for high beam and 80 watt for low beam. Enabling them to be on at the same time and then illuminating the foglights as well, you can have up to 560 watts blazing. The temperature increase in the H4 bulb (due to both filaments being illuminated) causes the filaments to shine brighter also.

— Disconnect ground (–) cable from battery terminal.

> **WARNING—**
> *Prior to disconnecting the battery, read the battery disconnection cautions given at the front of this manual.*

◄ Working in engine compartment at back of right headlight assembly, undo headlight cover metal clips and open cover to expose headlight wiring and connectors.

— Use accompanying illustrations (photo and wiring diagram) to identify headlight and foglight wiring.

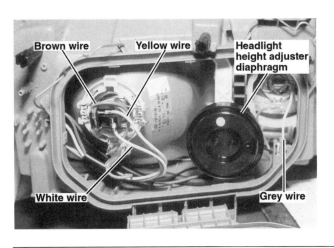

Brown wire Yellow wire Headlight height adjuster diaphragm

White wire Grey wire

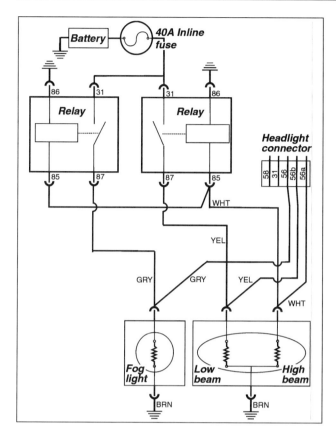

NOTE—

• *For reliability and maximum current transmission, use soldered-on connectors for the wiring procedure described below.*

• *Slip heat shrink insulating tubing onto the wires after cutting and prior to soldering.*

◄ Splice 8 to 10 inches of 14 gauge wire to high beam wire (**white wire**).

    • Attach a 2-inch jumper on end to go from terminal 85 on one relay to same terminal on the other.

— Splice 8 to 10 inches of 12 gauge wire to low beam (**yellow wire**) and foglight wire (**gray wire**).

— Connect ground wire from right headlight to existing ground connection behind headlight assembly or to any other convenient ground.

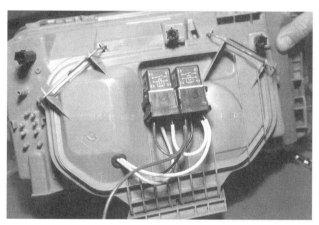

◄ Slot relay holders together and mount on right headlight assembly rear cover so they face upward with the terminals down (to keep out water and crud).

NOTE—

• *Work out the best spot and check clearances; the air-conditioner receiver / drier is close, as is the self-leveling hydraulic reservoir on the station wagon, on the left side.*

• *Reduce voltage drop at relays by keeping the wiring as short as possible.*

— Drill two mounting holes in cover, and bolt on relay holders.

— Drill and grommet a third hole for wires.

    • Pass previously soldered wires from headlight / foglight connectors through grommet and attach to relay holders.

— Mount relays on relay holders.

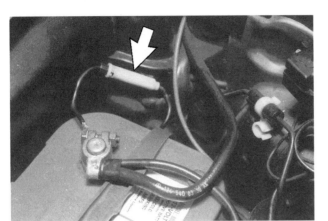

◁ Install 10 gauge wire from battery positive terminal to terminal 30 on both relays.

- Route it under cowl air intake.
- Install 40A inline fuse holder (**arrow**) next to battery.

NOTE—
- *A bulb warning lamp malfunction is part of the price of these improvements: the more powerful bulbs confuse the warning system enough to light that lamp, so you need to disable or modify it.*

- *The bulb warning module can be modified to work with the higher wattage bulbs by BergWerks in Van Nuys, CA, 877-230-5736.*

- *To disable warning light: Look at the instrument cluster face, determine location of bulb, then remove instrument cluster and remove the bulb from the back. Instrument cluster removal is covered in* **Chapter 11**.

— Reconnect battery, start engine, and turn on lights. If lights don't work properly, recheck wiring.

— Aim headlights with car at normal load. Park car on level surface, 25 feet from wall. Measure distance from ground to center of headlight lens. Mark the wall at this same height. The hot spot of the low beam should be at this height. Take a test-drive to make sure you can see and others don't flash you.

Headlight-leveling system, installing

This procedure explains how to install vacuum control tubing and the dashboard switch for the headlight-leveling system. Special parts necessary for this operation are listed earlier.

— Disconnect ground (–) cable from battery terminal.

> ***WARNING—***
> *Prior to disconnecting the battery, read the battery disconnection cautions given at the front of this manual.*

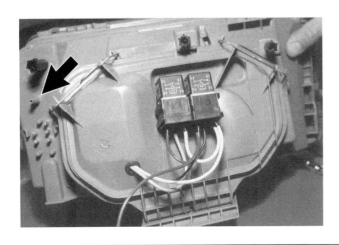

◁ Use a short piece of rubber hose to connect vacuum line to vacuum fitting (**arrow**) on back of right headlight assembly.

— Route vacuum tubing under fender joint back to battery, then underneath cowl air intake to brake booster area.

— Similarly, run vacuum line from back of left headlight to brake booster area.

◅ Join left and right vacuum lines with a Y or T-fitting (**arrow**).

— Working under cowl, on bulkhead just to right of brake booster, find rubber grommet with several vacuum lines through it.

  • Using needle-nose pliers, carefully pull out an unused vacuum fitting.
  • Feed a length of vacuum tubing from Y-fitting through grommet.

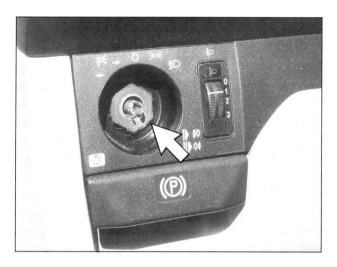

◅ Working inside car at dashboard, pull headlight knob off its shaft.

  • Undo 24 mm nut (**arrow**) holding trim panel
  • Wiggle out panel, left side first, and discard.

— Pull up floor mat behind brake pedal and unclip speedometer cable clamp so that cable has some slack.

— Remove instrument cluster:

  • Slip in wire hooks on each side of cluster and ease it part way out, right side first.
  • Unscrew speedometer cable connection.
  • Detach electrical harness connectors to back of cluster.

— Remove cluster entirely, then reach in (to right of speedometer cable) with long pliers to pull through new vacuum line.

NOTE—

This line must be long enough to reach new level control switch near headlight switch.

— Use fuel economy gauge vacuum line as source of vacuum. (This is one of connections to back of instrument cluster.)

• Install a vacuum T or Y-fitting in that line.
• Attach new vacuum line long enough to reach headlight switch area.
• Install check valve in new vacuum line to allow vacuum to work but to prevent backflow. Black side of check valve must be toward vacuum source. (Suck on it and see.)

NOTE—
If your car has no fuel economy gauge, use another convenient vacuum source.

— Reattach instrument cluster connections and reinstall cluster.

— Install level control switch into headlight switch trim panel

— Attach source vacuum hose to top connector (no. 1). Attach headlights vacuum hose to bottom connector (no. 2).

— Reinstall new headlight switch trim panel.

• Reinstall 24 mm trim retaining nut
• Reinstall headlight switch knob.

— Aim headlights using three black 13 mm aiming screws behind each unit.

• Outside screw controls left / right aim.
• Center screw controls height.
• Inner screw controls foglight height.

— Aim headlights with car at normal load with headlight level switch (on dashboard) at setting **1**. This assigns setting **0** a high position and settings **2** and **3** low positions for loads.

— If your car has self-leveling rear suspension, use setting **2** for normal load.

NOTE—
If the level control switch doesn't work, you may have reversed the vacuum connections to it, or you may have a vacuum leak in the new tubing.

MODIFIED CARS

AMG modified cars

The German tuning firm AMG had modified E-Class sedans as early as 1986 with the AMG Hammer. The Hammer was a W124 sedan with the AMG 4-camshaft 5.6 liter engine. The cars became very famous for their acceleration of 0 - 60 mph in approximately five seconds.

There were both station wagon and sedan versions with the 5.6 liter M117 engine bored to 6 liters and available with either 2 or 4 overhead camshafts. The 4-camshaft setups were very potent indeed. The twin overhead camshaft versions producing over 300 hp and around 400 ft-lb of torque were not bad either.

Ever since Mercedes-Benz purchased AMG in 1999 and brought the AMG product line into series production, there have been some rather astounding cars available at prices that are not unreasonable considering the performance. The C36, C43, E55 and M55 are good examples. There is a certain pleasure that comes from knowing your highly tuned, stiffly sprung hot rod can be worked on by any Mercedes mechanic, anywhere in the US, with good parts availability.

RENNTech modified cars

If you find the factory performance upgrades are insufficient, you can always contact RENNTech and have them take the AMG tweaks one step further. The C43, for example, is an approximately $50,000 C-Class with a 4.3 liter V-8 producing 302 hp and 302 ft-lb of torque. RENNTech would be more than happy to take your motor and modify it to a 6 liter, 408 hp, 468 ft-lb engine at a cost of $39,750 for the engine work alone.

12

Tuner contact information

- BergWerks
  www.bergwerks.com
  6318 Sepulveda Blvd.
  Van Nuys, CA 91411
  818-781-2770

- Brabus
  www.brabus.com
  Brabus North America Inc.
  4040 Campus Dr.
  Newport Beach, CA 92660
  949-797-0177

- Carlsson
  www.carlsson.de
  The Tire Rack
  777 W. Chippewa Ave.
  South Bend, IN 46614
  800-445-0179

- C.E.C
  www.cecwheels.com
  16200 S. Figueroa St.
  Gardena, CA 90248
  310-767-1111

- Lorinser
  www.lorinser.com
  C.E.C. East
  295 North St. #6
  Teterboro, NJ 07608
  201-727-1100

- RENNTech
  www.renntechmercedes.com
  1364 N. Killian Dr.
  Lake Park, FL 33403
  561-845-7888

Appendix A

Mercedes-Benz Heritage

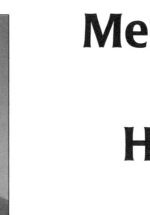

INTRODUCTION

◄ It all began with the granting of German patent numbers 28022 and 28243 to Gottlieb Daimler in December of 1883. These patents made possible the first high-speed, light weight internal combustion engines.

Patent 28022 described the use of tube ignition, which controlled the combustion of the new fuel. Patent 28243 described a technique of air-cooling engines that eliminated the weight of cooling liquids and the castings that held the liquid. The combination of these two patents opened up the possibility of motorized vehicles for the first time.

Prior to Daimler's work, stationary gas-vapor fueled engines had a maximum rpm of 180 - 200 and were extremely heavy. Daimler's new engine could reach 450 - 900 rpm and was fueled by liquid gasoline instead of natural gas.

◄ By 1886, Karl Benz was also involved in producing light weight, high rpm engines for motor vehicles.

1885 - 1940

Working separately until the 1920s, both Daimler and Benz put together an amazing string of firsts in automotive engineering.

◄ In 1885, Daimler put his first vertical engine in a two-wheeler, creating the first motorcycle. It was patented on August 29th.

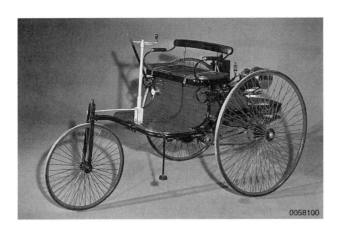

◄ In 1886, Karl Benz produced a three-wheeler, the first practical automobile. This was a fully integral design, patented January 29th.

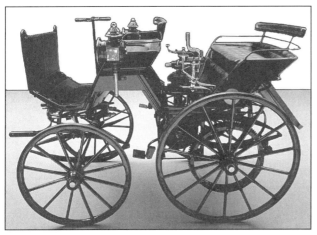

◄ Also in 1886, Daimler produced a four-wheel motorized coach. This was really a horseless carriage with drawbar steering, but functionally the first four-wheeled automobile.

◄ Gottlieb enjoyed promoting his powered transport inventions, which included boats and tram cars, by driving or riding in them. His son Adolph would sometimes handle the controls.

Over a period of years, Daimler and Benz continued their automotive innovations separately. Their names would not be formally associated until a quarter of a century after Gottlieb Daimler's death in 1900.

- 1888: Daimler engine used in first airship, a powered balloon
- 1890: Daimler develops first four-cylinder engine.
- 1894: Daimler powered cars share first place in the first road competition from Paris to Rouen.
- 1895: Benz develops first gasoline powered bus.
- 1899: Daimler develops the engine for first Zeppelin airship.
- 1901: First Mercedes built by Daimler-Motoren-Gesellschaft races in Nice, winning week-long event and introducing front-engined rear-wheel-drive automobile.

Emil Jellinek was a successful businessman living in Nice with his family, which included his daughter Mercedes. Jellinek ordered many cars from Daimler-Motoren-Gesellschaft. He promoted the cars, acting as a sales agent and entering races. He raced under the pseudonym Mercedes, coming to be known as "Monsieur Mercedes". In 1900, he signed a business agreement with DMG, which included using the Mercedes name for the cars. The name was trademarked in 1902.

- 1921: Mercedes introduces the first supercharged production cars.
- 1923: DMG and Benz pioneer diesel powered trucks.
- 1924: Daimler-Motoren-Gesellshaft and Benz & Cie entered into a cooperative agreement. In June of 1926 the two companies were formally joined together as Daimler-Benz AG.
- 1936: Mercedes-Benz introduces the 260D, the world's first diesel powered car.

◁ One of the best looking cars from the late thirties was the 170V Cabriolet.

On September 1, 1939, World War II began. All production of civilian automobiles was requisitioned by the government. Few cars were built, with production capacity devoted largely to trucks and aircraft engines. In 1940, racing circuits were closed. By 1944, car production had ceased entirely.

1945 - 1959

When the war ended in 1945, the factories were either in ruins or under allied occupation. It took several years to bring production back on line.

Postwar production began in 1946 using the prewar models, particularly the successful 170V, as a starting point. Right after the war, however, the greatest need was for commercial vehicles, so whoever was left from the design team joined up to develop these important aspects of the postwar economy. Parts that were found in the rubble were included in production.

Ambulances, police cars and delivery vans came first. Sedans would wait until late 1948, and it wasn't until 1949 that the first real postwar automotive products made their debut.

The postwar 170V was introduced as an evolution of the prewar car. Initially, the 1,696 cc in-line four-cylinder engine produced 38 hp (SAE). The engine was superseded by a new 45 hp (SAE), 1,767 cc in the 170Va in 1950. In addition to the larger more powerful engine, the 170Va chassis was fitted with revised springs, brakes and shock absorbers.

The string of engineering firsts continued:

- 1949: Safety peg door lock
- 1951: First safety bodywork with crumple zones for passengers
- 1954: First standard use of gasoline injection in a production car (300SL)
- 1957: First company to offer seat belts as an option
- 1959: First crash testing begins at the factory

0058104

The German driving public had always loved fast cars that handled well, so the factory was constantly pressured to provide sportier models. It responded with the 170 Super (S) in several versions. The basic sedan was fitted with the slightly larger body of the prewar 230 series and development of the engine raised the S version horsepower to 52 at 4,000 rpm from 1,767 cc. The 170V used an updraft Solex carburetor while the 170S was fitted with a downdraft Solex which gave more power at higher rpm.

The 170S had a top speed of 75 mph. This, according to the factory, made it the preferred car for police patrol work. Along with the sedan, the factory produced a two passenger convertible and a convertible sedan which sat four. The 170S marked the beginning of the of the midsized chassis.

In 1949 the 170D was introduced in Germany at the Hanover Export show. It remained in production until 1953 with total production topping 33,000. The 170D used a smaller version of the pre-war 2.6 liter diesel. This new diesel engine developed 38 hp (SAE) at 3,200 rpm. The engine used a prechamber combustion system which went a long way to quiet down the objectionable diesel "knock". In 1952, the diesel engine was fitted into the 170S chassis and the car became even more popular in part because the 170S brakes and road holding were so good for the time.

0058106

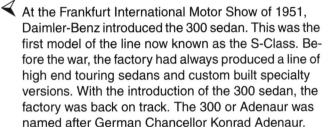

At the Frankfurt International Motor Show of 1951, Daimler-Benz introduced the 300 sedan. This was the first model of the line now known as the S-Class. Before the war, the factory had always produced a line of high end touring sedans and custom built specialty versions. With the introduction of the 300 sedan, the factory was back on track. The 300 or Adenaur was named after German Chancellor Konrad Adenaur.

0058105

The 300S was the "super" model, designed for enthusiasts. It was manufactured in coupe and convertible versions.

0058107

Meanwhile, the Frankfurt show also witnessed the introduction of the 220, which replaced the 170S. The 170S chassis was now fitted with a short-stroke 2.2 liter 6-cylinder engine which developed 80 hp (SAE) at 4,600 rpm and was capable of superior performance on the German Autobahns. The engine had an overhead camshaft for accurate valve actuation at higher rpm and the crankshaft assembly was specially balanced to aid smoothness at higher rpm. As an added benefit, it was quieter than its predecessors.

The fully synchronized 4-speed transmission featured a light and precise column change, which eliminated the need to remove the right hand from the steering wheel to change gears.

The 220 would accelerate from 0 - 100 kph (0 - 62 mph) in 21 seconds and featured a top cruising speed of 87 mph. Only 220 pounds heavier than the 170S and equipped with an additional 28 hp (SAE), the 220 offered significantly improved performance. Following the pattern set by the 300 series, the new 220 was offered in sedan, convertible sedan, 2- or 3-seat convertible and coupe body styles.

 On the racing circuit, Mercedes-Benz was achieving great success. The 300SL, not yet available as a production car, won the 1952 Carrera Panamerica.

In 1953, an entirely new chassis was introduced with very novel engineering. Up to this time, the 220 / 170S versions had a classic X-shaped, oval tube frame with body and suspension mounting points along the length of the frame so the suspension mounted directly to the chassis as did the engine, transmission and drive train.

0058108

0058109

 The new car, called the 180, was constructed as a platform chassis with areas of high cross-sectional density which gave the chassis great torsional strength and rigidity that increased the safety, improved the handling and lowered the noise level.

In the 180, the entire power plant including the transmission, the suspension and the steering were now mounted to a subframe. The subframe was then secured to the main frame using rubber mounts at three points. There were advantages both in manufacturing the car and repairing the chassis with this easily removable subframe. The isolation of the suspension and engine from the main chassis also reduced road noise and engine vibration. Road holding was improved by the use of a single pivot swing axle independent rear suspension.

In 1954 the new 220a was introduced. Essentially an enlarged version of the 180, it used its predecessor's 2.2 liter engine, which produced 85 hp (SAE) through a two-barrel downdraft Solex carburetor.

With the factory committed to maintaining a line of diesel passenger cars, the 180 chassis was fitted with an engine that was almost a carbon copy of the very successful engine from the 170D. Producing 43 hp (SAE) at 3,800 rpm, this diesel became the standard taxi in Europe. Its durability and reliability established a legend for Daimler-Benz diesel powered cars that exists to this day.

The factory had always believed that racing proves and improves the breed. Three 180Ds were entered in the grueling 1955 Mille Miglia race in Italy. The race distance was 922 miles over two lane narrow cliff side roads and through small towns and crowd-lined streets. The three cars finished 1st, 2nd, and 3rd in the diesel class with an average speed of 60 mph.

The 180D marks the start of the diesel chassis being slightly smaller than the gas chassis. This continued until 1968 with the introduction of the W114 / W115 chassis.

By 1954, Mercedes-Benz was able to offer the 300SL Gullwing sports car as a production model. The 300SL had huge brakes, a tubular chassis, an aerodynamic body, excellent handling and was expensive.

The three liter mechanically injected 6-cylinder motor produced 220 hp (SAE) at 5,800 rpm with the standard camshaft at 8.55 : 1 compression.

Introduced in 1957, the roadster version of the 300SL was available with up to 250 hp (SAE) at 6,200 rpm with 9.5 : 1 compression and the racing camshaft. This engine has a very high specific output of 79.8 hp (SAE) per liter. This is remarkable for a standard production engine, particularly considering there was tremendous flexibility throughout the power range. In comparison, the M119 engine (in the 400E) is a high tech 4.2 liter with 11 : 1 compression, four camshafts, 4 valves per cylinder, variable cam timing and knock sensing, producing 275 hp (SAE). This yields a specific output of 65 hp (SAE) per liter, significantly less than the much older, much smaller, much simpler engine.

By this time, racing was once again part of the daily routine at the factory. The 300SL went on to win many road races and rallies. Meanwhile, the formula cars (W196) were reigning supreme on the Grand Prix circuit.

In 1955, a 300SLR driven by Stirling Moss won the Mille Miglia.

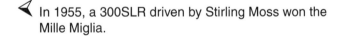

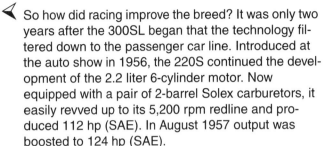 So how did racing improve the breed? It was only two years after the 300SL began that the technology filtered down to the passenger car line. Introduced at the auto show in 1956, the 220S continued the development of the 2.2 liter 6-cylinder motor. Now equipped with a pair of 2-barrel Solex carburetors, it easily revved up to its 5,200 rpm redline and produced 112 hp (SAE). In August 1957 output was boosted to 124 hp (SAE).

In 1958, only four years after the introduction of the 300SL, the factory fitted the 2.2 liter six-cylinder with mechanical fuel injection. Designated as the 220SE, power output jumped to 134 hp (SAE) at 6,000 rpm, while the 0 - 100 kph (0 - 62 mph) times dropped to under 13 seconds.

The 220SE injection system used a two element injection pump with each element feeding three cylinders through injection nozzles mounted in the intake manifold. This compared to the 300SL, which used direct cylinder injection from a six element pump. The 300SL pump had a manual warm up device that was managed with a choke cable from the dashboard. The 220SE warm up system was fully automatic making driving much more carefree by avoiding driving around with the choke on.

Both the 220S and the 220SE were available in sedan, coupe and convertible versions. The 220S was built from 1956 to 1959 while the limited edition 220SE was built from 1958 to 1960.

The two-door coupes and convertibles were delightful automobiles, with light and precise manual steering.

When the 220 series went out of production in 1960 there would not be a midsize series coupe or convertible until the E-Class coupe in 1988 and the convertible in 1990. Coupes were available in the W114 chassis in 1968 and the W123 chassis in 1977 but the complete lineup would not be offered again until the E-Class.

At the 1959 Frankfurt show, the factory showed several new models continuing the 2.2 liter engine series. This show marked the introduction of the finned body, which Mercedes called the "panorama body style." Known as the "b" series (W111), the 2.2 liter versions were designated the 220b, the 220Sb and the 220SEb.

There were no coupes or convertibles based on this midsized chassis. The coupe and convertible of the 2.2 liter series now had their own body configuration, which was the precursor to the later 108 sedan. The 220 "b" series would be followed in 1961 with a 3-liter version, but, otherwise the engines and transmissions remained unchanged from the previous models.

The factory began their extensive crash testing program in 1959 and the information gained was engineered into the new chassis. The dashboard featured an energy absorbing cover and the steering wheel had a large center pad for chest protection. The rear axle design was improved with the addition of a camber compensation spring that kept the rear wheels from going to positive camber (tucking up) while cornering and the rear shocks were relocated out towards the wheels which further improved the handling. These were fairly popular models with 69,691 220b, 161,119 220Sb and 66,086 220SEb models sold from 1959 through 1965.

1960 - 1985

Many evolutionary changes took place during the production cycle. Disc brakes replaced the front drum brakes in April of 1962 and dual braking circuits were introduced in August of 1963. The 1963 and later 220Sb with disc brakes was probably the most popular car among Mercedes mechanics of the era. The car was very simple to work on and had wonderful reliability.

More innovations appeared during this period:

- 1960: Safety steering column patented
- 1962: Diagonal three point seat belts offered as an option
- 1967: Safety steering column fitted to all models
- 1970: Three point inertia reels offered as an option. Anti-lock brake system development begins.
- 1971: Patent application for an airbag system for the driver
- 1973: Inertia reel three point seat belts installed as standard equipment in all models
- 1974: The beginnings of frontal offset crash testing
- 1976: New version of safety steering column in series production
- 1978: ABS (anti-lock braking) in series production

- 1979: Newly developed forked front member structure allowed the new S-Class to withstand the offset crash testing. Height adjustable front seat belts provided for a better fit.
- 1981: Seat belt tensioners and airbags available as special options. Traction control available in S-Class.
- 1984: All models equipped with seat belt tensioners for front seats. ABS braking standard equipment for S- and SL-Class.

◁ In 1961 the 300SE was introduced to the public. This was a very interesting derivation of the midsized chassis. Instead of a W111 chassis it was dubbed the W112, which indicated that in place of the springs at each corner there was an airbag that was kept inflated to over 150 psi from a compressor mounted on the engine. Level control valves were used at each of the two front wheels, while one valve handled duties for the rear axle.

The engine in the 300SE, listed as the M189, was a modified version of the 300SL engine. The 300SL engine, which is tilted on its side, was listed as the M198. Using a two element injection pump similar to the 220SE and manifold rather than direct injection, this 3 liter motor developed 185 hp (SAE) at introduction and was later increased to 195 hp (SAE). The car weighed 3,476 pounds and would reach 0 - 62 mph in 12 seconds with a top speed of 124 mph. This was a fairly expensive car in the US and only 5,202 (and an additional 1,546 long wheelbase models) were sold from 1961 to 1965.

The W111 coupes and convertibles were available with both the 2.2 liter and 3.0 liter mechanically injected engines. 220SE coupe / convertible sales figures for the period 1960 - 1965 totaled 16,902 units. Of the more expensive 300SE versions, 3,127 were sold for the period 1962 - 1967. At the end of their production the 300SE cost $11,500 - $13,000 compared to $8,000 for the 220SE.

◁ The W111 coupe / convertible line continued through 1971 and included some of the most famous and desired Mercedes-Benz models of all time, the V-8 powered 280SE 3.5 liter coupe and convertible.

In 1967 the Frankfurt show previewed the latest line-up. These cars would become known as the /8 (slash eight) series: Even though production began in 1967, they first appeared in the US in January, 1968. Also called the New Generation, this line included two very similar platforms, W114 and W115.

The W114 cars all had 6-cylinder gasoline engines. The W115 cars had 4-cylinder gasoline engines (220, 230) or 4-cylinder (220D, 240D) or 5-cylinder (300D) diesel engines.

The 230 sedan, built on the W114 chassis, had the 6-cylinder 2.3 liter M180 engine which produced 120 hp (SAE) at 5,400 rpm. A total of 221,783 of these cars were delivered from the factory.

◁ The 250 sedan, also built on the W114 chassis, was powered by the single cam 2.5 liter M114 engine from 1967 to 1972, and the single cam 2.8 liter M130 engine until 1976.

◁ The first two-door coupe version of the W114 chassis was called the 250C. It was given the single cam 2.8 liter M130 engine from 1968 to 1972. The second and last two-door coupe based on the W114 chassis was called the 280C and had the twin-cam 2.8 liter M110 engine.

The suspension for the new cars was completely new. Gone was the swing axle rear end of the W111 chassis, replaced with a differential that was bolted to a rear subframe assembly and half-shafts to each rear wheel. Semi-trailing arms, shock absorbers and springs rounded out the rear end. The front suspension was unequal length A-arms with anti-dive geometry. The A-arms were fitted with rubber bushings instead of bronze bushings and grease fittings.

The W114 also had disc brakes on all four wheels with a dual-diagonal braking circuit fitted so that if a brake hose tore or a caliper leaked there would still be 3 brake calipers available to stop the car.

The collapsible steering column had been developed during crash testing so that in a severe front end collision it couldn't come near the driver's chest. Three-point seat belts were made by the Kangol Company in Great Britain using a unique magnetic latching mechanism. In 1970 retractor belts were an option and rear seat belts were standard. By 1973, the standard front seat belts were retractor three-point harnesses.

In the first year of production for the US, the engine was a 2.5 liter 6-cylinder carburetor version called the M114, which produced 146 hp (SAE) at 5,600 rpm.

In 1968 the 2.8 liter M130 engine appeared. This produced 157 hp (SAE) at 5,700 rpm. It was installed in the 250 sedan and the 250C coupe until 1972.

In 1973 the M110 twin cam motor was introduced, producing 158 hp (SAE). This was installed in the newly badged 280 sedan and the 280C coupe until 1976.

In 1975 the US version of the M110 engine was equipped with catalytic converters which bolted directly to the exhaust manifold, forcing the exhaust gas through a very small opening. This slowed the exhaust flow over the catalyst to insure efficiency. Because of this significant exhaust back pressure the cars were very sluggish.

The W115 chassis included 220, 220D, 230, 240D, and 300D models.

The 220 model had a 2.2 liter 4-cylinder M115 engine that produced 116 hp (SAE) at 5,200 rpm, breathing through two Solex side draft carburetors. The car had a top speed of 100 mph and a 0 - 60 time of 14 seconds. Worldwide production numbers were 128,739 units, but few were sold here due to the car's lazy manners.

The 220D diesel was a rather different story, being one of the best selling cars the factory ever built. From 1967 until 1976 the car sold 420,273 units. Its popularity started with an indestructible 2.2 liter diesel engine which, when used in taxi service, was known to accumulate over 400,000 miles before being replaced. This "wunder-motor" developed 65 hp (SAE) at 4,200 rpm, delivered a top speed of 84 mph, and comfortable cruising along American highways at 70 - 75 mph. Some of the car's popularity in America at that time can be traced to fuel shortages and a 55 mph national speed limit.

A 4-speed manual transmission was standard equipment on the 220D with a 4-speed automatic available as an option. The manual transmission version was a delight to drive. The handling was light and precise and the braking excellent. A well equipped version of the 220D cost around $7,000 in the early 1970s, an excellent value for the money. The 220D helped to develop a legion of diesel drivers in a country where diesel powered automobiles were very rare.

Many 220D drivers went on to other Mercedes diesels over the years. In 1973 the 240D appeared on the W115 chassis, and production up to 1976 totaled 131,319.

The 240D displayed a few changes from previous models. The openable wing windows in the front doors of previous models were gone. In 1974 the bumpers were extended to accommodate the shock absorbers now required by the Federal government. The added displacement of 0.2 liter increased the top speed just slightly.

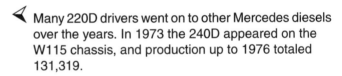

In 1975 the factory introduced a diesel engine that had a few people scratching their heads. The 3 liter 5-cylinder 300D had 72° crankshaft throws. This engine developed 79 hp (SAE) in its normally aspirated form and the later turbo versions would reach 125 hp (SAE).

The 300D was only available with an automatic transmission in the US, although in the rest of the world it was available with a 4-speed manual. The 300D was rated by the EPA at 31 mpg for highway driving and 24 mpg for the city driving which compared very favorably with the 240D. By the end of its production run in 1976 the 300D sold for $14,000. In 1976, with the fuel crisis fresh in buyers' minds, the diesel powered cars ac-

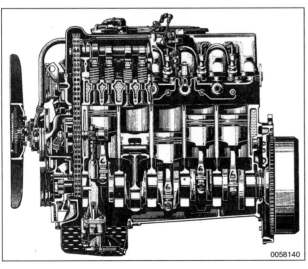

counted for 46.4 percent of Mercedes sales in the US. 300D production was 53,690 in three years, while the W114 / 115 chassis combinations sold a total of 1,919,066 units from 1968 through 1976.

At the Geneva Auto Show in 1976, Mercedes introduced the W123, the replacement for the W114 / W115 chassis. The W123 was available in both gas and diesel engines through the entire production. Models would include the 230, 280E, 280CE, 240D and the 300D in sedan, coupe and station wagon body styles, as well as the more powerful turbodiesel.

◀ The W123 cars introduced many new features. The instrument cluster was recessed and surrounded with padding which extended throughout the interior. The instrument numbers were large and easy to read. The heating and cooling systems were more efficient. The seating shape was improved to better hold the passengers during cornering. Height adjusters for the front seats were standard equipment, and front seat travel was increased for tall drivers. The exhaust system was manufactured from more corrosion proof materials, and the front brakes were equipped with a brake pad wear indicator. Lighting for the US market included a 7 inch round high / low beam headlight and a 5¾ inch foglight that was controlled separately via the headlight switch.

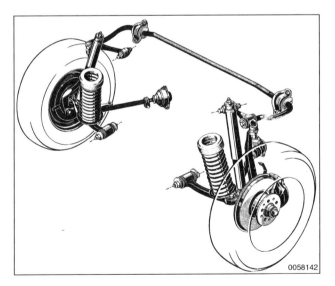

◀ The W123 front suspension was completely redesigned from the W114 / W115 setup. It was a slightly modified copy of the front suspension on the W116 S-Class cars that started production in 1973.

0058135

The 280E four door sedan and the 280CE 2-door coupe were powered by the M110 twin-cam engine with K-Jetronic fuel injection. Unfortunately, technology was still lagging behind environmental regulations. The worldwide version of this engine made 185 hp (SAE), but the US emission-controlled version produced only 140 hp (SAE). This was on a car that weighed a whopping 3,500 pounds. As a result, performance was described as just adequate when compared to the 3,200 pound European version with 185 hp (SAE). The 280 was dropped from the line in 1981.

With the new W123 chassis MBNA imported the 4-cylinder 240D and the 5-cylinder 300D, while the rest of the world also had the 200D and the 220D. The 240D was available with either manual 4-speed or automatic 4-speed transmissions, but the upscale 300D was only available with the automatic gearbox.

The 300D, 300TD and 300CD were powered by the normally aspirated 83 hp (SAE) 3 liter 5-cylinder engine. The turbodiesel, using the power unit from the S-Class 300SD, was introduced at the Frankfurt show in 1979 with production scheduled for the 1980 model year. By 1982 all of the 5-cylinder diesels imported to the US and Canada used the turbocharged 125 hp (SAE) engine. The turbocharger was built by AirResearch until 1984 when the German KKK unit was substituted. These engines have proven to be extremely reliable, easily going over 500,000 miles without the cylinder head being removed for service.

Along with the sedans, Mercedes imported the 300CD coupe and the 300TD station wagon. From the front seats forward, the wagon interior mirrored that of the sedan. The second set of seats were different as they could fold flat to make a large cargo area. With the seats folded, the rear cargo area was 9.3 feet long and could carry up to 1,540 pounds, thanks in part to the self-leveling rear suspension system.

The station wagon was quite popular in the US and, considering its price, sold quite well. With a price tag around $35,000, 36,874 were sold.

For the sedan, 75,261 of the turbo powered cars were sold. Worldwide production of the W123 chassis in all its variants totaled 2,696,914 cars.

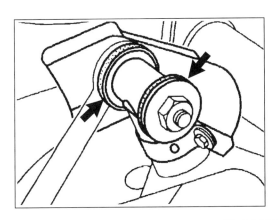

Appendix B

Problems and Repairs

GENERAL

There is a repair information system within the Mercedes-Benz network, available in several different formats. Aside from the printed repair manuals, there are also Diagnostic Trouble Code (DTC) manuals, electronic troubleshooting manuals and chassis and system diagnostic manuals.

The service microfiche system contains the diagnostic directories and the programmed repair sections along with service information and time guides.

The electronic Workshop Information System (WIS) for the professional technician contains most of the above, as well as a troubleshooting guide, within its large database of information.

Access to this information is expensive. At the time of this writing, WIS costs $2,500 plus an annual update fee. The electronic troubleshooting manual for the E-Class costs $370.45 (2000 price list) for the volumes and supplements. Dozens upon dozens of sheets of microfiche may be bought at $10 per sheet. Purchasing the Mercedes information system is usually beyond the means of the DIY mechanic or informed owner.

In this chapter you will find extracted repair information from all of the above sources. While it is not possible within the scope of this book to go into individual repair procedures, you may be able to use the data in this chapter to get detailed repair information from your independent repair shop or your Mercedes-Benz retail dealership. If the symptom fits your particular E-Class you can discuss the problem with your mechanic in a knowledgeable manner. Every mechanic has not heard of every solution for every problem and this chapter might save your mechanic some time and you some money.

INFORMATION TABLES

The tables that follow are arranged by repair group number as designated in the Mercedes-Benz information system.

Where possible, illustrations, photos or minimal repair hints have been included here. However, these are not repair procedures. For complete and correct repair procedures, consult Mercedes-Benz repair information.

Problems and Repairs

Group 01: Engine housings

Problem	Possible cause, suggested repair
M103, M104, OM606 engines Engine oil leak at rear main seal Old seal carrier New seal carrier	Defective seal. Replace rear main seal carrier, MB part no. 010 010 32 22 with updated part: M103 or M104 engine: Use MB part no. 010 010 42 22. OM606 engine: Use MB part no. 010 060 10 22.

Group 05: Engine timing

Problem	Possible cause, suggested repair
M103 engine Hard to start, vibrates at idle, engine cuts out or has no power	Perform compression and cylinder leakage tests. If compression pressure in any cylinder is less than 116 psi or cylinder leakage is greater than 25%, loosen and remove applicable rocker arm bearing bracket to see if compression pressure goes up or cylinder leakage drops below 10%. If so, check for intake valve pulling through seat. Reinstall bearing bracket and measure hydraulic element lift. If there is no lift intake valve is pulling through seat. Remove cylinder head and repair by machining or replacing valve seats and guides.
M103 engine Hard to start, vibrates at idle, cuts out or has no power	Hydraulic valve adjuster(s) jammed. Replace hydraulic valve adjuster(s).
OM606 engine Produces blue smoke or has high oil consumption	Cap on first camshaft bearing improperly machined on inside; excess oil sucked into combustion chambers via crankcase ventilation. Remove cylinder head cover. Remove shaped hose between crankcase pressure control valve and oil separator chamber in cylinder head cover. Run engine at 3,000 rpm and note whether separator fills with oil. If so: Remove cylinder head cover, actuate starter and notice if oil runs out between 1st camshaft bearing and camshaft drive gears. If so: Replace camshaft and all camshaft bearing housings and bearing caps. Remove prechambers and check for cracks in burner holes. If so: Replace prechambers.

Group 07: Fuel injection

Problem	Possible cause, suggested repair
M103 engine Does not start	a. Ignition control module malfunction. Install Siemens ignition control module. b. Formed hose between idle speed air valve and air guide housing fallen off due to backfire. Test air flow potentiometer position. Check rest position of air flow sensor. Center air flow sensor plate Check rubber hose between idle speed valve and air guide housing for tight fit. Replace if swollen,
M103 engine in 300E Poor performance, whirring noise from fuel pump, hesitation at high ambient air temperature	Fuel hose between fuel tank and fuel pump kinked near fuel tank. Replace fuel hose, MB part no. 124 470 31 75, and insure proper routing.
M103 engine Hesitates, cuts out or is difficult to start at times.	Crankshaft position sensor faulty. a. Check crankshaft position sensor for production date. Replace any with date earlier than code 642 (i.e. 640, 635). b. Check sensor for resistance (nominal value 680 - 1240 Ω). Test for short to ground and intermittent operation. Replace if required.
M103 engine (to 8/30/90) Shakes at idle.	Engine idle too low. Raise idle speed about 50 rpm on cars with automatic transmission: Remove violet wire from connector 26/3 and connect to ground.
M103, M104 engines with CIS-E Cuts out intermittently with instant restart.	Incorrect adjustment of transmission control pressure cable may be detected as hesitation. Adjust transmission control pressure cable correctly.
M103, M104 engines with CIS-E Hesitates, cuts out or is difficult to start at times	CIS-E control module or harness defective. If wiring harness tests OK, replace CIS-E control module.
M104.992 engine (to 3/31/94) Does not start at temperatures below -5°C (23°F)	HFM-SFI control module set too rich. Replace HFM-SFI control module. (Software rewritten as of 8/94.)
M104 engine with HFM-SFI Shakes, misses on acceleration, dies while idling	Defective hot film air flow sensor. Replace hot film air flow sensor. *Note:* Hot film air flow sensor may be damaged by sand and particulate matter passing through air filter assembly. When working on air filter assembly, make sure that: Air cleaner gasket is not damaged. Air cleaner housing cover is not distorted. Air cleaner and air cleaner housing are mounted properly. Intake manifold is clean.
M103, M104, M119 engines Cuts out, can not be restarted	Electrical lead of oxygen sensor comes into contact with driveshaft causing malfunction of fuel pump relay. Replace oxygen sensor. Check oxygen sensor wire routing. Replace fuel pump relay.
M103, M104, M119 engines Poor idling and poor warm-up characteristics	a. Air leaks around injector seals. Replace injector seals. b. Malfunction in EGR system, air injection system or fuel injection system. Perform emission system tests for applicable system. c. Idle speed and CO value too low. Test idle speed and CO mixture. Check idle air distribution hose for restriction. d. Check spark plug connectors for intermittent short circuit. e. Spark plug gap too small. Reset spark plug gap to 0.8 mm (.032 in).

Group 07: Fuel injection

Problem	Possible cause, suggested repair
M103, M104, M119 engines Hesitates, cuts out or is difficult to start at times	a. A/C compressor control module (KLIMA) circuitry defective due to moisture/corrosion coming in through vent bore. Make sure vent bore in relay is closed with dab of RTV. b. Defective tachometer. Disconnect tachometer to see if problem is resolved. Replace tachometer if necessary. c. Ignition spark jumps to ground inside distributor cap(s). Check for burn marks inside cap and replace. d. Loose engine coolant temperature sensor electrical connector. Replace sensor connector. e. Faulty engine management ground connections. Trace and repair ground connections at intake manifold. f. Loose connectors on CIS-E wiring harness. Check and repair. g. Loose fuel pump ground connection in trunk. Check and repair.
Engines with CIS-E fuel injection Stalls suddenly and restarts after brief period	Problems with electrical connections. a. Check ignition coil connections. b. Check tachometer signal wire for intermittent ground contact at diagnostic socket, tachometer, fuel pump relay, KLIMA relay. c. Check plug connections for looseness at fuel pump relay, over-voltage protection relay and KLIMA relay. d. Check electrohydraulic actuator for recovery after coasting fuel shut-off.
Engines with CIS-E fuel injection Cuts out during coasting.	Loss of tachometer signal. Connect digital VOM between CIS-E control module and ground (pin 6). Push vehicle forward and backward looking for 0.9V. Repeat test at Hall effect speed sensor (connector X26, pin 11) and check plug connector X53/5 for intermittent contact.
Engines with CIS-E fuel injection Stumbles or cuts out when coming to a stop, idle surges intermittently 	Loose solder connection in over-voltage protection relay (**arrow**). Measure resistance between relay pins 87E and 87L. Nominal value 0 Ω while wiggling pins. If resistance changes, resolder or replace relay.
Engines with CIS-E fuel injection Fuel pump noisy	a. Rubbing fuel lines. Check condition and routing of fuel lines. b. Contaminated screen in fuel distributor. Clean or replace screen. c. Fuel pump worn out or dirt in fuel tank. Replace fuel pump and clean tank screen.

Group 07: Fuel injection

Problem	Possible cause, suggested repair
Engines with CIS-E fuel injection Oxygen sensor system duty cycle not adjustable. Check engine light is illuminated	a. Oxygen sensor malfunction. 　Check oxygen sensor duty cycle while driving. Replace if sensor is sluggish. 　Check intake and exhaust system for tightness. 　Tighten fuel system electrical ground connections. 　Loosen and retighten oxygen sensor. b. Cable between oxygen sensor and CIS-E control module pin 8 shorted to ground. 　Unplug CIS-E control module and check resistance between sockets 7 and 8. Nominal value above 10 kΩ. If resistance is below 1 Ω, repair or replace harness. c. Loose, intermittent connection at connector sleeve Z within wiring harness in CIS-E control module plug. 　Open CIS-E control module plug and resolder connections.
Engines with CIS-E fuel injection Warm engine hard to start	Internal leakage of fuel system. Test fuel system for internal leakage and repair as needed. *Note:* Cranking time of four seconds is normal.

Group 09: Air cleaner, air injection, EGR operation

Problem	Possible cause, suggested repair
OM606 engine in E300 Diesel Engine bucks with rattling noises.	Resonance flap broken or shaft worn. Replace intake manifold (includes resonance flap).

Group 14: Intake and exhaust manifolds, catalytic converter

Problem	Possible cause, suggested repair
All E-Class Excessive heat in right front footwell	Catalytic converter too close to car floor. Measure distance between converter and floor. Minimum distance = 8 - 10 mm (0.3 - 0.4 in). Adjust if required. Install fiberglass insulating mat, MB part no. 000 989 18 10, available by the meter, under right side floor mat.
Models with M103 engine Exhaust manifold leak at exhaust flange.	a. Exhaust manifold loose. Reinstall with new gasket and lock nuts. b. Exhaust manifold warped. Check and replace as needed.

Group 15: Engine electrics

Problem	Possible cause, suggested repair
All engines Whining noise from alternator	a. Battery not well charged. Check battery. Recharge if required. b. If excessive whining still occurs, replace alternator. *Note:* Starting at approx. 3,000 rpm the alternator fan can cause a whining noise. *Note:* At very low temperatures the alternator may whine for the first minute of operation.
All engines Starter spins with engine running, electrical wires burned. Starter does not disengage and is spun by engine.	a. Heavy weights attached to key via key chain that prevent starter switch from returning to run position completely. Remove weights. b. Starter defective. Replace starter. c. Starter wiring burned. Repair as needed. d. If complaint continues, replace complete steering lock and ignition lock cylinder.
All gasoline engines Starter noisy	Bent gear teeth on ring gear. To diagnose, activate starter with ignition disconnected. Metallic noise should no longer be heard. Replace ring gear.
M103 engine Cold engine difficult to start	Incorrect spark plugs installed. Install correct spark plugs Bosch H9DC, H9DCO or ones with equivalent heat range
M103 engine Loud knocking noise from engine compartment	Iron cores of some Bosch ignition coils are poorly glued. Replace any coil with production code before FD845 or after FD847
M104.94x, M104.99x engines Engine operation erratic, missing, surging, bucking	Defective engine wiring harness in area of hot film air flow sensor. *Note:* Wiggle harness to test. Replace engine wiring harness. Change harness routing as follows: Position hot film air flow sensor electrical harness over air intake duct bellows. Position air flow sensor harness in bead below hood seal. Replace test coupling (16-pin X11/4) mounting screws with blunt screws if required. Attach air flow sensor harness with clips, MB part no. 000 546 67 43. Attach clips in front of and in back of stamped identification number on engine compartment rear bulkhead.
M119 engine Engine hard to start with long cranking period and/or starts and dies.	Clearance between crankshaft position sensor (L5) and segment on flywheel too small. Install 0.5 mm (0.02 in) shim between crankshaft position sensor (L5) and contact surface. (Use gasket paper for shim.)
M119 engine Engine cuts out prematurely in gear selector position D, cruise control does not function, exterior lamp failure indicator lamp comes on when brakes are applied.	Speed signal affected by radio. Malfunctions in various vehicle systems resulting from improper radio installation. Disconnect speed signal from radio plug A pin #1 (green/white) and insulate.

Group 18: Lubrication system

Problem	Possible cause, suggested repair
All engines Low oil level light illuminates, especially during left turns, with engine running and correct oil level. Oil level sender 15-pin connector Sensor wire	a. Oil level sender resistance too high. Measure resistance of oil level sender. Should be less than 0.1 Ω. b. Oil level sender harness resistance too high. Check continuity of wire between sensor and instrument cluster (pin 5 of 15-pin connector. Should be less than 0.1 Ω c. Instrument cluster defective. If both sensor and wire test ok, 60-second delay built into instrument cluster is not functioning. Replace cluster.
M103 engine After cold start: Humming, scraping noise from front oil pan at idle and up to 1500 rpm. Noise diminishes with increasing engine temperature and usually disappears when operating temperature is reached.	Noisy oil pump. Replace oil pump: 4MATIC cars, MB part no. 103 180 08 01 Non-4MATIC cars, MB part no. 103 180 03 0

Group 20: Engine cooling

Problem	Possible cause, suggested repair
M103 engine and M104 engine up to 1/32/95 Engine coolant loss at rear engine suspension eyes	Hardened sealing rings leaky. Replace sealing rings, MB part no. 012 997 51 48.

Group 22: Engine suspension

Problem	Possible cause, suggested repair
M103 engine Humming, droning or vibration when driving in curves.	Rear engine mount settled. Adjust for stress-relief or replace mount.
M103, M104, M602, M603 engine Rumbling noises coming from front engine mount area.	Engine mount bolts not retorqued correctly. Check bolt torque. Tightening torque for all engines 25 Nm (18.5 ft-lb)

Group 25: Clutch

Problem	Possible cause, suggested repair
All models with clutch Clutch pedal occasionally sticks when driving in mountainous roads.	Air bubbles in clutch / brake fluid reservoir and lines due to high thermal loads in brake system. Replace brake / clutch fluid.
All models with clutch Squealing noise when depressing clutch pedal	Poor friction between clutch master cylinder bore and primary piston seal. Disassemble clutch master cylinder. Clean piston and cylinder bore with alcohol. Apply silicone paste, MB part no. 000 989 84 51, to cylinder bore and primary cup seal. Reassemble and bleed.
All models with clutch Whirring or grinding noise when depressing clutch pedal	Throw-out bearing damaged due to high thermal loads (bearing loses lubricant). Install throw-out bearing prepacked with high temperature lubricant, MB part no. 001 250 23 15. (Production phased in 12/89.)

Group 27: Automatic transmission

Problem	Possible cause, suggested repair
All transmissions Howling and singing noises from area of torque converter and primary transmission pump	Transmission oil pump deflector cracked or broken. Remove valve body. Replace oil deflector on intermediate plate.
Transmission nos. 3297013 to 3316017 Noises when coasting or driving in reverse	Defective thrust bearing of K1 clutch. (First signs of wear are grinding noises in reverse.) Remove transmission oil pan and look for steel shavings. If shavings found, remove transmission, remove front cover and replace thrust washer, MB part no. 000 272 25 62, and thrust needle bearing, MB part no. 007 981 68 10. Measure axial play of K1 clutch and correct. (See MB service information.) Thoroughly clean torque converter and transmission cooler lines. If shavings not found in pan, remove valve body and intermediate plate and look for steel shavings. If steel shavings found, replace torque converter.
722.3 transmission / M103 engine Delayed 2 - 3 shift	Spring problem in accumulator K1. Remove valve body. Install modified spring pack, MB part no. 126 270 44 77, for accumulator K1.
722.3 transmission / M103 or OM603 engine Oil leak at one of three torque converter drive flanges	Crack in torque converter housing at drive flange. Replace torque converter and flex drive disk.
722.3 transmission from 1/1/92 Transmission slips when starting off in first gear.	Teflon ring on brake band piston B2 torn. Replace B2 piston with updated seal design, MB part no. 107 270 04 32.
722.3xx transmission / M103 engine When engine is cold transmission will not upshift until very high rpm. Transmission function normal within 90 seconds.	Transmission wiring harness is incorrectly installed on kickdown solenoid and upshift delay solenoid valve. Correct wiring harness connections on automatic transmission. (See MB service information.)
722.3xx transmission Hard 4 - 3 downshift at approx. 60 - 70 kph (37 - 43 mph)	Variation in friction materials in brake band B2. Replace brake band B2.

Group 27: Automatic transmission

Problem	Possible cause, suggested repair
722.4 transmission / M103 or OM602 engine to 5/1/91 Transmission does not shift out of first gear.	No governor pressure due to broken drive gear for centrifugal governor. Remove centrifugal governor. Remove secondary pump and inspect. If spiral spring has moved from correct location below cover between pump gears, remove bottom cover. Replace check valve with MB part no. 126 270 05 89. Replace drive gear for centrifugal governor. Replace helical gear on output shaft and replace centrifugal governor.
722.4 transmission / 260E and 300E 2.6 models from 9/1/88 Whistling noise when shifting into reverse	Noise emanates from bore in intermediate plate that allows filling of disc-brake B3. Remove valve body and intermediate plate. Chamfer throttle bore on valve body side. Ensure that release valve B3 is correctly seated in valve body. (See MB service information.)
722.4 transmission / 260E and 300E 2.6 models or OM602 or OM606 engine Hard 2 to 1 downshift when starting off	Intermediate pressure too low to switch off brake band B1. Remove valve body. Replace plate check valve with bore, MB part no. 124 270 02 89.

Group 29: 4MATIC

Problem	Possible cause, suggested repair
4MATIC 4MATIC function indicator illuminates briefly during hard acceleration, straight ahead position, dry pavement.	4MATIC function may be activated by low tire pressure or car equipped with snow tires. Adjust tire pressure. *Note:* Snow tire problem should disappear when tires have accumulated 1,000 - 1,500 miles of wear.
4MATIC 4MATIC function indicator illuminates intermittently while driving in curves, without slip.	Defect in steering angle sensor. Replace contact ring and steering angle sensor. *Note:* Be sure to install 4MATIC version of steering angle sensor.
4MATIC 4MATIC function indicator illuminates on small radius curves, without slip.	Front wheel speed sensor harness faulty. Replace speed sensor.
4MATIC Crackling noise when starting under normal acceleration, speed approx. 25 kph (15 mph). Crackling noise when letting off brakes after braking to a standstill.	Normal operating noise of solenoid valves in 4MATIC hydraulic unit. Check routing of hydraulic lines from hydraulic unit to transfer case. Make sure hydraulic lines do not rest on car floor.
4MATIC Strong vibration immediately after starting from standstill in a small radius curve (such as when parking)	Incorrect hydraulic system pressure. Check hydraulic circuits. Replace hydraulic unit or service valve if required.
4MATIC Vibration while driving small radius curves and strong vibration under hard acceleration straight ahead at 40 - 60 kph (25 - 37 mph)	a. Incorrect hydraulic pressure. Check hydraulic system for pressure loss. System should retain constant pressure for 40 seconds. Replace 4MATIC hydraulic unit if not. b. Incorrect friction values in multiple-disk clutch. Replace oil in transfer case and use special ATF, MB part no. 001 989 07 03. After installing special ATF, drive car in tight left and right curves for a brief period to get benefit of oil change. c. No known cause. Replace transfer case

Group 29: 4MATIC

Problem	Possible cause, suggested repair
4MATIC Vibration when applying brakes lightly (in curves, after starting off and accelerating 10 - 20 kph / 6 - 12 mph)	a. Air in hydraulic system. Bleed hydraulic system. For pre-1991 cars: Remove lines AV and ZS (see MB service information) at transfer case and place ends in a suitable container. Run engine and drain hydraulic oil until free of air bubbles. Correct hydraulic oil level in reservoir when completed. For 1991 and later cars: Use bleed screw. b. Incorrect initial pressure of multi-disk clutch. Check initial pressure. Nominal value = 1.2 - 1.3 bar (17.4 - 18.8 psi). c. Incorrect friction values in multiple-disk clutch. Replace oil in transfer case and use special ATF, MB part no. 001 989 07 03. After installing special ATF, drive car in tight left and right curves for a brief period to get benefit of oil change.

Group 30: Throttle control

Problem	Possible cause, suggested repair
M103 engine Cruise control surges going downhill.	Fault in deceleration fuel shut-off system. Disconnect idle speed microswitch and drive car. If condition is no longer evident, deceleration fuel shut-off system is cause. Reconnect idle speed microswitch, otherwise engine idle is poor and vehicle is not in federal compliance. No final remedy available at this time. Shortening throttle rod may reduce problem to an acceptable level.
M103 engine Car surges while holding cruise control in DECEL position.	Unknown cause. Shorten connecting rod to cruise control actuator by 2 - 3 mm (2 - 3 turns) from slack position.
Cars with cruise control Cruise control does not function following replacement or installation of new control module.	Pin 14 in 14-pin cruise control module connector has been grounded. Remove ground bridge from pin 12 to pin 14. *Note:* Connector 12 is ground. Pin 14 should not be used.
Cars with ASR ASR warning lamp comes on while driving and electronic accelerator operates in limp-home mode with increased pedal resistance.	Check accelerator control linkage. Perform diagnostic test. Replace accelerator pedal position sensor.
Cars with ASR Engine dies occasionally during deceleration and can be restarted immediately.	Defective safety contact switch M16/1s in EFP actuator. Replace EFP actuator.

Group 32 – 35: Suspension and drivetrain

Problem	Possible cause, suggested repair
All E-Class Front spring broken in area of first winding **(arrow)** 	Stress corrosion from environmental influences. Replace front springs. Install protective zinc plates (reactive anode, MB part no. 124 321 00 36) on both springs.
All E-Class Knocking noise in front sway bar mount 	a. Mounting surfaces for sway bar link to the front subframe wear. This causes link to loosen at subframe. Remove both sway bar links and inspect mounting surface on subframe for cracks. If no cracks are detected, retap threads in frame member. Reattach links with new bolts. Tightening torque 60 Nm (44 ft-lb) b. Reinforcing plate welded to subframe loose. Cracks detected under sway bar link mounts. Replace cracked frame members.
All E-Class Creaking noise in front end when driving on uneven road 	Front strut upper mount noisy due to settling. Loosen mounting nuts **(arrows)** on front strut upper mount. Spray contact area with wax preservative and retighten nuts. Tightening torque 20 Nm (15 ft-lb)

Group 32 – 35: Suspension and drivetrain

Problem	Possible cause, suggested repair
All E-Class Knocking noise at front axle	a. Insufficient pretension on front strut upper mounting nut. Replace loose self-locking nuts and tighten. Tightening torque 60 Nm (44 ft-lb) 4MATIC cars 80 Nm (59 ft-lb) b. Excessive play in strut piston rod due to premature wear of working piston guide ring on high mileage vehicles. Raise car, push down brake pedal, then push and pull on strut rod to determine play. If play is detected, replace strut. Check sway bar and control arm bushings. Check for play in idler bearing assembly.
All E-Class Vibration/shimmy at steering wheel	a. Defective steering damper. Test and replace steering damper. b. Tires not balanced, out-of-round or match points not aligned. Check tire vertical and lateral run-out. Check tire/wheel matching points. c. Balance wheels/tires. d. Front control art bushings faulty. Replace rear rubber bushings on front control arms and install at 90° to normal position. e. Steering gear frictional torque set incorrectly. Test frictional torque of steering gear. Must be higher than 90 Ncm (0.8 in-lb). Optimal frictional torque 120 Ncm (106 in-lb)
All E-Class Rumbling/humming in speed range from 110 - 150 kph (68 - 93 mph) 	Driveshaft (propeller shaft) out of balance. Balance driveshaft. If problem persists, install rear differential vibration damper, MB part no. 124 350 03 72 at rear subframe. Tightening torque 150 Nm (110 ft-lb)
All E-Class Oil leaks out rear differential vent	Under unfavorable operating conditions (severe service, extreme cold) oil can foam and get pushed out vent. Replace differential cover and vent, MB part nos. 124 351 30 08, 124 350 03 90. Rear cover to differential tightening torque 45 Nm (33 ft-lb) *Note:* Use anaerobic sealant, as there is no gasket.

Group 32 – 35: Suspension and drivetrain

Problem	Possible cause, suggested repair
All E-Class Grunting noise in rear suspension. Can occur when car is rocked while standing still.	Moisture between bolt shank and bushing surface of lower rear wheel bearing carrier bushing (**arrow**) causes corrosion. Install new bushing, MB part no. 201 352 00 27. Note: Use MB special tool 201 589 05 43 00 to replace bushing without removing wheel bearing carrier.
All E-Class Howling/whistling noises from rear	Rear wheel bearing seal not turning together with inner race. Replace rear wheel bearing(s) as necessary. *Note:* If bearing manufactured by FAG, before installation apply Loctite® Prism 401 to bearing seal and inner race at four locations (**arrows**) indicated in illustration. Turn inner race until sealing material is evenly distributed in seal groove. Repeat procedure on opposite side.
500E Front axle knocking noise when braking	Insufficient tightening torque on front axle reinforcing strut bolts (**arrows**). Replace washers, MB part no. 000 433 008 407, and retorque bolts. Tightening torque 33 Nm (24 ft-lb)

Group 40: Wheels, tires, alignment

Problem	Possible cause, suggested repair
All E-Class ABS warning light illuminates at highway speed.	Different-sized tires/wheels installed. Install correct, matching tires / wheels.
All E-Class Increased wear on outside shoulder of front tires	Excessive toe-in on front wheels. Check wheel alignment on front end and adjust as needed. *Note:* Set front toe correctly by using front end spreader bar. Spreader bar spring tension amounts to 90 - 110 Nm / 66 - 81 ft-lb.

Group 42: Brakes, ABS

Problem	Possible cause, suggested repair
All E-Class ABS warning light illuminates, ABS still operates brake system normally.	a. Alternator charges but not at full capacity. Check alternator output. Replace or repair as necessary. b. Alternator warning light illuminates but so dimly it is hardly visible. Check alternator output. Replace or repair as necessary.
All E-Class Soft brake pedal or insufficient braking at front or rear axle	Flow noises heard in check valve of brake booster vacuum line. Install new vacuum line with modified check valve (white/black), MB part no. 126 430 29 05.
All E-Class ABS warning lamp illuminates intermittently and goes out again while driving.	a. Electrical consumers switching on and off cause battery voltage to intermittently drop below ABS threshold of 10.5V. Check battery/charging system and repair as needed. b. Defective over-voltage protection relay or loose connection in ABS system power supply or ground. Test relay with ABS test adapter and check all connections for electrical tightness.
All E-Class Front brakes squeal when applied	Friction vibration from disks. Reface or replace brake disks.
All E-Class Shudder or droning at front while braking	a. Brake disks warping or excessive run-out. Replace brake disks and install brake pads with Textar® compound 298-41c, MB part no. 000 420 99 20/05. b. Vehicles with nonstandard running gear, (lowered, sport rims) have an increased tendency to warp brake discs because of reduced brake ventilation.
All E-Class Long brake pedal travel after replacement of front brake pads. Uneven wear of brake pads.	Caliper sliding bolt bent because partially disassembled caliper used to turn steering from lock to lock. Replace bolt, MB part no. 000 421 16 74. Check and make sure calipers moves freely on guide pins.
All E-Class Rattling noise at front brakes	a. Brake pad spring clip has insufficient tension or is incorrectly installed. Bend spring clip to increase tension and install correctly b. Caliper sliding bolt bent. Replace bolt, MB part no. 000 421 16 74.
All E-Class Parking brake does not release or parking brake warning light in instrument cluster does not go out.	Front parking brake (Bowden) cable binding. Replace cable. *Note:* Improved version installed as of 1989.
All E-Class Parking brake rattles in rear.	Play in brake shoe spreading lock. Replace parking brake shoes, MB part no. 124 420 07 20. *Note:* Improved version installed as of 7/92.

Group 42: Brakes, ABS

Problem	Possible cause, suggested repair
All E-Class ABS warning light illuminates intermittently.	Intermittent loss of contact in speed sensor wiring harness near coaxial connector of either front wheel sensor. *Note:* If harness is damaged within 0.5 meter (20 in) of speed sensor connector, repair using special MB repair kit.
All E-Class Pulsating brake pedal with light braking (not within control range of ABS). ABS warning light does not illuminate.	a. Defective wheel speed sensor or electronic control module causing return pump to operate. Check resistance of wheel speed sensor. Check sensor for metal chips on tip and clean if necessary. b. Open circuit in front wheel speed sensor electrical harness. Remove and check sensor harness. If colored tape is mounted inside or above harness mounting clip in wheel housing, harness could be stressed and damaged when road wheel moves downward. Stretch and flex near fastening clip. Remove sensor from steering knuckle and simulate front wheel going through turns and over bumps.
Cars with diesel engines Loss of brake assist	Damaged vacuum pump roller bearings. Check for pitted or worn cam at injection timer. Replace vacuum pump and cam at injection timer. *Note:* Remove broken bearing pieces from oil pan or timing chain cover.
E-Class with ASR Intermittent knocking noise from left front fender within 10 - 30 seconds after starting engine.	Noise from ASR pressure reservoir. Check routing of lines between hydraulic unit (ABS / ASR) and pressure reservoir (under fender).
E-Class with floating front calipers Rattling noise from front on uneven roads	Play in brake pad carrier bushing. Partially disassemble floating caliper. A bushing is pressed into one hole in pad carrier, recognized by groove on pad carrier (**arrow**). Replace pad carrier with this hole at top.
E-Class to chassis no. 384627 ABS or ABS / ASR warning light illuminates after engine is started and stays lit until ignition is switched off.	a. Open circuit in front speed sensor electrical harness near mounting clip or bracket. Replace defective sensor harness. b. Missing and / or false wheel speed sensor signal. Check resistance of speed sensors. Stretch and flex electrical harness, looking for breaks.
4MATIC ABS warning light illuminates while driving and remains lit until ignition is switched off.	Left front speed sensor cannot be tested with ABS test unit. See model year 1990 introduction to 124.230 / 290 4MATIC for diagnostic instructions.

Group 46: Steering

Problem	Possible cause, suggested repair
All E-Class Central locking can be engaged at right front door even though key is in steering lock position 1 or 2.	Warning buzzer switch S8/2 on steering lock defective. Replace switch.
All E-Class Clacking noises from impact absorber in steering wheel	Loose Torx screws for steering wheel electrical contact plate. Remove airbag unit. Tighten contact plate Torx screws. Tightening torque 5 Nm (3.6 ft-lb)
All E-Class Scraping noise when turning steering wheel	Additional brushes and slip ring have been installed in steering wheel hub for SRS system. No action required. Noise will diminish as the brushes wear in. *Note:* Never apply lubricants to slip ring brushes. Keep surfaces dry and clean.
All E-Class Insufficient power steering assist when turning steering wheel to left quickly	Trapped air in steering gear. Drive car until power steering reaches operating temperature. Raise car and turn wheels to full right lock. After waiting time of approx. 5 minutes, idle engine. Turn steering wheel to full left and right lock repeatedly. *Note:* Steering gear is not faulty if slight resistance continues to be present when turning steering wheel quickly. With normal driving, remaining trapped air will be bled in time.
All E-Class Knocking noise in right front when driving on irregular road surfaces 	a. Play in steering idler arm bushings (**arrows**). Replace bushings. b. Insufficient lubricant in idler arm bushings. On low mileage cars, lubricate with silicone grease, MB part no. 000 989 84 51 (100 g can). *Note:* Apply silicone grease only to bore of rubber bushings. After installation, remove excess grease to prevent dirt accumulation. Do not expose car paint to grease. Wash hands immediately after using silicone grease.
All E-Class Oil leak at adjustment screw on power steering gear 	Polyamide ring on counter nut (**A**) does not seal. Replace counter nut, MB part no. 001 990 70 51. Gasoline powered cars: Remove steering gear. Diesel powered cars: Remove air filter housing. Mark position of adjusting screw (**B**) Replace counter nut without turning adjustment screw. Tightening torque 65 Nm (48 ft-lb) *Note:* If adjusting screw is accidently turned, reset steering gear frictional torque to 120 Ncm (106 in-lb).

Group 46: Steering

Problem	Possible cause, suggested repair
All E-Class Rattling / knocking noises at wheel lock with engine idling, at operating temperature	Modified pressure plate in power steering pump. (Only applies to LUK pump from 20/7/1992 through 23/8/1992, production date code20 G.) Replace power steering pump. Install ZF power steering pump or LUK pump with production date code before 20 G or after 23 H.
All E-Class Knocking noises in steering tie rods on poor roads	Too much play in left tie rod ball joint (left hand drive cars). Install left tie rod with "hard" ball joint, MB part no. 000 338 54 10.

Group 47: Fuel system

Problem	Possible cause, suggested repair
260E, 300E 2.6, 300E 2.8, 300E, E320 coupe, cabrio, wagon, 300TE, all 4MATIC Fuel tank leaky or collapsed	Insufficient ventilation through activated charcoal canister. Replace charcoal canister. Check vent lines in front of and in back of canister. Replace any collapsed lines.

Group 54: Electrical

Problem	Possible cause, suggested repair
All E-Class Battery discharged, electronic components damaged.	a. Starting with battery jump from second car may cause high voltage spikes and damage electronic components. Diagnose / repair / replace components as necessary. b. Crossing jumper cables when starting from second car will blow fuse in over-voltage protection relay (**arrow**). Replace fuse. *Note:* Over-voltage relay is in electronics box at right rear of engine compartment. 10A blade fuse is on top of relay. c. Charging battery in car without disconnecting cables may cause high voltage spikes and damage electronic components. Diagnose / repair / replace components as necessary.
All E-Class Brake wear and / or low coolant level warning light illuminated. Right side headlight wiper/washer not working.	Corrosion at right headlight ground. Check for damage to brake pad wear indicator ground wire. Clean and tighten grounds and electrical harness connectors. Apply a coat of spray paint to ground W2. *Note:* W2 is on chassis next to right headlight wiper motor.
All E-Class Radio does not turn on or off in conjunction with ignition switch.	Fuse 1 for circuit 15R is blown. Investigate cause of blown fuse and repair. Replace fuse 1.

Group 54: Electrical

Problem	Possible cause, suggested repair
All E-Class Cruise control operates intermittently or not at all. 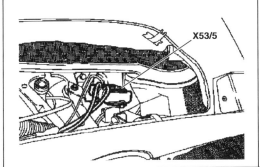	Contacts in 6-pin connector X53/5 are temporarily or completely interrupted. This will also affect A/C blower speed at higher vehicle speeds. Install new 6-pin connector with manufacturing date code 4985 or later, marked with green dot. *Note:* Connector X53/5 is behind instrument cluster, slightly to right of center.
All E-Class Bulb failure indicator light illuminates after actuating directional signal switch quickly from right to left turn or vice versa even if no bulb is defective.	Problem in bulb failure control module. No repair solution as of 4/28/99
All E-Class A/C compressor occasionally does not operate or does not operate at all. 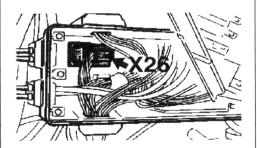 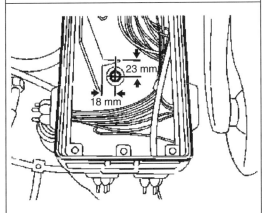	a. Corrosion due to moisture at engine wiring harness connector X26, located in fuse box under fuse and relay carrier. (Connects push-button A/C control panel or power supply wire to A/C compressor control module.) Remove and dry out or replace fuse and relay carrier and other damaged parts, as needed. *Note:* To Make sure water corrosion problem does not recur, drill 6 mm (¼ in) diameter drain hole in lowest spot of fuse box bottom (see illustration). Check all rubber boots on fuse box for leaks and seal with sealing compound as required. Check fusebox cover for leaks and replace cover and gasket if required. b. Printed circuit traces in KLIMA (A/C) module and / or pins in KLIMA module connector are corroded. Water gets into electronic components via cover panel below windshield. Replace KLIMA module. Clean module connector if needed. Use RTV to plug vent hole in KLIMA module.

Group 54: Electrical

Problem	Possible cause, suggested repair
All E-Class Brake lights come on intermittently or stay on continuously without actuating brakes.	a. Return spring for brake pedal is not connected. Reconnect or replace. b. Brake light switch travel too short. Adjust. c. Brake light switch defective. Replace.
All E-Class Outside temperature indicator does not display temperature or display is intermittent.	Temperature sensor harness is routed too tightly. This can result in break in harness or at temperature sensor solder points. Install new temperature sensor. *Note:* Route harness properly. Point of entry to fusebox is marked on harness with tape. Make sure tape is on outside of fusebox to allow maximum harness length.
All E-Class Speedometer needle vibrates or jumps.	Route speedometer cable correctly. Replace cable if necessary. NOTE: Lubricating a speedometer or cable will always result in failure of the unit.
E-Class with electric seats Electric seat adjustment does not function with either front door open. Radio or SRS warning light illuminate when either front door is open.	Defective diode because of missing or blown fuse 9. *Note:* Fuse 9 blows due to short in front dome light. This short-circuit will overload and blow seat adjustment diode. Repair short, replace fuse, replace diode.
E-Class from 6/1/92 Fuse 6 blows occasionally.	a. Connections to fuses 6 and 7 mixed up when originally connected. Check connections for fuses 6 and 7 and correct according to wiring diagram. b. Ground wire for horns too small. Upgrade to separate ground wires for each horn (at least 1.5 mm^2). *Note:* Horn ground wire runs from right front footwell (generator / battery harness noise suppressor) to horns.
400E, 500E Transmission kickdown and A/C cut-out at full throttle does not operate. 	KLIMA (A/C) module (**arrow**) from production code 01/00 up to and including 37/00 defective. Replace with MB part no. 011 545 97 32.

Group 62: Body structure

Problem	Possible cause, suggested repair
All E-Class Clacking noises at A-pillars near engine hood hinges. Panel ─── A-pillar 40 mm 20 mm	a. Weld seams between reinforcement panel and A-pillar missing. Weld panel to A-pillar. *Note:* Top seam weld = 40 mm (1.6 in); bottom seam weld = 20 mm (¾ in). b. Check wheel house paneling behind reinforcement panel for cracks (**arrow**). MIG weld cracks.
All E-Class Tension cracks on front control arm brackets	On vehicles with high mileage or under certain operating conditions stress cracks can occur on front control arm brackets. These stress cracks have no effect on operational stability. Contact MBUSA field engineering.

Group 72: Doors

Problem	Possible cause, suggested repair
All E-Class Bezel behind inside door handle protrudes from door panel.	Distance between door sheet metal and door trim panel is too large. Make special tool from mild steel flat bar stock 10 x 20 x 240 mm (0.4 x 0.8 x 9.45 in). Deform rectangular holes (**arrows**) for inside door handle mounting towards vehicle center (there are three holes in all). Glue 2 mm (.08 in) felt pads at contact area of inside door handle bezel.

Group 72: Doors

Problem	Possible cause, suggested repair
All E-Class Clicking noise in door lock 	Noise from plastic components in door latch assembly, near pivoting latch which rotates into striker eye. Lubricate both sides of pivot point where latch rotates (**left arrow**). Lubricate lock assembly through slot in plastic housing (**right arrow**). Use graphite oil, MB part no. 001 989 03 03.
All E-Class Knocking noise from door check strap 	Door check strap screws loose. Remove interior door trim panel. Remove check strap screws (**arrows**), examine threads for damage. Retap threads, replace screws if damage is found. Tightening torque 10 Nm (7.2 ft-lb) Note: Replace screws using thread sealant, MB part no. 002 989 94 71.
All E-Class Wind noise at doors	Inside window seal does not rest against window glass correctly. Localize noise by taping closed water drains at bottom of the door. Remove inner door panel and seal. Carefully bend inner door sheet metal toward window glass with chock of wood. *Note:* Seal is positioned correctly if strip of paper cannot be pushed between glass and inner window seal.
All E-Class Rear doors difficult to open from outside when hot	Friction of zinc coating on door latch parts increases when hot. Remove door latch. Lubricate door latch parts with molybdenum-disulfide grease (Moly-spray).
All E-Class except coupe and cabriolet to 10/31/92 Cracking noise in area of door lock on uneven roads	Unfavorable material matching between rotary catch and striker. Replace striker using MB 140 720 00 04. Adjust doors. If doors cannot close with new part remove shim plate.

Problems and Repairs

Group 72: Doors

Problem	Possible cause, suggested repair
E-Class from 01/9/89 Crackling noise from door trim panel. 0058744	Fastening nuts on wooden trim (**arrow**) loose. Remove door trim panel. Remove wooden trim fasteners. Apply thread-locker (Loctite®) to screws and reinstall. Tightening torque 0.8 - 0.9 Nm (7 - 8 in-lb).

Group 77: Sunroof

Problem	Possible cause, suggested repair
All E-Class Rattling noise with sunroof open or closed	Four attachment clips for sunroof headliner are loose. Fasten clips to sunroof headliner using double-sided adhesive tape
All E-Class Rattling noise with rear of sunroof raised	Excessive vertical play of water drain channel. Eliminate play by adjusting both stops.
All E-Class Sunroof does not close or open completely.	Control module on drive motor (actuating cam for microswitch) adjusted incorrectly. Perform basic adjustment and, if needed, fine adjustment.
All E-Class Sunroof cannot be adjusted or adjustment must be corrected constantly.	Guide tube is loose on sunroof frame. Disconnect rear of sunroof headliner and retighten guide tube. *Note:* In some cars a wrong sheet metal screw nut (nut-clip) was installed. Correct MB part no. is 123 994 00 45.
All E-Class Chattering noise when closing or opening sunroof	a. Incorrect height adjustment of sunroof. Adjust correctly. b. Guide tube and runout tube do not line up with drive motor or are incorrectly installed. Align guide tube and runout tube or install correctly. c. Guide tube is bent at connection to sunroof or is dented. Replace guide tube.
All E-Class Movement of sunroof is reversed when actuating sunroof switch.	Sunroof is installed upside down. Install correctly.
All E-Class Sunroof does not open or close.	Guide tab on end piece of sunroof drive cable not properly installed in mounting plate. Guide tab binds in guide tubing. Before installation, coat drive cable with lubricant, MB part no. 001 989 14 51. Make sure guide tab at front end of drive cable is securely located in mounting plate, pointing upwards. Remove drive cable and check for damage. Replace if necessary. If guide tube has been spread apart because of incorrect mounting of drive cable, squeeze guide tube together to its original shape Make sure mounting plate moves freely in slot of guide tube. Replace guide tube if required.

Group 77: Sunroof

Problem	Possible cause, suggested repair
All E-Class Sunroof does not operate.	Friction clutch on sunroof motor is adjusted too tight. Nominal toque 6 - 7 Nm (53 - 62 in-lb). Motor current draw is excessive (approx 30A) causing 16A fuse to blow. *Note:* Friction clutch maximum draw = 18A. Check adjustment of friction clutch and correct if necessary. If friction clutch operates correctly and sunroof binds, check free movement of sunroof.
All E-Class Rattling noise in roof panel	Too much free play between drive cable on sunroof and guide tube. Install new drive cable in roof panel. *Note:* Current production cables are surface treated electrostatically and coated. Part number remains same.
All E-Class Sunroof hard to move or locks up. Roof paintwork scratched.	Sliders on holder for sunroof cover are worn or bent so that roof cover is pressed upward out of sliding position when it closes and hits against reinforcement frame. Replace sliders on holder for sunroof cover. *Note:* If slider holder is bent, replace tilting bracket.
All E-Class Sunroof squeaks when opening and closing 	a. Sunroof sliding brackets adjusted too tightly. Loosen brackets, press outward slightly and retighten. Tighten brackets in sequence **1** to **8**. b. Sliders not greased. Remove sliders and lubricate, MB part no. 001 989 14 51. c. Channel for sliders too narrow. Remove sliders and glue strip of textile tape along entire length of screw attachment surface on sunroof frame.

Group 80: Central locking and networked systems

Problem	Possible cause, suggested repair
All E-Class Heated windshield washer nozzle fuse 7 blown	Short in the heated windshield washer nozzles. Replace windshield washer nozzle. *Note:* Check current draw of new nozzle before installation. Initial current draw of approx. 300 mA must go down to 100 - 150 mA after nozzle heats up. Newer nozzles have fixed resistance value of 200 mA.
All E-Class Battery discharges, possibly in a short period of time.	Microswitch in front door locks or in trunk lock sticks open or wire to microswitch is shorted to circuit 31, thereby activating convenience control module. Current draw with car unlocked is approx. 200 - 800 mA. If car is locked via central locking system current draw at fuse G or H is approx. 15 - 20A. When temperature switches in power window motors are activated the current is reduced to approx. 200 mA. To test microswitch: Unplug connector D on convenience control module (under left seat cushion). Use multimeter to measure resistance between socket 4 of connector D and circuit 31 (ground). Nominal value > 20 KΩ. If measured value is less than nominal value, disconnect microswitch connectors at door or trunk (or tailgate) locks one at a time. If nominal value is attained when disconnecting a connector then that microswitch is defective. Inspect and replace lock if necessary.

Group 80: Central locking and networked systems

Problem	Possible cause, suggested repair
All E-Class Alarm cannot be armed or disarmed from trunk or tailgate. 	Male connector X43 (white plastic) may have been accidentally connected to female connector M14/1x2 (clear plastic). This will disconnect alarm system from central locking system and turn off alarm system arming from trunk / tailgate. Connect X43 to central locking system harness and M14/1x2 to central locking system pump (M14/1 or M14/2). *Note:* Central locking system pump and connectors are located under rear seat on passenger side.
All E-Class Alarm comes on while driving.	a. Ground connection, terminal 2, of alarm system control module 14-pin connector is spread apart and has poor or intermittent contact. Carefully tighten socket with pliers. Do not replace door lock switches for this problem. *Note:* Alarm control module is located in passenger footwell under floorboard. b. Trunk lock element out of adjustment causing central locking system to arm alarm system. Stepping on brake pedal or turning on ignition switch sets off alarm. Adjust trunk lock element properly.
All E-Class Alarm intermittently arms by itself.	Moisture in alarm system electrical connectors in harness channels under front floor mats causes short-circuits. Clean connectors and relocate to pillar areas.

Group 82: Chassis electrical

Problem	Possible cause, suggested repair
All E-Class Combination (turn signal/headlight dimmer) switch does not turn off after driving through curves.	Defective switch manufactured by Kostal. Replace combination switch. *Note:* Production changeover date code is 23/93.
All E-Class Front dome light not operating with switch in time delay position	Short circuit in dome light due to excessively long contact spring. This can result in damage to power seat diode, blown fuse 9 and inoperative seat belt warning buzzer. Replace dome light unit.

Group 82: Chassis electrical

Problem	Possible cause, suggested repair
All E-Class Crunching or grinding noises over entire wiper sweep (Bosch windshield wiper system) 	Insufficient lubrication of rubber bellows (**arrow**) between motor crank and wiper linkage. Remove rubber bellows. Grip with pliers, pull out and cut off with cutting tools.
All E-Class When activating windshield washer system, unwiped areas of windshield become dirty and smeared. Low coolant level indicator lamp on.	Thermovalve in heated windshield washer heat exchanger leaks, allowing engine coolant to enter washer reservoir. Replace heat exchanger using updated MB part no. 124 830 17 61. *Note:* Replace engine coolant and clean out windshield washer reservoir.
All E-Class Windshield streaks, poor wiping in one direction 	a. Microedge of wiper blade damaged by dirt, grit. Inspect edge and replace wiper insert if needed. b. Washer fluid not mixed to prescribed ratios. Refill reservoir and adjust ratio to specifications. c. Undefined, hard to remove deposits on windshield glass (possibly hot wax from car wash). Wipe windshield with cleaner, MB part no. 000 986 40 71. d. Wiper arm is skewed. Bring wiper arm to center position on windshield. Remove wiper blade. Place wiper arm carefully on windshield. Wiper arm must lie parallel to windshield glass. Correct by twisting arm. e. Excessive play between wiper claws and wiper blade. Replace wiper blade. f. Insufficient clearance between wiper gear head and windshield. Make 5 mm (0.196 in) thick gauge out of plastic, wood or similar material. Check clearance **A** between windshield and wiper gear head. If gauge cannot be inserted wiper must be adjusted. Loosen nuts for wiper gear head and move gear head up until gauge can be inserted. If needed, add washers between rubber blocks and wiper gear head. g. Insufficient clearance between wiper blade and wiper arm (unwiped area in wiper field). Bring wiper arm to center position on windshield. Check clearance **B** with 5 mm (0.196 in) gauge. If clearance is less than 5 mm bend wiper arm toward windshield until gauge can be inserted.
E-Class with heated exterior mirrors Crackling interference noise in radio with ignition on	Interference may be caused by CIS-E control module. Unplug control module for test. Interference-free control module has current part number plus suffix 05.
E-class cabriolet up to chassis no. 841132 Rear window heater does not function.	Mount for electric wire for heated rear window not stable enough in area of convertible top frame. Rear side windows on left and right can catch in electric wire for heated rear window in convertible top frame when opening and damage or tear wire(s). Check both sides and replace damaged wire(s) with modified parts. Left wire: MB part no. 124 543 34 27 Right wire: MB part no. 124 440 06 08 Mounting screws: MB part no. 000 966 006 018

Group 82: Chassis electrical

Problem	Possible cause, suggested repair
E-Class sedan, coupe Cracking, ripping noises from rear of car	Taillight reflector housing rubbing against body. Noises begin after some time. Place caulking compound, MB part no. 001 987 56 46, on body mating surfaces for reflector housing and body.

Group 83: Heating, ventilating, air conditioning (ACC or automatic climate control)

Problem	Possible cause, suggested repair
All E-Class Rubbing noise from blower motor fan	a. Fan wheels located incorrectly on motor shaft. Replace blower motor with fan wheels attached. Note: Exercise care when replacing blower motor without fans wheels attached. Position fan wheels on the motor's shafts correctly. b. Blower motor is not properly attached to bracket. Reattach blower motor properly. c. Plastic blower housing is deformed. Minor deformation can be corrected by scraping area of housing where fan wheel is rubbing. d. Major deformation of heating/A/C housing (box) at front bulkhead. Reinstall correctly or replace housing.
All E-Class Sweet smell when operating A/C system in heat mode	Slight coolant seepage in heater core (between header plate and tubes). Replace heater core. Note: Leak may be so small that coolant loss at engine coolant reservoir is not noticeable. Note: Production improvements were phased during the 1988 and 1990. Service suggestion: Remove dashboard and upper heater box cover only. After disconnecting coolant lines heater core can be pulled out toward top.
All E-Class A/C blower does not function.	Bad contact at fuse 12. High temperature can cause fuse contact to fail. Install separate fuse for blower motor.
All E-Class Automatic climate control provides only maximum heating unless temperature wheel is set to MIN. 	Current draw of auxiliary coolant pump (M13) is above 0.8A or pump is seized. This triggers short circuit protection feature in A/C control panel. Current to auxiliary coolant pump and coolant monovalve is interrupted. Turn ignition on and set temperature wheel to MAX. a. Touch auxiliary coolant pump to check if pump is running. If not, replace pump. b. Check current draw of auxiliary coolant pump. If current draw is above 0.8A, replace pump. Note: Auxiliary coolant pump is to right of battery in engine compartment component compartment.
1991 E-Class Noise when A/C compressor switches on (sounds like a fan speeding up)	Production error at Siemens when evaporator was converted to aluminum. Replace evaporator. Note: Heating / A/C housing has sticker "Fabrikat Siemens" on right, visible through glove compartment. Siemens evaporator marked with white dot on expansion valve are OK. Replacement parts only available from Behr.

Group 88: Body components

Problem	Possible cause, suggested repair
All E-Class Trunk lid does not open when pressing lock button in.	Plastic parts of upper and lower trunk lock halves are sticking together. Coat lock striker sides (**arrows**) with thin layer of lubricant, MB part no. 001 989 14 51.
E-Class Trunk lid does not stay open. Hole 2 Hole 1	Trunk lid hinge spring tension low. Increase tension by moving spring end from **hole 1** to **hole 2**.
E-Class to 3/90 Clicking noise from rear window area when driving over rough roads	Trim piece (**arrow**) covering center seam of rear window molding loose, creating noise. Install modified trim piece, MB part no. 124 678 42 37, with teflon coating on inner surface.

Group 88: Body components

Problem	Possible cause, suggested repair
E-Class sedan Noises at C-pillar trim molding 	a. Molding rubs against body sheet metal as body flexes. Remove molding and apply special lubricant, MB part no. 000 989 26 58. *Note:* Application of foam material under molding is not recommended (may cause molding to protrude out of C-pillar). b. Lower edge of plastic trim cover is touching rear fender. Install rubber buffer (**arrow**), MB part no. 201 987 02 39, under plastic trim.

Group 91: Seats

Problem	Possible cause, suggested repair
All E-Class Electrostatic charge on seats	Electrostatic charges can occur at relatively low humidity when non-conducting materials rub against one another or are separated from one another. Shoes with insulating plastic or rubber soles increase this effect. To reduce effects of electrostatic charge: Apply antielectrostatic agent, MB part no. 000 986 42 71. Apply leather care agent, MB part no. 000 986 05 71, sparingly with clean rag and polish lightly with soft clean cloth after drying. Effect lasts for approx. 3 to 4 weeks. Unfortunately there is no effective anti-static charge treatment for M-B Tex seats. Touch conductive metal such as door handle before getting out. Position and fasten anti-static velour mats available from MB accessories.
All E-Class Cover of front seat backrest or front seat cushion loose	a. Backrest cover mounting strip is not tight enough in retaining channel. Install four clips, MB part no. 000 986 14 78, into mounting strip of each backrest cover and press into retaining channel. b. Seat cushion mounting strip is not tight enough in retaining channel. Install one clip, MB part no. 006 988 12 78, into front and rear retaining channels.
All E-Class Front seat cushion has insufficient side support when driving through turns. 	Insufficient side support of seat cushion frame. With extreme weight on front seat, cushion cover can be pinched at front seat tilt adjust mechanism. Install two foam blocks (**arrows**), MB part no. 124 910 16 75, in seat cushion padding on left and right side between two front seat springs.

Group 91: Seats

Problem	Possible cause, suggested repair
All E-Class SRS (supplemental restraint system) warning light flickers intermittently, Code 3 stored in memory of control module.	Steering wheel contact slip rings have broken wire or damaged solder joint. Remove steering wheel and replace slip rings.
All E-Class except coupe and cabriolet Front seat backrest readjusts itself without apparent reason.	Rentrop brand mechanism installed in backrest hinge defective. Replace backrest frame with one manufactured by Keiper-Recaro, MB part nos. 124 910 84 34 (right) and 124 910 83 34 (left).
260E and 300E 2.6 with manual seat adjusters Noise from manual seat adjustment mechanism on winding roads	Plastic bushings in cross pipe of lateral adjustment lever noisy. Remove seat and lubricate left and right plastic bushings (**arrow**).
E-Class to 1/90 Front seat head restraint cannot be removed.	Head restraint release button installed 180° reversed. Remove backrest cover from rear of seat. Replace left head restraint guide rail, MB part no. 124 970 00 15.

Group 91: Seats

Problem	Possible cause, suggested repair
E-Class sedan Noises in the seat belt height adjuster.	Excessive play in height adjuster slide in B-pillar. Glue felt to end piece of the slide (**1**). Install 2 clamps, MB part no. 124 988 93 78, in center of slider guide (**2**).

Groups 94 – 97: Body sealing

Problem	Possible cause, suggested repair
E-Class sedan Wind noise at triangular window in rear door.	Sealing problem at triangular window. It must be seated completely and make full contact in window frame. If sealing lip does not make optimum contact fill triangular area (**arrow**) between sealing frame and window frame with universal sealant, MB part no. 003 989 01 71. *Note:* Replace highly deformed sealing frames.
E-Class from 7/93 Water leakage at trunk lid.	Leaky license plate light fixture at trunk lid handle. Remove handle and apply 3 mm (⅛ in) bead (**arrows**) of universal sealant, MB part no. 003 989 01 71.

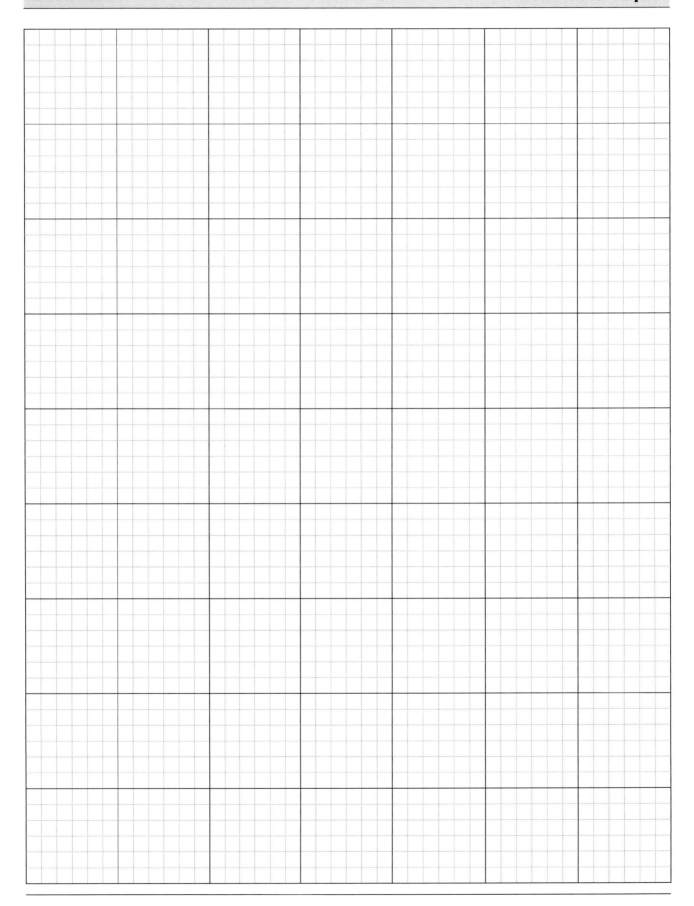

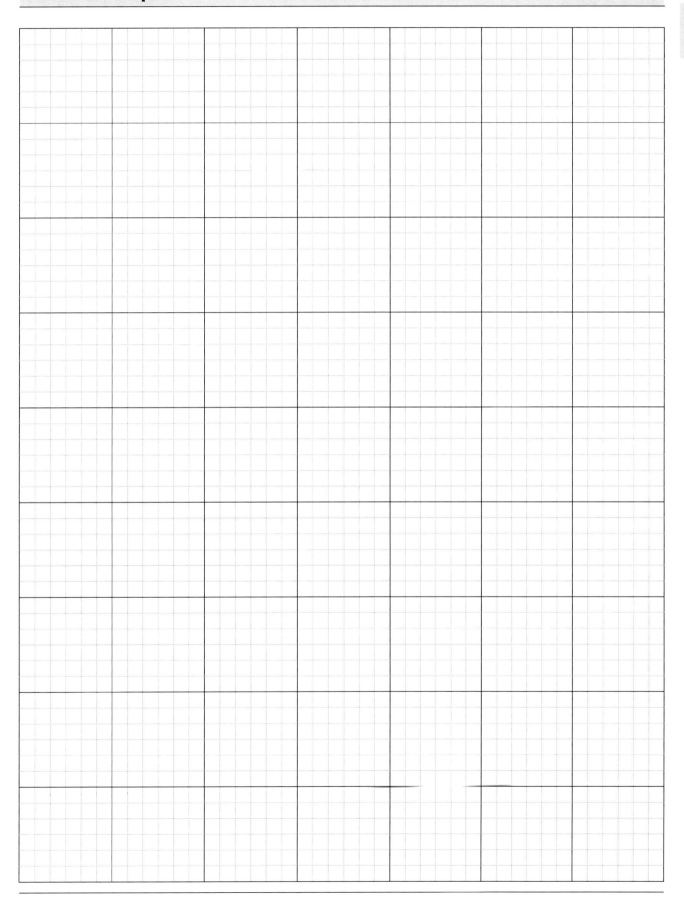

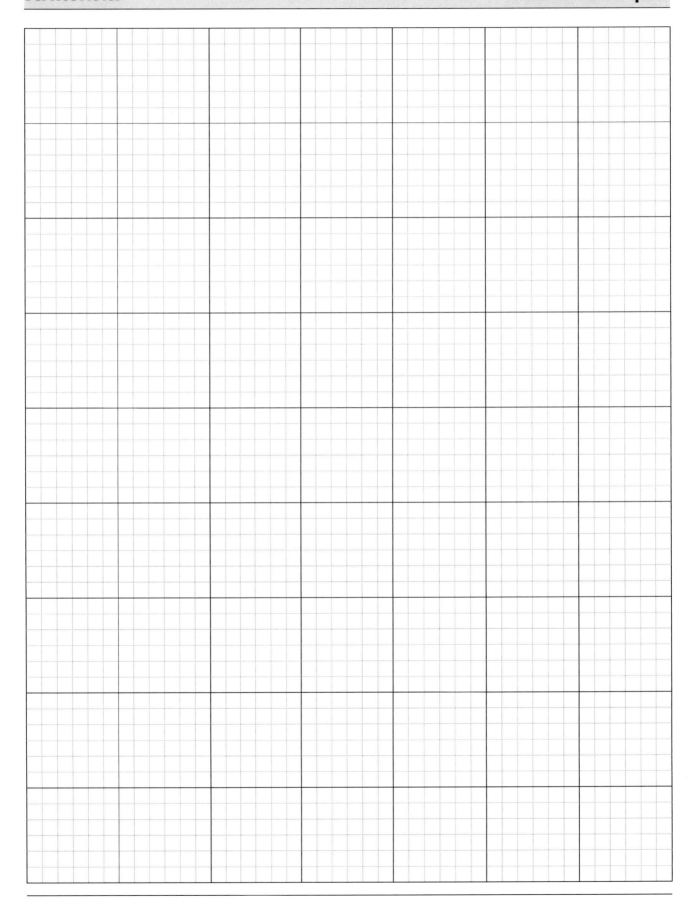

Afterword

The hook was cast in 1957. I was sixteen. My cousin Norman brought back a 1957 300SL roadster purchased during an army stint in Germany. When the car arrived at the port in New York City, my father and I went with Norman to uncrate and drive it home. Somehow I was shuttled into the subway for the trip home as dad waved merrily from the passenger seat of the beautiful white roadster. My revenge was to come later.

One early Sunday morning, Norman came by to take me for a ride. "Let's go get a glass of orange juice," he exclaimed. I thought it a little strange, but went along for the open-air ride. As we headed into New Jersey and onto the turnpike heading south, I knew this wasn't any ordinary glass of OJ we were after.

"Norman, where are we heading for this glass of orange juice?" I asked. He had cleared it with my mother (it was summer vacation) and we were on our way to sunny Florida.

My *real* experience with Mercedes-Benz began on those back roads of the eastern seaboard. Once the hook grabbed, it was unimaginable to think about driving any other automotive brand.

I finished college and tried my hand at the corporate world, but it never worked for me. I soon learned that I more enjoyed lying under my cars and tinkering.

One day I walked into a Mercedes-Benz dealership and asked for a job as a mechanic. I spent the next five years working at various Mercedes-Benz dealerships around the US. In 1975 I decided to open my own shop to service the cars in a manner that was satisfactory to me. *Stu Ritter Mercedes-Benz Technician, Inc.*, continues to this day. I sold the business to my shop foreman in 2000 after a very pleasurable twenty-five years. I enjoyed my time as both mechanic and shop owner.

Lately I've been teaching people about their cars and making technical language understandable to non-technical people. Educating people about their cars has always been a fun challenge for me.

In 1995 I started answering questions on the Internet from interested do-it-yourselfers (DIYers) and in 1997 started an email list. That same year I presented a seminar at StarTech, the national technical gathering of the Mercedes-Benz Club of America. In 1999 I was asked to write for *The Star,* the club's magazine, and in 2000 became their technical editor.

Having driven thousands of Mercedes-Benz automobiles over the past thirty years I've become quite fond of the 1986 to 1995 E-Class. I presently own a 1993 400E and my wife owns a 1994 E320 Station Wagon. Prior to the 400E I owned a 1988 300E Sportline for ten years.

I sincerely hope you enjoy this book as much as I enjoy my E-Class cars.

–**Stu Ritter**

Selected Books and Electronic Editions From Bentley Publishers

Driving

The Unfair Advantage
Mark Donohue
ISBN 0-8376-0073-1 (hc); 0-8376-0069-3(pb)

A French Kiss With Death: Steve McQueen and the Making of *Le Mans*
Michael Keyser ISBN 0-8376-0234-3

The Speed Merchants: A Journey Through the World of Motor Racing 1969-1972
Michael Keyser ISBN 0-8376-0232-7

Going Faster! Mastering the Art of Race Driving
The Skip Barber Racing School
ISBN 0-8376-0227-0

The Racing Driver
Denis Jenkinson ISBN 0-8376-0201-7

Sports Car and Competition Driving
Paul Frère with foreword by Phil Hill
ISBN 0-8376-0202-5

Engineering

Maximum Boost: Designing, Testing, and Installing Turbocharger Systems
Corky Bell ISBN 0-8376-0160-6

Bosch Fuel Injection and Engine Management
Charles O. Probst, SAE ISBN 0-8376-0300-5

Race Car Aerodynamics
Joseph Katz ISBN 0-8376-0142-8

Reference

Road & Track Illustrated Automotive Dictionary
John Dinkel ISBN 0-8376-0143-6

Audi

Audi A4: 1996–2001 Service Manual 1.8L Turbo, 2.8L including Avant and quattro
Bentley Publishers ISBN 0-8376-0371-4

Audi A4/S4: 1996–2001 Official Factory Repair Manual on CD-ROM
Audi of America ISBN 0-8376-0833-3

Audi A6: 1998–2002 Official Factory Repair Manual on CD-ROM includes Sedan, Avant, S6 Avant, allroad quattro
Audi of America ISBN 0-8376-0836-8

Audi TT Coupe, Roadster: 2000–2002 Official Factory Repair Manual on CD-ROM
Audi of America ISBN 0-8376-0839-2

BMW

Complete Roundel 1969–1998
8 CD-ROM set: 30 Years of the Magazine of the BMW Car Club of America, Inc.
BMW Car Club of America ISBN 0-8376-0322-6

BMW 3-Series (E30) Service Manual: 1984–1990 318i, 325, 325e(es), 325i(is), and 325i Convertible
Bentley Publishers ISBN 0-8376-0325-0

BMW 3 Series (E36) Service Manual: 1992–1998, 318i/is/iC, 323is/iC, 325i/is/iC, 328i/is/iC, M3
Bentley Publishers ISBN 0-8376-0326-9

BMW 3 Series (E46) Service Manual: 1999–2001, 323i/Ci, 325i/Ci/xi, 328i/Ci, 330i/Ci/xi Sedan, Coupe, Convertible and Sport Wagon
Bentley Publishers ISBN 0-8376-0320-X

BMW 5-Series (E28) Service Manual: 1982–1988 528e, 533i, 535i, 535is
Bentley Publishers ISBN 0-8376-0318-8

BMW 5-Series (E34) Service Manual: 1989–1995 525i, 530i, 535i, 540i, including Touring
Bentley Publishers ISBN 0-8376-0319-6

BMW 7 Series (E32) Service Manual: 1988–1994, 735i, 735iL, 740i, 740iL, 750iL
Bentley Publishers ISBN 0-8376-0328-5

BMW Z3 Roadster Service Manual: 1996–1998, 4- and 6-cylinder engines
Bentley Publishers ISBN 0-8376-0328-5

BMW Enthusiast's Companion™
BMW Car Club of America
ISBN 0-8376-0321-8

BMW 3 Series Enthusiast's Companion™
Jeremy Walton ISBN 0-8376-0220-3

BMW 6 Series Enthusiast's Companion™
Jeremy Walton ISBN 0-8376-0149-5

Unbeatable BMW: Eighty Years of Engineering and Motorsport Success
Jeremy Walton ISBN 0-8376-0206-8

Chevrolet

Camaro Exposed 1967–1969: Designs, Decisions and the Inside View
Paul Zazarine ISBN 0-8376-0876-7

Chevrolet by the Numbers 1955–1959: The Essential Chevrolet Parts Reference
Alan Colvin ISBN 0-8376-0875-9

Corvette by the Numbers 1955–1982: The Essential Corvette Parts Reference
Alan Colvin ISBN 0-8376-0288-2

Corvette 427: Practical Restoration of a '67 Roadster
Don Sherman ISBN 0-8376-0218-1

Corvette From The Inside
David R. Mclellan ISBN 0-8376-0859-7

Corvette Fuel Injection & Electronic Engine Management: 1982–2001
Charles O. Probst, SAE ISBN 0-8376-0861-9

Zora Arkus-Duntov: The Legend Behind Corvette
Jerry Burton ISBN 0-8376-0858-9

Ford

Ford Fuel Injection and Electronic Engine Control: 1988–1993
Charles O. Probst, SAE ISBN 0-8376-0301-3

The Official Ford Mustang 5.0 Technical Reference & Performance Handbook 1979-1993
Al Kirschenbaum ISBN 0-8376-0210-6

Harley-Davidson

Harley-Davidson Evolution V-Twin Owner's Bible™
Moses Ludel ISBN 0-8376-0146-0

Jeep

Jeep Owner's Bible™
Moses Ludel ISBN 0-8376-0154-1

Porsche

Porsche Carrera 964 1989–1994 Without Guesswork™: Technical Data
Bentley Publishers ISBN 0-8376-0292-0

Porsche 911 Carrera Service Manual: 1984–1989, Coupe, Targa and Cabriolet
Bentley Publishers ISBN 0-8376-0291-2

Porsche 911 SC Service Manual: 1978–1983, Coupe, Targa and Cabriolet
Bentley Publishers ISBN 0-8376-0290-4

Saab

Saab 900 16 Valve Official Service Manual: 1985–1993
Bentley Publishers ISBN 0-8376-0312-9

Saab 900 8 Valve Official Service Manual: 1981–1988
Bentley Publishers ISBN 0-8376-0310-2

Volkswagen

Jetta, Golf, GTI Service Manual: 1999–2002 2.0L Gasoline, 1.9L TDI Diesel, 2.8L VR6, 1.8L Turbo
Bentley Publishers ISBN 0-8376-0388-9

Jetta, Golf, GTI, Cabrio Service Manual: 1993–1999, including Jetta*III* and Golf*III*
Bentley Publishers ISBN 0-8376-0366-8

Passat 1998–2002: Official Factory Repair Manual on CD-ROM
Bentley Publishers ISBN 0-8376-0837-6

New Beetle: 1998–2002 Official Factory Repair Manual on CD-ROM
Bentley Publishers ISBN 0-8376-0838-4

Volvo

Volvo 240 Service Manual: 1983–1993
Bentley Publishers ISBN 0-8376-0285-8